Economic Calculation
in the
Socialist Society

Trygve J. B. Hoff

Economic Calculation
in the
Socialist Society

Trygve J. B. Hoff

Liberty Fund

Indianapolis

⌈※⌉ 𝔼𝔸⤳

The cuneiform inscription that serves as our logo and as the design motif for our endpapers is the earliest-known written appearance of the word "freedom" (*amagi*), or "liberty." It is taken from a clay document written about 2300 B.C. in the Sumerian city-state of Lagash.

Originally published as *Økonomisk kalkulasjon i socialistiske samfund* by H. Ashekovg, Oslo, in 1938. English translation published by William Hodge and Company, Limited, London, in 1949.

Translated from the original Norwegian by M. A. Michael.

The publisher acknowledges the cooperation of the Institute for Humane Studies. This book is included in the Institute's Studies in Economic Theory Series.

Library of Congress Cataloging in Publication Data

Hoff, Trygve J. B.
    Economic calculation in the socialist society.

    Translation of: Økonomisk kalkulasjon i socialistiske samfund.
    Reprint. Originally published: London: W. Hodge, 1949. With new introd.
    Bibliography: p.
    1. Marxian economics. I. Title.
HB97.5.H5613   1981   335.4   80–83795
ISBN 0–913966–93–2   AACR 2
ISBN 0–913966–94–0 (pbk.)

85 84 83 82 81 C 5 4 3 2 1
02 01 00 99 98 P 6 5 4 3 2

Contents

Introduction

In 1940, two years after the publication of Trygve J. B. Hoff's *Okonomisk kalkulasjon i socialistiske samfund* (Oslo: H. Ashehovg, 1938), the original Norwegian version of the book you are about to read, the socialist economist, H. D. Dickinson wrote in a very favorable review article:

> The problem of economic calculation in a social system where the ownership of all means of production is, in the ultimate analysis, vested in a single organ of social administration has been a live issue among economists for some years. It seems now to have reached a stage in which none of the disputants has very much new to say. Consequently, it is now ripe for a comprehensive survey and a judicial summing-up. This has been very successfully attempted by a Norwegian scholar in the work before us. The author has produced a critical review, at a very high level of theoretical competence of practically everything that has been written on the subject in German and English. [*Economic Journal*. 50 (June-Sept. 1940): 270–274.]

The controversy that is the subject of Hoff's book was exactly twenty years old when Dickinson wrote his review. It was a controversy that raged first in the German and later in the English economic literature. During its twenty-year life span, there was lively and sometimes acrimonious debate in which both sides to the dispute brought up issues that are fundamental to the understanding of both the socialist and the market economy and of the models which economists use to describe them. At the time, the participants in the discussion perceived the question to be which form of economic organization yields the most desirable economic consequences, capitalism or socialism. For most of the participants, the criterion for evaluating the two economic systems was the maximization of social welfare in the technical economic sense, and the question they tried to resolve was whether socialism or capitalism could satisfy the wants and needs of consumers more efficiently.

While the early socialist writers had simply asserted the superiority of their system by claiming its historic inevitability, the genuine debate about the problem of economic calculation began in 1920 with the publication of Ludwig von Mises' article, "Die Wirtschaftsrechnung im socialistischen Gemeinwesen" in the *Archiv fur Sozialwissenschaften;* translated as "Economic Calculation in the Socialist Commonwealth" in F. A. Hayek, *Collectivist Economic Planning* (London: George Routledge and Sons, Ltd, 1935). Here, Mises pointed to the vagueness of the socialists' economic programs and to the unreliability of their claims for economic superiority, and argued that far from being a superior economic system, socialism in fact was totally incompatible with rational economic behavior. The essence of Mises' argument was that in order to make rational economic decisions (that is, to produce the greatest valued output for the smallest use of resources), producers and consumers need to know the market prices of producer goods and consumer goods. Market prices are data that permit producers to determine whether or not they have produced their product most economically, and profits are the signals that tell them if they have performed as well as other producers in the economy. Without prices, there is no possibility of calculating costs or revenues or profits, and therefore, no way of knowing if the products most highly valued by consumers have been produced. Here, Mises was arguing that the same economic logic must be applied to any system that aspires to satisfying consumer wants efficiently. This argument was not new; it had been made in an article published in 1902 by a Dutch economist, N. G. Pierson (translated as "The Problem of Value in a Socialist Society" in *Collectivist Economic Planning,* cited above) whose work was at the time not very well known and also, by Enrico Barone who in a 1908 article ("The Minister of Production of a Socialist State" also later published in *Collectivist Economic Planning*) that followed up some suggestions originally made by Vifredo Pareto, showing that the same economic logic which led to a rational allocation of resources in a capitalist economy would also apply to a socialist one. What distinguished Mises' arguments from those of Pierson and Barone was his vehement assertion that the information necessary for economic calculation could be obtained only through market-determined prices.

Partly because of the certainty with which he stated his argument, and partly because his argument was repeated independently by Max Weber in his book, *Wirtschaft und Gesellschaft* in 1921, reaction to Mises' article produced a quick response in the German literature. Much of the initial reaction consisted of attempts to deny that under socialism there would be any necessity of calculating in the same way as under capitalism; some of the alternatives to economic calculation presented by the socialists in answer to Mises were non-monetary exchange, valuing according to labor input, and distribution from public store houses at no cost to consumers. With a few notable exceptions, the thrust of the early German responses to Mises were aimed at eliminating "bourgeois" economics and replacing it with some sort of ill-conceived utopia. (Accounts of some early socialist programs can be found in Hoff, Chapters 4, 5, and *Collectivist Economic Planning,* Chapter I.)

More promising answers to Mises' criticisms began to appear in the late twenties and early thirties when the discussion of socialism was taken up by English-speaking economists. What distinguished the English contributions to the discussion from most of the earlier German ones was the admission of one of Mises' basic points that prices were as important for rational calculation in a socialist economy as they were in a capitalist economy. With few exceptions, all the English contributors were neoclassical economists who agreed that the equilibrium position described by the model of perfect competition represented maximization of human welfare. Their programs for socialism were aimed at reproducing this beneficial result of perfect competition without the defects they believed to be inherent in capitalism: monopolies, externalities and inequalities of wealth. They attempted, therefore, to find methods by which central planners could arrive at a set of economically rational product and factor prices that did not rely on free markets and the private ownership of the means of production.

Interestingly, one of the first of the schemes to overcome

the deficiencies of capitalism through market planning was presented by H. D. Dickinson, the reviewer of the Norwegian edition of Hoff's work. In an article entitled "Price Formation in a Socialist Community" (*Economic Journal,* 43 [June 1933]; 237–251), Dickinson described an economic theory of socialism which set the outline for the many socialist models to follow. In direct response to Mises' challenge, Dickinson constructed a model of a socialist economy with the following characteristics: personal goods were private property, there was common (that is, state) ownership of natural resources and the means of production, and most importantly, there was a large sector of individualized consumption for which cost calculation would have to be carried out using prices. To obtain these prices, Dickinson proposed that the central planners estimate statistical demand curves and production functions and solve for equilibrium prices through a series of successive approximations. Essentially, Dickinson proposed the construction of a mathematical model of the economy much like some modern computer simulation models. Since in 1933, computers of the sophistication required to do the formidable job of simulation certainly did not exist (and still do not exist), Dickinson actually supposed that the mathematical system could be solved manually.

While Dickinson's solution for obtaining prices in an economy without markets was crude and unconvincing to the profession (he, himself, abandoned the technique in his 1939 book, *The Economics of Socialism* [Oxford, Oxford University Press, 1939]), his description of the general aim of a socialist economy was widely accepted: to provide for maximum satisfaction of private consumer demand. For many supporters of socialism such as Oskar Lange,

Abba Lerner and E. F. M. Durbin, this was the raison d'être for planning in a world where capitalism fell short of the goal. These so-called "market socialists" proposed solutions to the pricing problem in a socialist economy that were designed to duplicate the relevant characteristics of a competitive capitalist economy operating under ideal conditions. In fact, the only prominent English economist to enter the debate who explicitly disagreed with the "market socialists" was Maurice Dobb.

In 1928, Dobb published his *Russian Economic Development* (London, George Routledge and Sons, Ltd) in which he agreed with Dickinson that ". . . the categories of economic theory are equally valid in a socialist as in an individualist order" ("Economic Theory and the Problems of a Socialist Economy" in *Economic Journal,* 43, [Dec. 1933]; pp. 588–598.), but by 1933 when he wrote the above cited article he had decided that his former position was invalid. There he claimed that those who touted the importance of having prices with which to calculate costs and profits were really making an implicit value judgment; they were assuming that consumer preferences were somehow "sacred" and that the sole aim of socialist economic planning should be to satisfy these preferences. Dobb then attacked both the intelligence of consumers and the morality of permitting them to have free choice about the commodities they consume. He claimed that consumers are manipulated by advertising, do not always know what is best for themselves and are essentially short-sighted in their saving and investment decisions. Hence, it would be more in keeping with socialist ideals to have the planning board make at least some of the consumers' consumption decisions for them. While Dobb's attitude was both paternalistic and authoritarian, he did notice something the market socialists overlooked in their enthusiasm for the model of perfect competition. As Dobb put it sometime later, "Either planning means overriding the autonomy of private decisions or it apparently means nothing at all" (*Political Economy and Capitalism,* [London, George Routledge and Sons, Ltd, 1937] p. 279.) For Dobb, socialism was not just tinkering with the system to remove the imperfections of the market, it meant replacing the system completely with a new set of values to guide production and distribution in which the satisfaction of the consumer was no longer a primary element.

Dobb's position was extreme and unpalatable to his more liberal colleagues, among them Abba Lerner who was provoked into writing a scathing criticism of Dobb in which he pointed out the major flaw in the argument ("Economic Theory and Socialist Economy," *Review of Economic Studies,* 2 [Feb. 1935], pp. 51–61). Lerner, a former student of Friedrich Hayek at the London School of Economics was also favorably disposed toward socialism, yet perhaps because of Hayek's influence he recognized the analytic importance of Mises' claim that without prices, economic calculation is impossible. He therefore argued that Dobb's criticism that consumer preferences should not necessarily guide the planning board's decisions was beside the point. Regardless of whose preferences were going to be satisfied, those of the consumer or the central planners, prices are still needed to determine whether resources are being used most efficiently to achieve the goals the planners set for themselves and society.

During the early thirties, the debate about socialist planning was being carried out almost exclusively by those favorable to socialism. The major exception was Lionel Robbins who showed that market prices were needed in order to calculate efficiently and who criticised schemes that relied on systems of equations or fictitious markets to arrive at proxies for actual market prices. (See his *The Great Depression* [London, Macmillan and Company, 1933], pp. 145–155.) While Robbins' arguments were well taken, they did not represent a substantial advance over Mises' original work. It was not until 1935 when Hayek published *Collectivist Economic Planning* that the pro-capitalist writers presented substantially new arguments against socialist planning. Hayek included in this volume an English translation of Mises', Pierson's, and Barone's original articles that had touched off the debate in the first place, an original essay by George Halm reviewing the German literature, and, in addition, Hayek included two essays of his own that constituted the most important novel contributions to the volume. The first was a review of the controversy until 1935, and the second was a critical article entitled, "The State of the Debate," in which he expanded upon Mises' original contention that economic calculation is impossible without market prices to provide relevant information. In many respects, the publication of *Collectivist Economic Planning* should have been a turning point in the debate. That it was not, reflected the inability of the socialists to deal with Hayek's arguments.

While by that time there was no longer any doubt that prices were necessary ingredients in any system of rational economic calculation, the contention of Dickinson, Dobb (in 1928) and Lerner was that these prices could be determined in the absence of free markets and private ownership of the means of production. Hayek, however, argued from Mises' position that non-market prices were simply not substitutes for market prices, and attempts to use non-market prices to duplicate the results of the market were doomed to failure. In the course of his essay, Hayek stressed several aspects of the market that he believed had not been taken into account by the socialist planners. He argued that while the models used by the socialists to arrive at solutions to the pricing problem were not logically contradictory, they bore no relationship to the manner in which prices were formed in the real world. In constructing their models, the socialists left out important relationships that if included would surely alter the conclusions they sought. Thus the market socialists had constructed models that were in a practical sense irrelevant to the problems they wished to solve. Incredibly, Hayek's sophisticated insight was misinterpreted to mean that, unlike Mises, Hayek conceded that socialism is possible, but that he was just raising practical objections to its implementation. Oskar Lange later called this position the "second line of defense" implying that the critics of socialism were in retreat. ("On The Economic Theory of Socialism" in *Review of Economic Studies,* 4 [Oct. 1936, Fcb. 1937], pp. 53–71; 123–142). For some reason, this improper characterization of Hayek's attitude was accepted by the profession as correct with the unhappy result that the substance of Hayek's criticisms was lost.

In both this essay and in his later one, "The Competitive Solution" (Economica N.S.7 [May, 1940], pp. 125–149. Reprinted in *Individualism And Economic Order* [Chicago, University of Chicago Press, 1948], pp. 181–208), Hayek engaged in a point by point refutation of the socialist programs for duplicating the efficiency of the market. There were several themes that characterized both critiques, but the two principal ones were the role of information in a market economy and the inapplicability of static equilibrium models for setting policies for a dynamic world. For example, the major reason he objected to the Dickinson-style mathematical solution was not primarily because of the practical difficulties involved in solving the equations (although that was part of it), but that it would be physically impossible for a planning board to acquire the information necessary to specify those equations.

As Hayek saw it, the information that individuals use to guide their economic activity is vast, detailed and necessarily incomplete. It is not neatly summarized in objective demand and cost functions which need only be revealed to the central planners in order for them to take over the task of economic decision making. Economic activity is the process of discovering alternatives which improve profitability and hence, resource efficiency. It is part of entrepreneurship to identify superior resources and to combine them in more imaginative ways to produce a product, and it is this activity which adds to the information available in the market place. Furthermore, even if the information available to economic actors were objectively determinable apart from their actions it is also decentralized. It is through the process of buying and selling in markets that all the decentralized bits of knowledge can coalesce into a coordinated whole. Hence, market prices result from the interaction of individuals with unique and fragmental knowledge and are not simply data available to passive "price takers" as Lange believed.

Hayek attributed much of the error in the arguments

of the proponents of socialism to their "excessive pre-occupation with the conditions of a hypothetical state of stationary equilibrium," (*Collectivist Economic Planning,* p. 226). Both Mises and Hayek believed that while equilibrium states are an aid to the understanding of how an economy functions, they are not the subject of economic inquiry. The real world never reaches a position of static equilibrium because the data constantly change. Hence, any administrative solution to obtaining relative prices whether it be statistical techniques or a process of trial-and-error, cannot be effective because the prices arrived at will be obsolete before they can be announced.

In addition to discussing the existing published work on socialism, Hayek also anticipated some of the programs which would be offered by the socialists after the appearance of his volume. These programs he called "competitive socialism" because of the attempt to restore some kind of competition in a basically centrally planned economy. That is, managers of socialist enterprises would be instructed to act as if they were perfect competitors in their production decisions. There were two objections to this in Hayek's opinion. The first was that it did not take into consideration "whether decisions and responsibility can be successfully left to competing individuals who are not owners or are otherwise directly interested in the means of production under their charge" (p. 219). That is, will managers who are not owners or whose income does not directly depend upon the efficient operation of their businesses behave in as aggressively competitive a manner as those whose livelihood is at stake? Thirty years later this same issue would be explored in the growing literature on property rights economics, the economics of how different allocations and specifications of property rights affect economic incentives and therefore economic behavior. (For a survey of the growing literature on property rights economics, see Furubotn and Pejovich "Property Right and Economic Theory: A Survey of Recent Literature" *Journal of Economic Literature,* 10 [Dec. 1972], pp. 1162–1337).

The issue of property rights was only hinted at in the early literature on socialist economics. Mises, both in his 1920 article and in his more ambitious book, *Die Gemeinwirtschaft* ([1922]. Translated as *Socialism* [London, J. Cape, 1936]) argued that one could not play at being an entrepreneur, that one had to risk one's own income on the outcome of the decisions one makes if the market is going to yield the most efficient outcome. Hayek further contended that under socialism, a manager's decisions would not be subject to the objective test of profit or loss to determine their correctness, and his livelihood would therefore depend upon convincing the planning board that the decisions he made were the best ones at the time. As a result, managers would be less likely to make risky decisions regardless of their potential profitability because their major task would not be to achieve success *ex post,* but to convince someone else that they had made reasonable choices *ex ante.* While the actual distribution of risk taking depends upon the constraints facing individual managers (an argument can be made that they will be either more or less prone to risk taking than private entrepreneurs), the problem of the effects of property rights on individual economic behavior was an important issue neglected by the socialist during the debate.

Perhaps an even more fundamental criticism of the socialist programs was Hayek's suggestion that they erroneously believed costs to be objective entities that exist independent of the decision-maker. In fact, the costs incurred in the production of anything equal the value of the foregone alternatives. But at the time a production decision is made, the values of the foregone alternatives depend upon the decision-maker's expectations about future prices, which are necessarily largely subjective. Planners would have to engage in detailed audits of public firms not only to ascertain that current outlays were being covered by revenues—a relatively simple matter, but also to determine whether or not managers had made the "best" choices in the past without competition in markets to reveal *ex post* what constituted the "best." [James Buchanan has argued perhaps too sweepingly that the entire controversy hinged on the question of the subjective nature of costs. See his *L.S.E. Essays on Cost* (London: London School of Economics and Political Science, 1973) pp. 3–10, and *Cost and Choice* (Chicago, Markham Publishing Co., 1969), pp. 20–23.]

One year after the publication of *Collectivist Economic Planning,* Oskar Lange published his two-part article "On The Economic Theory of Socialism" (cited above, p. 9) which was the most complete elaboration of socialist economic theory until that time. It was intended to be a final refutation of Mises' claim that socialism was impossible because of the absence of market prices, yet it showed remarkably little appreciation of Mises' early arguments, and it benefited not at all from Hayek's important insights. Lange began his essay by facetiously thanking Mises for pointing out the problem of economic calculation under socialism and forcing socialists to devise a solution. The solution, he claimed, had been hinted at by Wicksteed in

1910 when he described the dual nature of prices. Prices are both exchange ratios determined in the market and, in a more general sense, they are the terms on which alternatives are offered. Thus, socialist planners could set prices which would represent the terms on which alternatives are offered to the industry managers and could assure that these were equilibrium prices by appropriately adjusting them in response to any observed surplus or shortage of goods. This "trial and error" method of discovering market clearing prices had actually been proposed eight years before by Fred Taylor in his Presidential Address to the American Economic Association. Taylor, in a somewhat simplistic and dogmatic manner, claimed that socialism was not only possible, but actually preferable to free markets as long as the price controllers followed two simple rules: when goods are in short supply, raise price, and when there are surplus goods, lower price. This would assure that all prices are in equilibrium and would obviate the need for a system of mathematical equations to arrive at equilibrium prices. Lange likened the process to a Walrasian tâtonnement, with the central planning board acting the part of the auctioneer. To complete the analogue to Walrasian general equilibrium, producers would be instructed to produce at minimum average cost and at a point where price equals marginal cost assuring thereby the allocative efficiency of perfect competition. The system would work, Lange explained, because managers would be told to act "as if prices were independent of decisions taken" [p. 81] and prices would thereby be treated as parameters rather than independent variables.

It is instructive that Lange decided to quote Wicksteed's formulation of the meaning of price in the beginning of his article; instructive primarily because it reveals Lange's complete lack of understanding of exactly what Wicksteed was trying to show. In the *Commonsense of Political Economy* [London, Routledge & Kegan Paul, 1910], Wicksteed described the essentially subjective nature of the opportunity costs that faced anyone attempting to make a rational economic decision. That is, when one considers making a purchase, the price represents the market exchange value, but the "terms on which alternatives are offered" includes not only the market price, but all the subjective elements that must be calculated in one's choice, the subjective value of all the foregone alternatives (p. 28). Obviously, this has nothing to do with the distinction Lange was trying to make between market prices and centrally planned prices. The prices which Lange's planning board would set, far from providing a more encompassing kind of price, would figure in an individual's subjective calculus in exactly the same way as market prices more conventionally do. Individuals would still have to personally evaluate the whole range of alternatives, the "terms on which alternatives are offered" to them, but the administered price would substitute for the market price. The real problem, then, of how legislated prices would be made to represent actual relative scarcities of the commodities available for exchange, could not be exorcised with an impressive incantation. Lange had still to show that the tâtonnement he prescribed could be made to yield measures of relative scarcity as well as market exchanges. This, he did not accomplish.

Even if one were to grant that relevant prices could be determined by the central planning board, it was essential to Lange's plan that managers of firms and industries treat these prices as parameters and, in effect, duplicate the behavior of perfectly competitive firms. The problem here is that socialist managers would not really be perfect competitors, and while there might very well be many firms in an industry with firm managers making output decisions on the basis of given prices, Lange's plan also required the existence of industry managers who would make decisions regarding the growth or decline of their industries as a whole. The industry manager, then, would really be in the position of a monopolist who knows his output decisions will affect the price of his produce. Lange never explained how one might convince a manager in this position to ignore the influence he has on prices when making plans for future industry production.

After the publication of Lange's articles, the problem of what set of rules would induce managers to make decisions that would lead to desired consequences in a planned economy replaced the problem of pricing in the literature on socialist economics. By this time, the socialists agreed that the problem of pricing had been solved by the Taylor-Lange trial and error process (Hayek's objections notwithstanding), and what remained to be decided was how these prices should be used in the actual production of goods and services. One contribution to the solution of the problem was offered by E. F. M. Durbin ("Economic Calculus in a Planned Economy." *Economic Journal,* 46 [Dec. 1936], pp. 676–690). Durbin claimed that all one had to do to assure efficient production on the part of managers was to instruct them to make "normal profits"; that is, to instruct them to produce the largest output possible in any existing plant that is consistent with making normal profits, and where normal profits cannot be earned, instead to equate price to marginal cost. Durbin never mentioned the problem of obtaining prices with which to calculate costs because he intended only to provide a set of practical rules to guide production in a socialist economy where prices were already given.

Durbin's article elicited a response from Abba Lerner which showed some appreciation for one of Hayek's important criticisms of socialism. In his article, "Statics and Dynamics in a Socialist Economy" (cited above), Lerner criticized economists for trying to duplicate the symptoms of perfect competition in socialism instead of "going direct to the more fundamental principle of marginal opportunity cost" (p. 251). The real goal of socialist economies, according to Lerner, is the maximization of the value of production, and this can be achieved by assuring that no resources are used to produce a commodity which can be used to produce a more highly valued commodity elsewhere. That is the essence of rational use of resources and the aim of all production plans. If price represents the marginal valuation of the product sold and marginal cost represents the value of the foregone alternatives, one should simply instruct all socialist managers to produce that output which equates price to marginal cost for any planning period under consideration. It is unnecessary to insist that managers make normal profits since normal profits are only a symptom of static equilibrium when what is really needed is a rule that will guide the allocation of resources in a dynamic world.

Given his assumptions, Lerner's rules for managerial efficiency are logically unassailable. Prices are determined through the Lange trial and error process, and managers are told to produce where marginal cost equals price. Any change in data will show up as a price change which will cause managers to alter their production accordingly. As long as costs are objective elements which can be identified apart from market evaluations, rational decisions can be made. However, if costs are subjective estimates, as Hayek (and Wicksteed) argued, the rules for managerial efficiency are no longer clear cut; the marginal cost estimates of managers will not be the same as the marginal cost estimates of the central planners and some additional behavioral rules will be needed. Lerner never confronted the problem of the subjectivity of costs, just as he never touched on such questions as what incentives would exist for managers to follow the instructions given them by the planning board, or how skilled planners would be at perceiving the need for adjusting the parameters of the system, questions he considered to be in the province of sociology rather than economics.

It was at this point in the theoretical development of the debate that Hoff published the Norwegian edition of *Economic Calculation in the Socialist Society*. As Dickinson indicated in his review, by this time the disputants had reached an impasse. The proponents of socialism had developed a theoretical apparatus to guide the socialist state which satisfied them, while the critics still maintained that this theoretical apparatus missed the point and was inapplicable to the kind of human beings populating the world. Dickinson himself was to publish one year after Hoff's book appeared a more comprehensive treatment of socialist economic theory which followed much the same outline as Lange's earlier work and improved on it very little. And one year after that, Hayek was to publish his last article dealing specifically with the problem of economic calculation under socialism in which he reiterated most of his earlier objections. Not only had neither side anything substantially new to say, but neither side had succeeded in converting the other. The time was ripe, to paraphrase Dickinson, for a "summing up."

Trygve Hoff had been interested in the problem of socialist calculation for several years before he began his systematic investigation of the problem. He had been intrigued by Mises' contention that rational economic calculation under socialism was impossible, and he viewed with dismay the actual development of the one self-proclaimed socialist economy in existence, the Soviet Union. He had studied economics at Harvard where he was subject to the quasi-Austrian influence of the young Joseph A. Schumpeter, and his investigations into the problem of socialist economic calculation earned him a doctorate from Oslo University (no small feat with a faculty which was predominately sympathetic to socialism).

Hoff at this time was by no means an impartial observer of the passing scene; he was an enthusiastic advocate of the free market both on efficiency and on moral grounds. Furthermore, Hoff put his philosophy into practice by serving as editor of the well-known Norwegian business journal, *Farmand*. Yet when he set out in his book to make sense of all the arguments for and against socialism to determine to his satisfaction whether or not a socialist economy could make rational economic decisions, he did so in a spirit of impartiality that is the epitome of good scholarship. His conclusions were with those who criticized socialism, but only because he believed that those were the conclusions consistent with his analysis.

Hoff arrives at his conclusions in a notably organized

manner. He begins his critical analysis of the economic calculation debate by trying to bring some order into the often imprecise terminology used by socialists and non-socialists alike. Hence, after an introductory chapter stating the problem to be confronted, he spends two very useful chapters setting out definitions of the terms he will use and assumptions upon which he intends to base his analysis. To Hoff, a socialist economy is one where private property in the means of production is replaced by a central authority which directs industrial activity. In such a society, however, the central authority is only able to judge whether or not it is achieving its goals when it knows what the production of various goods costs either in terms of effort or in opportunity costs. Here, then, is where the problem of economic calculation begins.

Hoff begins his critical discussion of socialist economics by showing the absurdity inherent in any scheme to operate an economy without the aid of money. While to the modern reader, the discussion in Chapter 4 might seem unnecessary, proposals for abolishing money from circulation once formed the heart of many early Marxist economic plans. By the time the debate reached England, plans to have an economy operate "in natura" were ignored by the socialist economists, but they were still sometimes advocated by non-economists who did not perceive the magnitude of the economic problems this would entail. Having established the necessity of operating within the framework of a money economy even under socialism, Hoff goes on to show the impossibility of calculating economically on the Marxian basis of labor time, and then shows that all of the costs elements common to capitalist accounting methods will also be necessary to socialist accounting. Once again, while this was taken for granted by the English participants in the debate, it was not taken for granted by the early German socialists, and it was this group that Hoff (and Mises before him) was answering. Hoff then uses the last five chapters to engage in a critical analysis of the various plans for socialist economies presented during the course of the debate.

While there is no reason to engage in a detailed description of the contents of a book which the reader is about to confront directly, it is appropriate to point out some of the major themes in Hoff's analysis. In general, Hoff's perception of the market is more Austrian than neoclassical. He agrees with Mises and Hayek that market prices are necessary to accurate economic calculation and that prices decided upon by non-market means are not adequate substitutes. He dismisses Lange-Taylor style trial and error prices as being impractical and naïve attempts at duplicating what the market does more efficiently and points out the vast number of problems this supposed solution ignores. For instance, Hoff asks what initial prices should the planning board set, who will be responsible for altering prices and at what intervals, how much should prices be altered in response to excess demands or supplies, and how will the planning board assure that supplies alter in response to demand changes? Throughout, Hoff emphasizes the necessity of adjusting all prices simultaneously to arrive at the general equilibrium solution the trial and error process aims for, and the extreme practical difficulties involved in trying to accomplish this.

Even if one grants that relevant prices can be established, Hoff still sees many problems that arise when trying to run a centrally planned economy efficiently. In making decisions about production, the planning board will find it necessary to calculate values for profits, interest, rents and depreciation without the aid of markets. While he thinks that little damage will be done by assuming some arbitrary rate of interest to coincide with the planning board's desired rate of growth (and on this issue he disagrees with Mises and Hayek), Hoff sees many difficulties inherent in attempting to deal with profits. Hoff defines profit as the residual income that falls to the entrepreneur for combining resources and assuming risk. Supposedly in a centrally directed economy, there will no longer be a class of entrepreneurs, but there will still be risk. Under capitalist institutions, those who choose to own assets bear the risks involved in their use, but under socialism, the entire community must bear the risks associated with decisions made by the central planners. While this may or may not be a defect of socialism, there is no question that it will alter the behavior of economic decision makers, and especially that of managers of firms who no longer bear personal financial responsibility for their actions. Even more important, since the central authority must bear all of the risk of the production decisions they make, they must have reliable data to make correct estimates of the future, but they will be in a less favorable position to obtain such data. Following Hayek and Mises, Hoff notes that private entrepreneurs have market prices to tell them what relative scarcities are now, and they have discounted asset values to indicate what the opportunity costs of various decisions are likely to be. A central planning board necessarily lacks this vital market information and is, therefore, even less likely to make correct decisions than the private entrepreneur.

Hoff is somewhat less concerned than is Hayek about the

problems of calculating depreciation in a socialist economy. He argues that depreciation is at best an estimate in the private market, and not much will be lost by having central planners do the estimating. He sees that the most likely result will be that planners will miss some profitable production opportunities through inappropriate depreciation estimates, but that the loss may be small. Hayek, on the other hand, thought that the inability to calculate depreciation accurately would be a major source of error in a centrally planned economy (*Collectivist Economic Planning,* pp. 232–236].

It is interesting to note that Hoff's critical analysis of socialism bears a striking resemblance to both Mises and Hayek. Again and again, he criticizes the socialists for basing their plans on wholly unrealistic assumptions that make their models inapplicable to the problems they are trying to solve. He singles out their reliance on static equilibrium analysis when the real world is dynamic; their assumption that all magnitudes are capable of instantaneous adjustments; and their neglect of the problem of how information about economic variables is obtained and transmitted through an economy. Hence, he finds with Mises and Hayek that the socialist schemes for running a planned economy as efficiently as capitalism are doomed to failure. However, unlike Mises, Hoff does not claim that this means socialism is impossible, only that it cannot result in the "maximum satisfaction of human needs." He concludes that socialism can exist, but at a lower level of production and consumption because many opportunity costs will not be counted in making economic decisions.

At the time of publication, there was much in *Economic Calculation in a Socialist Society* that could have shed light on the current controversy, but it failed to have any impact on the main disputants for the simple reason that it was available only in Norwegian, a language inaccessible to most of the scholarly community. In Dickinson's very favorable review of 1940, he asked whether it would not be possible to find some financial support for having Hoff's work translated into English, but before that could be accomplished, World War II broke out, and Norway was occupied by the Nazis. One of the unfortunate consequences of this cruel turn of history was that the English edition of which the following is a reprint was not available until 1948, ten years after its original date of publication. By that time, the economic calculation controversy was no longer a topic of scholarly debate, and most of the original contributors had moved on to other areas of study.

Hayek wrote one more article on the topic of economic calculation in 1940 ("The Competitive Solution," cited above) in which he reiterated many of his earlier criticisms that simply had been ignored by the socialists. He then went on to explore the problems of knowledge in economic theory, a problem he raised during the debate. In 1944, Lerner, although still sympathetic to the aims of socialism, concluded in his *Economics of Control* (New York: Macmillan, 1944) that the political consequences of socialism could too easily be anti-individualistic and authoritarian, and he then began to concentrate on the economics of regulating a basically capitalistic society. Lange and Dickinson considered all the major theoretical problems to be solved and felt that no further theoretical defense of socialism was necessary (although Lange continued to study the practical problem of running a socialist economy). This attitude was also held by Joseph Schumpeter who wrote in his *Capitalism, Socialism and Democracy* (New York, Harper and Row, 1950 [originally published in 1942]), "as a matter of blueprint logic it is undeniable that the socialist blueprint is drawn at a higher level of rationality" (p. 196). While Schumpeter warned of political problems in the socialist society, his judgment of the superior economic logic of socialism seemed to be shared by the majority of economists by the late 1940's.

A good illustration of this attitude of the profession toward the socialist position can be found in an essay written by Abram Bergson for the American Economic Association's *A Survey of Contemporary Economics* entitled, "Socialism" ([Homewood, Illinois, Richard D. Irwin, Inc., 1948], pp. 412–448). This article was intended as a summary of the advancements in the development of an economics of socialism from the late nineteenth century to the present, and as such, it summarized the general consensus of opinion among economists regarding socialism. Naturally, Bergson examined the debate of the twenties and thirties which began with Mises, but his attitude is perhaps best summarized when he states, "By now it seems generally agreed that the argument on these questions advanced by Mises himself, at least according to one interpretation, is without much force" (p. 412), and then hints that those who challenge socialism on the grounds that it limits freedom are engaging in a "tactical maneuver, to bolster a cause which Mises' theories have been found inadequate to sustain" (pp. 412–413). While most of the rest of Bergson's discussion is well-balanced and fair to the contributors to the debate, it is clear that he believed that the critics of socialism had not proven their case, and that the economic problems associated with socialism are minor ones. It is not so much that he denied the theoretical relevance of Mises and Hayek's arguments, but rather that they will be very important in the actual day to day operation of the socialist economy. For Bergson in 1948, the only issue in the debate not settled was which system is more likely to be most efficient, and here he believed political issues would dominate since the economic ones were for the most part settled.

Bergson's article appeared the same year as the English translation of Hoff's book: the two writings covered much the same ground and explored many of the same issues. However, where Hoff's work was more of a treatise on some unresolved problems in the economics of socialism and relied heavily on quotations from original sources to support the arguments made, Bergson's work was a short article that effectively summarized an issue that for most of the profession seemed to be closed. Hoff made a contribution to an ongoing debate while Bergson summarized a debate of the past. In addition, the terminology used by Bergson was more familiar to the American and English members of the profession while Hoff's terminology, due to the difficulties of translation seemed a bit old-fashioned and cumbersome. Hence, anyone in 1948 wanting to learn about the economic calculation problem in socialism would be unlikely to pick up Hoff's book when Bergson's article was available. In this way, an excellent piece of scholarship that made some valuable observations about the relative merits of socialism and capitalism was virtually ignored by most of the economics profession.

It is now over thirty years since the publication of the English version of *Economic Calculation in the Socialist Society,* and forty since the appearance of the Norwegian original, yet because of the peculiar nature of its subject, the book can still be read with profit. From an historical perspective, it presents an admirable summary of the state of the debate circa 1938. One of Hoff's strong suits is his ability to marshall all the arguments both pro and con on a subject and exposit them in a thoroughly logical manner. His extensive use of quotations from original sources, once considered a small defect by a reviewer of his work in 1950 (*Times Literary Supplement* [Feb. 2, 1950]), turns out to be a real bonus to the modern reader who is likely to be unfamiliar with the original literature. For the reader limited to the English language, the detailed accounts Hoff gives of the early German literature are especially useful. In addition, the reader's attention is called to Appendix C, "A Comparison between Our Conclusions and Experiences in Soviet Russia." While this is not part of the logical development of Hoff's analysis, it nevertheless lends some perspective to the historical milieu in which his ideas were formed. The economic performance of the Soviet Union during the 1920's and 1930's can only be described as dismal, and the appendix is a good reminder to the modern reader that the economic theories of socialism presented by essentially neoclassical economists during the 1930's had absolutely nothing to do with actual practice in the Soviet Union during that time. The reader is also advised to pay close attention to Appendix A, "The Price Mechanism in a Private Capitalist Society" and Appendix B, "Alleged Defects of Capitalist Societies and the Chances of Eliminating Them in Socialist Societies" where one finds an excellent summary of the operation and advantages of free market. In both these appendices, Hoff demonstrates the clear understanding of the nature and function of prices in a market economy that informs his entire analysis. Both are excellent pieces of analysis of more than just historical interest.

While the primary attraction of Hoff's valuable book is in elucidating a particularly important chapter in the history of twentieth-century economic thought, this by no means detracts from the interest it generates. Indeed, the chapter in history of which this book is a part has recently again become important to contemporary economic debate.

The economic calculation controversy of the 1930's, we have seen, was a debate over the relative efficiency of socialism and capitalism. It is not surprising that in 1980, after more than thirty years exposure to the dubious achievements of actual socialist economies, one hears few serious claims for the obvious superiority of socialism on any level, theoretical or practical. That issue does appear to be closed among Western economists. Moreover, as early as the 1960's economists in their effort to reassess the grandiose claims of the early neoclassical socialists, began to take more seriously Hayek's early criticisms, many of which were descriptive of practical problems frequently encountered in Eastern Europe. By now, Hayek is generally recognized to have made important contributions to economic theory during the course of the original debate. It is only within the last decade, however, that the Austrian view of markets and competition which was the foundation of Mises and Hayek's (and to a lesser degree, Hoff's) work is being vigorously explored and extended. Among the problems now in the forefront of Austrian economic thought which are also having an impact on the mainstream of the profession are the meaning and role of entrepreneurship, the role of markets in communicating knowledge, the subjective nature of the choice process, and the institutional variation in market structures, all of which were central to Mises and Hayek's early criticism of socialism. In so far as Hoff shared these concerns, with the reissue of this book, he finds himself once again in the center of an important theoretical investigation, but this time in a more strategically favorable position.

KAREN I. VAUGHN

George Mason University, 1980

Translator's Note

My grateful thanks are due to Mrs. Vera Lutz and to Dr. Arthur Birnie for their invaluable guidance through the maze of economic terminology.

M. A. M.

Preface

The purpose of this book is to investigate the possibilities of economic calculation in socialist societies.

Such an investigation is of *practical* value in a period when the trend in most countries is towards planning and socialism. It also has its attractions from a theoretical point of view, because the elimination of markets and prices (determined by demand and supply) means that the very basis of economic theory is disintegrating. It is also pertinent to enquire to what extent existing economic theory is valid under present circumstances and to what extent economics —and economists—are of any use when dictators and civil servants determine the economic course.

During the last few decades, criticism has been directed at "value judgments" and "hidden political and ethical assumptions" in economics. I agree that such assumptions should be stated. Thus, although the problem of economic calculation in socialist societies is one that it should be possible to discuss objectively irrespective of one's political views, I wish to say here that my original sympathy for socialist ideals has given place to an ever-growing doubt as to the political, cultural and economic consequences of socialism. I hope and believe, however, that this scepticism has not made my arguments illogical, nor my conclusions worthless.

In the text, I have made no reference to existing socialist societies such as Soviet Russia, as reference to this country often seems to introduce emotional elements into a discussion. However, in Appendix C I have attempted to compare the actual developments in Soviet Russia with the conclusions I have deduced.

In Appendix A non-economists will find a short description of a market economy.

In Appendix B is given an enumeration of objections made against (private) capitalism, and a brief subjective assessment of their validity. In this appendix is also discussed how far these alleged defects may conceivably be eliminated in socialist societies.

The translation into English has been delayed owing to the war, but except for a few minor corrections the English edition is identical with the Norwegian, which appeared in 1938.

TRYGVE J. B. HOFF

Economic Calculation
in the
Socialist Society

1

Statement of the Problem–
Earlier Treatment of the
Subject–Possibility of
"Objective" Discussion

Discussion of the feasibility of practical socialism has so far been mainly confined to its ethical and psychological aspects. The more technical question of the possibility of economic calculation under socialism, though not entirely neglected, has received relatively little attention. As early as 1854 the German pioneer of the theory of marginal utility, H. H. Gossen, declared that only private ownership could give a yard-stick for determining how much might suitably be produced of different goods according to existing resources.[1]

Professor Vilfredo Pareto broached the question on several occasions,[2] and in 1902 the Dutch economist N. G. Pierson wrote in a polemic[3] against Karl Kautsky that even

---

[1] *Entwicklung der Gesetze des menschlichen Verkehrs und der daraus fliessenden Regeln für menschliches Handeln,* 3rd Edn. With a foreword by F. A. von Hayek, Berlin, 1927.

[2] See among others *Cours d'Économie Politique,* II, Lausanne, 1897, pp. 364–71.

[3] In the Dutch periodical *De Economist,* 1902, pp. 423–56, later printed in the author's *Verspreide Economische Geschriften,* Haarlem, 1910, and *Collectivist Economic Planning,* edited by F. A. von Hayek, London, 1935.

a socialist society will have its value problems and that the socialists will have to show how they are going to have a price system. In 1904 Professor Maurice Bourguin[4] criticized the socialist economy and drew attention to a number of the difficulties which existed. In 1908 the Italian Professor Enrico Barone treated the problem from the mathematical aspect along the lines indicated by Pareto.[5] The problem was touched on in 1919 by Dr. O. Neurath, who took the point of view that in a socialist society one could manage with a moneyless economy,[6] an idea which was similarly put forward by Dr. O. Bauer in the same year.[7]

The economist who has done more than any other to bring the problem up for discussion is Professor Ludwig von Mises. In an article written in 1920[8] he maintained that before there could be economic calculation there must be prices expressed in terms of money, prices not only of consumer goods, but of semi-manufactured articles and capital goods. Professor Mises has laboured this point in several treatises and books. As markets for capital goods and production-factors—*ex definitione*—cannot exist in socialist communities, Professor Mises maintains that calculation in socialist economies is an impossibility. (For references

---

[4] *Les Systèmes Socialistes,* Paris, 3rd Edn., 1933, p. 18. (First Edn., 1904.)

[5] In an article "Il ministro della produzione nello stato collettivista" in *Giornale degli Economisti,* 1908, II. The article was translated and reproduced in *Collectivist Economic Planning.*

[6] *Durch die Kriegswirtschaft zur Naturalwirtschaft,* Munich, 1919.

[7] *Der Weg zum Sozialismus,* Vienna, 1919.

[8] In *Archiv für Sozialwissenschaft und Sozialpolitik,* Vol. 47, I, April, 1920, later included in Professor Mises' *Gemeinwirtschaft,* Jena, 1922 (translated into English from a new edition of 1943 under the title of *Socialism,* London, 1936). There is also a translation of the article in *Collectivist Economic Planning.*

see p. 129.) Independently of Professor von Mises the German sociologist Max Weber[9] maintained that calculation *in natura* could not give a rational solution of the problems which would confront a planned economy.[10] Weber emphasized that conservation and rational employment of capital could only be secured in a society based on exchange and the use of money, and that the loss and destruction which would result were rational calculation not feasible in a completely socialized society, could make it impossible to maintain the present population in densely populated areas.

Of particular interest is the statement made in the summer of 1920 by the Russian Professor Boris Brutzkus during a series of lectures (given in Russia), that rational calculation in a centrally directed society, where there were no prices, was an impossibility.[11]

In addition to the arguments of N. G. Pierson, von Mises and Barone, already mentioned, *Collectivist Economic*

---

[9] *Wirtschaft und Gesellschaft* (*Grundriss der Sozialökonomik*, Part III), Tübingen, 1922, pp. 9–14, 55–56. Translated into English as *Theory of Social and Economic Organization,* London, 1947.

[10] It may be noted that Karl Marx realized that "the distribution of resources" would constitute a problem in the socialist society. Karl Kautsky has stressed the necessity of a monetary system and of "a free choice" for consumers. This latter was also realized by Engels, in as far as he said that the socialist society's plan must be based on the "profit" of the different consumer goods. (For further quotations see Chapter 5.) Neither Marx, Kautsky nor Engels have, however, discussed the present question of the possibility of economic calculation. Marx has evidently been aware of the importance and necessity of economic calculation (see p. 181).

[11] These lectures were reproduced in the Russian financial paper *Economist,* 1921–22, and later appeared separately (Berlin, 1923). They were translated into German in 1928 under the title of *Die Lehre des Marxismus im Lichte der Russischen Revolution* and included in the author's *Economic Planning in Soviet Russia,* London, 1935.

Planning contains a report by Professor Georg Halm of Würzburg, and an introductory and concluding chapter by the editor, Professor F. A. Hayek. Up to now this book, together with the English translation of Brutzkus' lectures which appeared at the same time, is the most important contribution to the discussion which has been made by those who are sceptical of the possibility of economic calculation in the socialist society, and it will presumably remain the standard work on the subject.

There have also been many contributions, chiefly in the form of articles and treatises, from those on the other side. First and foremost of these must be mentioned Dr. Eduard Heimann, Dr. Cläre Tisch, Dr. H. Zassenhaus, H. D. Dickinson, Dr. Maurice Dobb, Dr. E. F. M. Durbin, Dr. A. P. Lerner, and Dr. Oskar Lange.

In Scandinavian countries there has been to all intents and purposes no public discussion of the question of economic calculation in a socialist society. Nor did this question crop up during the discussion on "planned economy" during the Inter-Scandinavian Economic Congress held in Oslo in the summer of 1935. It is also significant that the problem did not even figure in the discussion on *Central Planning Production in Soviet Russia,* held during the meeting of the American Economic Association in Chicago on 28th December, 1928, in spite of the fact that the president of the congress, Professor Fred. M. Taylor, had the previous day chosen *The Guidance of Production in a Socialist State* as the subject of his opening speech.[12]

That the question of economic calculation has not been more ventilated is due to the fact that but few have been

---

[12] See *American Economic Review,* 1929, p. 1.

aware of the existence of such a problem. The explanation of this is partly that in our capitalist (i.e. *private* capitalist) society there are, or at any rate, have been, markets with a relatively free price formation and relatively free competition on both the buying and the selling side. The markets themselves have provided the data needed for economic calculation, while competition together with the necessity for accounting have created the need for economic calculation. Thus the question of economic calculation has never existed as a "problem" in countries with relatively free markets, and it was only individual economists, those particularly interested in the socialist order of society, who discovered that here was a problem of wide implication.

The importance of this problem is fully recognized by those who have taken part in its discussion, irrespective of their sympathies. One of the few economists of Marxist leanings who have occupied themselves with the question, Dr. Otto Leichter, wrote:

> The mere admission that such a question exists and the understanding of the tremendous importance of its solution, are so hard to achieve, that one can well understand the paucity of the attempts made to solve it. To Max Weber and Ludwig Mises really belongs the merit of having so energetically drawn the attention of socialists to this question. However little it was the intention of Mises to contribute by his criticism to the positive development of socialist theory and praxis, yet honour must be given where honour is due.[13]

Dr. Oskar Lange ironically expressed the same appreciation when writing that:

---

[13] *Die Wirtschaftsrechnung in der Sozialistischen Gesellschaft,* Vienna, 1923, p. 74.

> A statue of Professor Mises ought to occupy an honourable place in the great hall of the Ministry of Socialization or of the Central Planning Board of a socialist state . . . both as an expression of recognition for the great service rendered by him and as a memento of the prime importance of sound economic accounting.[14]

The non-Marxian socialist Dr. Eduard Heimann wrote of the lack of understanding of the problem's existence:

> Blindness to this problem is responsible for the general poverty of the literature of socialization which despite excellent individual performances, gets no further than a semi-scientific and optimistic social policy, and ignores the actual economic, the theoretic character of its task.[15]

Professor F. A. Hayek is of the opinion that the chief reason for the problem having been neglected,[16] is that Karl Marx himself omitted to discuss the question of how the socialist state would work in practice, and that he kept others from doing so. Those of his disciples who went into the question were derided and stamped as "unscientific," the most awful malediction to which members of "the scientific school" could be exposed.[17]

The historical and "institutionalistic" viewpoint which characterizes every modern socialist movement has also had

---

[14] "On the Economic Theory of Socialism" in *Review of Economic Studies,* October 1936, p. 53.

[15] *Mehrwert und Gemeinwirtschaft,* Berlin, 1922, p. 178.

[16] For example, Hayek mentions that even in publications like *Annales de l'Économie Collective* and the material laid before the World Social Economic Congress at Amsterdam in 1931 (published by the International Relations Institute under the title *World Social Economic Planning,* 2 vols, The Hague, 1931–32) the problem is not discussed at all.

[17] See *Collectivist Economic Planning,* pp. 13–14.

its effect outside the Marxist camp and has hindered attempts to study the problems which a constructive socialist policy will have to solve. It was outside criticism which first made the socialists take up the question.[18]

A third explanation is that many economists have deliberately refrained from subjects touching on socialism, so as to avoid being accused of having prostituted science in the cause of politics, a point of view which, in the author's opinion, is untenable. In the first place, if economists are to refrain from every question which nowadays is brought into politics, their field of activity would be absurdly restricted, to the detriment both of themselves and of the treatment of important problems. Secondly, as far as the problem in question is concerned, it is really one of the few which should be capable of discussion without politics being brought into it.

It can, of course, be maintained that the result of a discussion of the socialist society is capable of being exploited, but this is an objection which cannot be sustained in a period when practically speaking any statement and any form of artistic, and much of scientific, activity, is sought to be politically exploited (or repressed, so as not to be politically exploited).

As far as our problem is concerned, it comes within the very narrow boundaries which Professor Lionel Robbins has set for pure economic science:

---

[18] "Professor Mises' challenge has had the great merit of having induced the socialists to look for a more satisfactory solution of the problem, and it is only too true that many of them became aware of its very existence only after this challenge" writes Dr. Oskar Lange in "On the Economic Theory of Socialism," part 2, in *Review of Economic Studies,* February, 1937, p. 142.

Economics is the science which studies human behaviour as a relationship between ends and scarce means which have alternative uses.[19]

Professor A. F. Pigou[20] wrote that the distribution of resources (a problem closely related to that with which we are concerned) is in a socialist society a "technical problem." The question of economic calculation in the socialist society should, therefore, be capable of being solved independently of any political or philosophic prejudice. Recognition of the fact that much of that which goes by the name of "bourgeois economics" has really been based on hidden political or philosophical assumptions,[21] gives subjects without such assumptions and prejudices an exceptional attraction.

The accusation that "bourgeois economics" is politically prejudiced is often followed (see, among others, Dobb and Vogt) by a recommendation of socialism as an economic

---

[19] See *An Essay on the Nature and Significance of Economic Science,* London, 1935, p. 15. See also Robbins' *Economic Planning and International Order,* London, 1937.

[20] *Socialism versus Capitalism,* London, 1937.

[21] See Max Weber: "Die 'Objektivität' sozialwissenschaftlicher und sozialpolitischer Erkenntnis" in *Gesammelte Aufsätze zur Wissenschaftslehre,* Tubingen, 1922; *Wirtschaft und Gesellschaft;* English translation: *Theory of Social and Economic Organization;* Professor Gunnar Myrdal: *Vetenskap och politik i nationalekonomien,* Stockholm, 1930: Johan Vogt: *Dogmenes sammenbrudd innenfor den socialökonomiske videnskap,* Olso, 1937; Professor L. M. Fraser: *Economic Thought and Language,* London, 1937; and Dr. Maurice Dobb: *Political Economy and Capitalism,* London, 1937. As early as 1923 Professor Wilhelm Keilhau made an attempt to free economics from existing tendentious points of view and old dogmas in *Die Wertungslehre, Versuch einer exakten Beschreibung der ökonomischen Grundbeziehungen,* Jena, 1923.

system. This is yet another reason for investigating its practicability.

Even when discussing a subject which seems capable of objective treatment, one can scarcely expect to escape charges of writing with political bias. These charges have now taken on such ingenious forms that they are hard to refute. No longer is the primitive objection made, that a statement is contrary to the truth; it is also old-fashioned to say that an opponent is mistaken, though subjectively honest. Nowadays the opponent's point of view is accepted as a point of view, but is dismissed on the grounds that the person concerned is not in a position to argue objectively by reason of his belonging to a certain social class, or because he has grown up in a certain milieu.[22]

Dr. Johan Akermann made an interesting commentary on this in a book,[23] where he mentions the Marxist belief that all economic research is completely tendentious, and adds:

> Were this idea to be carried to its logical conclusion and accepted in that form, it would mean the complete victory of the anti-intellectual forces and the ruin of social science.[24]

That those who take part in the discussion of the possibility of economic calculation in the socialist society do not escape the charge of basing their work on latent political prejudices, can be seen from Dr. A. P. Lerner's ironical

---

[22] See amongst others Karl Mannheim: *Ideologie und Utopie*, Bonn, 1929.
[23] *Das Problem der sozialökonomischen Synthese*, Lund, 1938.
[24] *Op. cit.*, p. 99.

introduction to *Economic Theory and Socialist Economy.*[25]

> . . . they (the socialists) simply denied both the relevance and
> validity of the 'Mises' arguments, and considered them as base-
> less and calumnious inventions for turning the mind of the mul-
> titude away from the socialist path. The arguments were de-
> nounced as meaningless anti-socialist propaganda, produced by
> reactionary professors sacrificing their interest in scientific truth
> at the altar of class interest. They might be the victims of a
> class ideology which made it impossible for them to envisage
> a society in which their class had lost its place or they might
> be mercenarily selling their theories to the capitalist for cash.
> In either case their arguments were just part of the spate of
> anti-socialist propaganda, but did not deserve serious discus-
> sion. The department to deal with 'Mises' was not the 'Gosplan'
> but the OGPU.

To characterize the problem of economic calculation as
completely free from value-judgments, would be too categorical. Any statement can ultimately be said to rest on a
value-judgment. If one accepts this point of view, then there
is all the less reason for deriding the classical economists'
hidden prejudices, hidden from them, but not necessarily
by them.

As far as the present problem is concerned, it is not assumption free from value-judgment, if, for example, one
substantiates the need for economic calculation by referring
to the necessity of arriving at a "rational" allocation of resources. Rational for what? For maximizing production,
for maximizing satisfaction of needs, or for what? Here the
end must be known. The rationality of a statement, action
or enterprise cannot be judged unless its objective is known,
and the ends we have mentioned are neither necessarily
compatible, nor acceptable to all.

---

[25] *Review of Economic Studies,* 1934–35, p. 51.

It must be recognized that the terms "rational" and "rationality" are in themselves nominative,[26] but if the term "rational" is applied, not to the objective, but exclusively to the means and methods used to attain it, irrespective of its character, then one is on safer ground.[27] Go a step further and maintain that economic policy at any given moment must be *consistent* and that one must employ means which are compatible and do not prevent the given end from being attained, and one is, presumably, on the safe side.[28]

One is also on safe ground—*in casu* free from value-judgments—when one says that economic activity in any society, irrespective of its framework and form, must follow "the economic principle," by which is understood that one seeks to attain the greatest possible result in relation to the expenditure, or to attain a given result by employing the least possible expenditure (the least possible sacrifice).

Finally one is on safe (objective) ground in maintaining that *survey* is indispensable both in order to follow "the economic principle" and in order to judge if the economic policy, which is being followed, is consistent. Accept these principles and you also accept the necessity for economic calculation.

In discussing the possibility of economic calculation in

---

[26] For further comments, see L. M. Fraser: *Economic Thought and Language*, p. 39.

[27] The object here is not to discuss the conception of rationality in its different connections. On this see Sven Helander: *Rationale Grundlagen der Wirtschaftspolitik*, Nürnberg, 1933.

[28] Professor Oskar Morgenstern writes in *The Limits of Economics,* London, 1937, that *"the principle of the freedom of inconsistency* of economic policy is the only scientific economic principle which can be formulated without passing value-judgments," p. 53 (author's italics).

the socialist society, it has also been said that "marginalism" is such a principle free of value-judgments and one which will and must assert itself in any society whatever, irrespective of its political form. The correctness of this assertion depends on how one defines "marginalism." If by that is meant the same as "the economic principle" (see Professor Knight's definition below), then marginalism is free from value-judgments. If, however, one translates marginalism as the principle of marginal comparison, then the matter becomes a little more doubtful. If one says that the principle of marginal comparison expresses the praxis of adding and subtracting small quantities when making technical, emotional and mental comparisons, then this principle is capable of being employed in nearly every field of life. If, however, marginal utility is defined as increase in utility in relation to increase in quantity of the commodity concerned, when both the increase in profit and in quantity are minimal or infinitesimal (the marginal sacrifice being correspondingly defined), this presupposes a subjective and individual judgment, which cannot be brought into such a discussion as this without certain reservations. It is true that the individual in a socialist, as well as in a private capitalistic state will act (within the scope of existing possibilities) with regard to marginal profit and marginal sacrifice. However, it is possible that in the socialist state regard for the wants and needs of the individual will be replaced by official scales of requirements and that the extent to which individuals can practice the marginal principle will be strictly limited or entirely eliminated. If it is the central authority, and not the individual, which exercises the function of determining the society's savings and investments (for definitions see Chapter 8) the universal application of the principle of marginal comparison becomes still more doubtful.

The relationship of "marginalism" to our theme was discussed at the American Economic Association's meeting in March, 1936, when Professor F. H. Knight gave a paper on *The Place of Marginal Economics in a Collectivist System*.[29] There appeared many different interpretations of the idea. Professor Knight's definition of marginalism coincides with that of "the economic principle" given above:

> For the principles of marginalism are the largest, mathematical and universal principles of economy, i.e. of maximizing the return from any resources used in accordance with any technique, to secure any form of return.

Nevertheless, in the course of the discussion Professor Knight[30] was attacked by Professor William Orton for employing "the marginal principle" and for insisting that it is only the individual's estimate of satisfaction and cost which should count.[31] This Professor Knight did not do, but the objection shows how the mere word "marginalism" is associated with the concepts of subjective marginal utility and marginal sacrifice, but these we will leave out of the discussion for the time being.

We will, therefore, content ourselves with demonstrating the necessity of economic calculation on the grounds that we thus achieve "survey," and because such a comprehensive picture is a necessary prerequisite before one can determine whether the economic principle is being followed

---

[29] See *American Economic Review*, 1936 Supplement.

[30] *Op. cit.*, p. 253.

[31] *Ibid.*, p. 287.

and whether one is acting consistently so as to attain a given end.

As far as we have been able to ascertain, these principles have been accepted by all who have taken part in this discussion, both by those who doubt, and by those who maintain, the possibility of economic calculation in the socialist society. The reader is referred to the quotation from Professor F. H. Knight (one of the doubters) given above. In his paper he said that "marginalism" (by which he understands "the economic principle") is valid in theory and in practice, irrespective of whether the collectivist society allows individuals to determine their requirements or whether this is done by governmental fiat.

Professor Boris Brutzkus has said:

> No economist would willingly dispute the correctness of the proposition that every economic activity—whether it be carried on within the framework of a natural, a capitalist or a socialist economy—must obey the principle that its results must correspond to the cost expended upon them. Not in vain is this principle deemed to be an essential characteristic of economic activity. . . .[32]

Dr. Cläre Tisch, who is one of those who believe that economic calculation in a socialist society is possible, has the same estimate of the subject's significance:

> If there is any truth in this objection (that the socialist economy is not capable of rational administration and calculation), this destroys the possibility of any socialist economy; in such a case a socialist community is, it is true, perhaps conceivable,

---

[32] *Economic Planning in Soviet Russia,* p. 9.

but it is no longer an economy, that is to say, it is no longer able to dispose of the means at its command.[33]

Dr. Tisch refers to Professor Gustav Cassel who regards it as a matter of course that there must exist conformity between cost and result, if there is any question of economic activity.[34]

Dr. Otto Leichter, who likewise is one of the champions, is also of the opinion that the question

goes to the essence of things. It is neither more nor less than a question of the possibility of socialist economy as such, for an economy in which it is not possible to compare expenditure and result, to say nothing of bringing them intentionally into a certain, desirable relationship, is irrational. Such an economy . . . is in the long run impossible, for it must soon become bankrupt and sink into a state of complete unsurveyability. The question of whether or not economic calculation is possible in a socialist society, is, in fact, one of the questions on which depends the fate of socialism.[35]

A third participant in the discussion, Dr. Oskar Lange, who also is of the opinion that economic calculation is possible in a socialist society, writes:

The rules of consistency of decisions and of efficiency in carrying them out are in a socialist economy exactly the same as those that govern the actual behaviour of entrepreneurs in a purely competitive market.[36]

---

[33] *Wirtschaftsrechnung und Verteilung im zentralistisch organisierten sozialistischen Gemeinwesen,* Wuppertal-Elberfeld, 1932, p. 2.

[34] *Theoretische Sozialökonomie,* p. 5.

[35] *Op. cit.,* p. 12.

[36] *Review of Economic Studies,* February, 1937, p. 123.

A fourth and further champion, Dr. Maurice Dobb, goes so far as to say:

> because of the light it (economic accounting and calculation in planned economies) throws on the significance of economic concepts, the issue may well be a crucial one on which the whole future of economic theory may turn.[37]

---

[37] "Economic Theory and the Problems of Socialist Economy" in *Economic Journal,* December, 1933, p. 598.

2

Definitions and Assumptions

In principiis latet error, latet veritas

It saves both time and words, if concepts are clearly defined and their boundaries distinctly traced. For the sake of clarity it is usually helpful to go back to the origins of the concept, while for its delimitation one must consider adjacent spheres.

The word *calculation* comes from the Latin *calces* (chalk used in the Greek and Latin abacus). In a number of languages *calculation,* or rather the corresponding foreign word of the same origin, means computation in its wide sense, while in others it is used not only of computation of objects or relationships capable of quantitative measurement, but also in the sense of judgment and conjecture. In trade and economics calculation generally means a computation of what a commodity will cost collectively or as a unit, at purchase or sale.

The need for calculation arises partly out of competition and partly from the demand and the necessity for survey. In *trade* the basis of calculation is the purchase price of the commodity (foreign currency being converted), to which

is added freight, packing, insurance (where goods are
bought c.i.f.), duty, loss of interest, wastage and other
charges. In *industry* the object of calculation is to determine
what the commodity produced costs the producer. Here the
basis is the purchase price of the raw or semi-manufactured
materials used, to which is added all the costs connected
with its manufacture: wages, power, wear and tear, amortization and wastage, together with the general charges of the
producer himself. The size and nature of these depends
on whether the concern in question sells through wholesalers or direct to the public. In any circumstances there
are the additional charges of interest on capital, property taxes, administration, office, warehousing and des-
patching. In the last few years much work has been done
on cost accounting and the classification of the various
items. The foregoing enumeration of costs pretends neither
to be complete nor to coincide with the latest authorized
terminology, but is given merely to show that in a society
based on private economy calculation is built up of many
different data. This does not mean to say that in a socialist
society the same data are necessary in order to be able to
undertake a calculation.

We have already said that calculation signifies "computation of what a commodity will cost, collectively or as a
unit, at purchase or on sale." Can this be used as a definition? It does not appear that there need be any hesitation in
using the word "computation." The word "commodity" has
in Marxist literature been given a special definition which
makes the term ambiguous, especially when it has to be
used in a treatise on "the socialist community." Let us then
substitute for it "economic good or service," leaving aside
for the moment what is meant by economic.

The word "cost" is ambiguous and therefore undesirable in itself; it is especially so for our purpose. In ordinary speech "cost" is usually expressed in money and represents an exchange value. However, we do not know whether our socialist society will use money or, therefore, whether money-prices will exist. It is not even permissible to assume the existence of "commodity prices" and "relative barter prices," as we do not know, so far, whether markets and barter will be allowed in a socialist society.

Now, in economic theory "cost" has other meanings. The economist distinguishes between "money cost" and "real cost." This is in reality not a distinction, but only two ways of expressing "cost." "Cost" may be conceived to mean either (1) the efforts and resources which go to produce a thing (also called "pain costs" or "embodied costs") or (2) what is given up to produce (also called "displacement costs," "alternative costs," or "opportunity costs"). The term "sacrifice costs" can be used both of "embodied costs" and of "displacement costs."[1]

"Embodied costs" tend to be expressed in real terms. They would, therefore, seem to be well suited to our purpose, but this is not the case. Some forms of physical energy and some physical quantities are capable of being measured exactly in real terms, e.g. electric energy and some materials with an unvarying and standard quality, but in most

---

[1] See L. M. Fraser, *Economic Thought and Language*, p. 92. Chapter VI *op. cit.*, *Costs*, gives an excellent survey and also a good illustration of the difficulty in limiting the concept. Professor Fraser clearly shows the importance of the cost-concept for the value theory and points out—very rightly—that "the tacit adoption of a cost conception of value, and of a money-embodied conception of cost, decided the range of classical value-theory" (p. 96).

cases quality is not only variable, but very difficult to express in real terms. As an example may be mentioned the general fertility of a piece of land. When it comes to such cost factors as physiological quantities (e.g. human labour, skill and knowledge) the existence of a varying degree of quality is obvious. So is their importance and the difficulty in expressing exactly in real terms the differences in physiological quality.

Even if we concentrate on the second meaning of "cost," i.e. what is given up to produce a thing (the "displacement costs"), the difficulties are not avoided. In the first place "displacement costs" are usually expressed in money or as an exchange value, the existence of which we have no right to assume in a discussion of socialist economy. If, secondly, we try to measure "displacement costs" in real, nonmonetary terms, they are determined by the varying degrees of "disutility" per unit of work done. We cannot go into all the questions raised by the introduction of this concept; the main thing is that the disutility is a variable factor measured differently by the different contributors to the productive process. It means that costs are determined in psychological and subjective terms, and this means that we have introduced an element of value.

It is possible that such an element is unavoidable in this discussion. The concept of value always has been, and presumably always will be, the central and most debated one in economics, and one which continually recurs in any discussion of "economic calculation." However, this is reason enough to avoid the concept in definitions and particularly so in a book on socialist theory. If, e.g., we define calculation as "computation of a commodity's value" and then later give a "subjective"[2] definition of the concept of value, we undertake *a priori* an inadmissible limitation of the scope of our investigation, in that by doing so we preclude solutions based on an "objective" (Marxist) theory of value. If, on the other hand, we give an "objective" definition of the concept of value, we exclude the possibilities of calculation which have to be based on subjective value-reactions.

To sum up: "costs" is a motley and undesirable concept to introduce in definitions and especially in a discussion of socialist economy. If we analyze the concept we find that it implies and refers to the existence of factors such as money, prices, exchange, markets, quality and value. It is possible that some of these factors are unavoidable in any society which is based on division of labour and is working towards an end, but it is preferable not to include them when one is still at the definition stage of the discussion. In spite of its undesirability, however, there seems to be no better term at hand, and we are, therefore, reluctantly forced to use "cost" even in our definition. To avoid any misunderstanding it must be emphasized that the term, as it is used in the definition, does not necessarily imply the existence of money, exchange, prices or markets; nor is it implied that the cost elements are reduced to a common denominator; nor is any definite way of determining quality or value prescribed. We do not by definition exclude the possibility of calculation *in natura* and accept preliminarily

---

[2] "Subjective" is here used as the antithesis to the classical theory of value (carried to the extreme in the Marxist "objective" theory of value) and does not indicate any qualitative definition in the word's meaning of one-sidedness.

any cost in any form of efforts, resources and disutility, ir-respective of how measured.

After this the following definition of calculation will be adopted: *By calculation is understood computation of what an economic good, acquired or self-produced, collectively or as a unit, "costs" in its acquisition (or will "cost" at the moment of its disposal) irrespective of how the costs are measured.*

Wilhelm Keilhau gives a special definition of calculation in his *Wertungslehre,* where he speaks of (1) Valuations *in pre-time* of the economic activity. (2) Valuations *in co-time (status valuations).* (3) Valuations *in post-time (statements of results).*[3]

Incidentally, Professor Keilhau here draws attention to two concepts which, thanks to the "Swedish school," have in recent years been much used in the terms "ex-ante" and "ex-post." (These concepts have, besides, a deeper significance than those of prospective and retrospective estimates, but this is a question which it would take too long to discuss here.) Professor Gunnar Myrdal similarly speaks of "calculations concerning future development," while on the other hand he speaks of analysis of cost and *post facto* analysis.[4] It is very useful to distinguish between advance analysis and *post facto* analysis. There is a great difference between a *post facto* computation with known data and an advance computation where a number of factors will of necessity be uncertain. By dividing them into advance and *post facto* analyses there is introduced a factor which, consciously or unconsciously, has always played a large part

---

[3] Pp. 192–193 (author's italics).

[4] *Prisbildningsproblemet och föränderligheten,* Uppsala, 1927.

in industrial computations, namely, expectations, a factor which in recent years has assumed an honoured place even in theoretical literature.

The writer is not inclined to restrict the meaning of calculation to advance computation. In the first place it is not in accordance with the general use of the word in the Scandinavian and English-speaking countries, and in the second place such a special definition is all the less appropriate in view of Dr. Erik Lindahl's expressions "ex-ante" and "ex-post." Particularly in this treatise, where we are concerned with investigating whether in the socialist community there is any possibility at all of economic computation, irrespective of whether for the future or for the past, there is little reason to define calculation so as merely to cover budgeting and advance computation. What we shall investigate is the basis itself, both for advance computation and for what Keilhau and Myrdal respectively call statements of results and analysis of cost.

The concept of socialism is a controversial one. Disputes have, and presumably always will, rage as to what shall be understood by socialism[5] and as to how the socialist society shall be organized. There are, however, two main criteria for socialism which are generally accepted in scientific discussions: that the State owns the means of production, and that the State controls industrial life. Here the following definition will be adopted: *A socialist society is a society in which* (1) *the private ownership of means of production is*

---

[5] For a survey of this see, *inter alia,* Professor F. J. C. Hearnshaw: *A Survey of Socialism,* London, 1929. Dan Griffith gives in *What is Socialism?* London, 1924, 261 definitions. Werner Sombart in *Deutscher Sozialismus,* Berlin, 1934, gives the subject elaborate treatment and the concept a very wide definition.

abolished, and (2) *business initiative is invested in a central authority which alone directs industrial activity.* By "means of production" is understood both manufactured means of production, such as tools, machinery, factories and means of transport, and "natural" means of production such as land, mines and water power. The term resources will for the time being be used in the sense of material *means of production,* and the term *factors of production* in the sense of material *means of production plus labour.*

As we have spoken of *economic* calculation and in defining calculation have used the term *economic* (of services and goods), it may be asked what is meant by "economic." Practically every economist who has discussed economic theory or written economic textbooks, has given his own definition of what he understands by economic activity (and by the *subject* of economy, also called "economics"). It lies outside the scope of this book thoroughly to discuss these various concepts, but it may be briefly mentioned that these definitions fall into two main groups, the first of which associates economy with prosperity, riches and welfare, and lays the main stress on the production, interchange, distribution and in part consumption of commodities. The second group connects economy with scarcity.

Dr. Johan Akermann gave a neat, comprehensive definition when he wrote:

> . . . in order to complete the schematic representation, we shall say that the central question of political economy amounts to a systematic causal analysis of the repetitive phenomena which occur when individuals or groups—through consumption, interchange, production and trade—adopt an attitude to scarce material goods.[6]

---

[6] *Das Problem der Sozialökonomischen Synthese,* p. 16.

For Professor Myrdal economy as a subject is taboo. In his opinion it is not only unnecessary, but evidently *the* unforgivable sin for an economist to occupy himself with this question. He writes:

> Any attempt to define political economy as a science, does violence to reality . . . they want to have a definition which will make it possible to smuggle a normative content into the scientific experiment.[7]

and later:

> The only concept which an economist does not need to worry about trying to define, is just that of political economy.

It would be thought that particularly those economists who are of the opinion that economics is misused and turned into a normative branch of knowledge, will appreciate a clear-cut formulation and a limitation of the provinces within which an economist *qua* economist has the right to speak. This does not mean that the economist cannot and may not encroach on adjacent provinces and borrow from other sciences, least of all psychology.

Of the definitions which can be relegated to one or other of the two main groups, those of the first group make the limits of the economist's scope flexible.[8] The concepts pros-

---

[7] *Vetenskap och politik i Nationalökonomien,* pp. 230–231.

[8] Professor A. C. Pigou uses a less flexible definition in as far as he says that economic welfare is a part of social welfare which directly or indirectly can be brought into relation with money as a yard-stick. (*Economics of Welfare,* 3rd Edition, London, 1929.) This restriction cannot be accepted in our case, since we do not want to presuppose the use of money in a socialist society.

For analogous reasons we must reject the definition of economics which is based on economic theory as the study of market processes

perity, wealth and welfare are in themselves questionable and capable of definition in different ways. The first group gives to the concept of "economic activity" a functional significance, in as far as it is not the activity as such which determines whether it is economic or not economic, but what is intended by it. A round of golf can be an uneconomic employment of time, but it can also be an economic factor for a business man wishing to keep fit and increase his economic efficiency. The same can be said of such seemingly uneconomic activities as playing bridge or reading detective stories.

The other group of definitions, as we have said, associates economics with scarcity. According to these the economic problem is that of how to economize, or of how to be economical. The typical representatives of this school are Professor Gustav Cassel and Professor Lionel Robbins, the basis of whose argument is that in a society composed of individuals with different desires and needs there are not sufficient resources—meaning capital goods *and* natural assets—to cover all the requirements of all individuals, and that it is therefore necessary to make a choice between alternative uses.

Robbins' point of view, which is shared by many economists and among them many followers of the Vienna School, has on the other hand been fiercely attacked by both economists and others. Thus the biologist Professor Lancelot Hogben said in a Conway Memorial Lecture in

---

(formulated—but not accepted by Barbara Wootton among others—in *Lament for Economics,* London, 1938). We cannot assume the existence of markets in a socialist society. The above definition involves an unwarrantable and unrealistic restriction which—as a definition—robs economic theory of its general validity.

May, 1936, during a violent attack on economists in general, that Professor Lionel Robbins offers "a barren dialectic of scarcity . . . as a substitute for a genuine science of the wealth of nations."[9] Professor Edwin Cannan also criticized Robbins' chief point of view when reviewing his book[10] and it has similarly been the subject of an attack by Professor L. M. Fraser.[11] If the economists retire to their own selected areas and restrict their activity to studies of prices, the problems will be treated by demagogues and fanatics with no interest in logical reasoning and no knowledge of economic technique. Fraser throws some light on the matter when he writes that according to Robbins' definitions even discussions as to the nature and significance of economic science might be supposed to belong not to economics, but to logic or philosophy.

It may be said for Professor Robbins' definition, that it has a precision and a clarity, which those of the first group lack, and it must be admitted that it is inspired by a sympathetic desire to make economics a theoretical, nonnormative science; yet there is no denying that it makes economic theory very formalistic and that it seems doubtful whether economics can be given scientific status on the basis of such a limitation of its subject matter.

It may be noted that our problem, the investigation of the possibility of *economic* calculation, fits equally well into either group of definitions. Calculation is concerned with the state of production and distribution, thus agreeing with

---

[9] See *The Retreat from Reason,* London, 1936, p. 19.
[10] See *Economic Journal,* September, 1932.
[11] "How Do We Want Economists to Behave?" in *Economic Journal,* December, 1932.

the first group, and represents precisely the study of the distribution of limited resources of the second group. Since the term "economic good" is used in the definition of calculation, it may be remarked that here, too, the element of scarcity comes in. *By "economic good" is here understood material objects or services of any kind, which are desired and which exist in limited quantity or number.* Since the term "economic good" has been introduced into the definition of calculation, it is strictly speaking unnecessary to characterize calculation as "economic," but it is done to show that calculation is not only concerned with production and distribution, but with conditions which presuppose scarcity, such as necessitate a choice between alternative uses if it is desired to ensure that the sacrifice does not become greater than the result ("the economic principle"). Actually it is the scarcity of resources which enforces the necessity of economic calculation and is its *raison d'être.*

It is necessary to emphasize that two fundamental assumptions are implied in our interpretation of "economic good." The first is that a good, in order to earn the designation "economic," must be needed, which in fact means that the factor of value is introduced. If, as is usual, one maintains that the utility of a good must be determined subjectively—by subjectively meaning that the utility is decided by the individual—it can be doubted whether it is justifiable to introduce the concept of utility into a discussion of the socialist state, since socialism is based largely on the Marxian, or so-called objective, theory of value. It must, therefore, be expressly stated that we have *not* said that utility must be decided by the individual member of society. Karl Marx and his adherents have themselves had to concede that there may be produced commodities which are "useful,"[12] adding that the commodities produced must be useful socially and for the society. It may be noted that the decision is subjective whether it is made on behalf of oneself or of the other members of society, and whether it is made by an individual or by a group of individuals. The crucial point in this connection is that we accept that utility can be determined by the leader (or leaders) of the socialist community and not necessarily by the individual members of the community. Consequently references to "utility" do not imply that one has quietly introduced an assumption which conflicts with the socialist theory of value.

The other fundamental assumption implied in the definition is that, mentioned earlier, of scarcity of resources. This assumption has been generally accepted by all economists, even by those whose definitions belong to the first, or functional, group. This assumption of the scarcity of resources is so generally accepted that it may seem unnecessary to discuss it further. However, one cannot overlook the fact that lately doubts have been expressed as to its validity.[13] That these doubts can arise in the minds of the general public is understandable, and they are natural, for example, in times when there are unutilized factors of production (including labour) and large unsold stocks of commodities. These doubts are also caused by technocratic propaganda and calculations made by engineers, bio-technicians and agrarian physiologists regarding the *technical* possibilities

---

[12] For further quotations, see Chapter 6.

[13] See, *inter alia*, H.R. 7188. *Monetary Policy of Plenty instead of Scarcity.* (Hearings before the Committee on Banking and Currency, House of Representatives, July–August, 1937; January–February–March, 1938.) U.S. Government Printing Office, Washington, 1938.

of production (when the aspect of costs is forgotten or disregarded). There would be little reason for discussing these tendencies, if some economists had not—indirectly, it is true—begun to support these doubts.

Thus Mrs. Barbara Wootton writes:

> . . . yet the odd thing about actual economic life is that miracles apparently can happen—that the basic assumption of scarcity does not always hold.[14]
>
> And it cannot be too strongly emphasized that the non-fulfilment of this condition (assumption of scarcity of resources), renders inoperative, irrelevant and unreal the *whole* corpus of economic studies as defined by Professor Robbins and as embodied in the classical analysis and its contemporary elaborations and refinements.[15]

Mrs. Wootton says elsewhere that under the given assumption:

> the whole of the traditional theory of international trade, e.g. as elaborated at length by Professor Taussig, becomes ridiculous.[16]

Mrs. Wootton is logically *in salvo* as these statements are made on the assumption of non-scarcity. It is, nevertheless, astounding that she should make such categorical statements on that basis, not least since she had previously[17] given a clear and witty description of the significance of price mechanism which obviously accepted the assumption

---

[14] *Lament for Economics,* London, 1938, pp. 92 and 93.

[15] *Ibid.,* p. 106.

[16] *Ibid.,* p. 95. A footnote refers to Professor Taussig's *Theory of International Trade.*

[17] *Plan or No Plan,* London, 1934.

of scarcity. Yet in her last book Mrs. Wootton labels the theory of scarcity with the words—to-day so dreaded—"fundamentally orthodox." Her inspiration has come from Professor J. M. Keynes' *General Theory of Employment, Interest and Money,* with its strong emphasis on involuntary unemployment. She is of the opinion that Professor Keynes' argument "undermines the whole assumption of scarcity."[18]

The strong emphasis laid by Mrs. Wootton on non-scarcity can possibly be explained by her desire to show how sharp is the antagonism between leading economists, and thus to demonstrate the necessity of "lamenting" theoretical economics. When it comes to the point, however, Mrs. Wootton herself makes various reservations. That she calls the assumption of scarcity "the most fundamental of all his (the economist's) fundamental postulates"[19] cannot be laid against her, since she obviously dissociates herself from this point of view. On the other hand she seems to be expressing her own opinion when she writes:

> In that sense a commodity remains scarce as long as the supply of it is not sufficient to satisfy all conceivable demands without any price whatever being charged for it—a condition which is hardly anywhere in sight of being realized, even if we imagine all monopolistic restraints upon production to be removed. Everything which has a price is by that very fact demonstrated to be in some degree scarce, even if its physical output is reckoned in astronomical figures.[20]

She also seems to be giving her own opinion when she writes:

---

[18] *Ibid.,* p. 96.
[19] *Ibid.,* p. 90.
[20] *Lament for Economics,* p. 93.

. . . gluts are quite easily explicable in terms of the orthodox market mechanism for distributing scarce means, even though they may appear temporarily and superficially to belie the fact of 'scarcity'.

Thus Mrs. Wootton is quite aware what non-scarcity implies and she speaks ironically of the possible consequences of digging holes in the ground and filling them up again— a reflection which presumably most of those who have read Keynes' book will have made. She also draws the logical conclusion from the assumption of non-scarcity and points out that those who build on it must stop criticizing "pump-priming," unproductive middlemen, the construction of warships and the maintenance of unproductive classes of society,

for what more effective way of spending is there than the maintenance of an unproductive class?[21]

In the best Veblen style she says that both unproductive middlemen and warships are "conspicuous forms of supposedly prosperity-bringing waste."[22]

In spite of all her reservations and despite the fact that some of her comments almost reduce the assumption of non-scarcity to absurdity, the upshot is that Mrs. Wootton has placed this assumption on an almost equal footing with that of scarcity. In doing so she refers to Professor Keynes' *General Theory* and to Professor Hayek's *Prices and Production*. Whether Keynes and Hayek will accept this implication we do not know, but that such an implication *can* be made, has necessitated this review of the question and

---

[21] *Ibid.,* p. 101.
[22] *Ibid.,* p. 101.

forces us to state expressly that this book is based on the assumption of scarcity of resources. The periodical non-utilization of available factors of production is no proof at all that we have left the stage of scarcity. Such periodical non-utilization can to a great extent be explained as a natural link in the process of adaptation, which from time to time is necessary in an industrialized, dynamic society with a monetary economy and a highly developed division of labour. The permanently unsold stocks of commodities (and the consequent deliberate destruction of stocks) can be explained as a natural consequence of the price mechanism having been put more or less out of action, partly through the establishment of private monopolies and partly owing to public intervention which both restricts foreign trade and prescribes high minimum prices which stimulate production and reduce the number of buyers.[23]

Irrespective of whether or not one shares these points of view, it is a decisive objection against accepting the assumption of non-scarcity, that it—and this is of importance in discussing the question of calculation—implies that there exist resources sufficient to satisfy all requirements of all individuals. This is obviously not the case and is scarcely likely ever to be so in view of man's capacity both for developing fresh needs and the almost infinite elasticity of certain needs. This means that when employing resources a choice *must* be made between alternative uses, that one *must* economize, that economic calculation *must* be undertaken.

---

[23] Mrs. Wootton is besides fully aware of the existence of these interfering factors and their importance. See several passages in *Plan or No Plan* and *Lament for Economics,* p. 139.

3

Procedure–Additional Assumptions–The Aim of Social Economic Activity

There are various forms of socialism imaginable within the framework of a socialist society as we have defined it, ranging from that of a moneyless economy with compulsory labour to a community with an elaborate monetary economy and free choice of occupation and goods. It is possible that the need and possibility of economic calculation will be the same whatever the form of society, and that an investigation of each individual form would not make any fresh contribution to theory. This, however, is not probable, and we shall therefore examine the individual forms.

This can be done in one of two ways: we can either eliminate all irrelevant factors and establish so many simplifying assumptions that our conclusions become logically unassailable, or we can assume conditions which are likely to exist in reality.

The first method, an abstraction from reality, might not be unnatural in our case, seeing that we have already renounced (see preface) recourse to empirical material. Yet the practical value of the conclusions will be small if the conditions assumed are completely at variance with reality, as is the case with most assumptions used when discussing static societies. The following examples of such assumptions are typical: (*a*) that means of production are everlasting and that production does not take time (in order, if possible, to avoid the problem of interest and the interrelation between various changes in time);[1] (*b*) that the community in question is completely isolated and does not require imports from outside (in order, if possible, to avoid problems connected with international trade); (*c*) that no alteration takes place in the size or age-composition of the population, in the amount or rate of growth of savings, in technical development and in the tastes and customs of the people (in order, if possible, to avoid the problems of the trade-cycle and certain other difficulties).

One can, of course, gradually abandon those assumptions which are unrealistic and so get nearer to reality, but the more factors are introduced, the more uncertain and less logically unassailable the results tend to become. These remarks involve no criticism of economic theories based on static conditions in general. Abstraction from reality may be a first necessary step towards tackling problems from the world of reality. What, however, is a mistake—and a danger—is to apply the results of abstract experimental studies to everyday life.

It may be asked whether there is any need to aim at conclusions of practical significance. There is, of course, no necessity to do so. There is nothing to prevent us aiming merely at a theoretical, abstract solution, but since it is the socialist society which we are examining, it is nevertheless reasonable to look for conclusions which are also tenable

---

[1] The question of time's greater or smaller importance in the problem of interest is broached later.

in real life, and presumably no one will dispute the advantage of reaching conclusions which also have their practical value. (The question of theoretical *versus* practical conclusions is discussed more thoroughly in Chapter 15.)

The second method of procedure, that of accepting the fact that economic life is dynamic[2] and subject to constant change, is all the more natural in a treatise on the socialist society, as the protagonists of socialism promise more rapid economic progress. This, then, is the method we shall adopt, although in doing so we shall encounter more theoretical pitfalls and run a far greater risk of arriving at untenable conclusions.

The choice of dynamic analysis introduces a factor which is as confusing as it is important, namely, that of time. There are many interpretations of the distinctions between the static and the dynamic in economic theory. In

---

[2] The author does not mean that a static society is unreal—an antithetic conclusion some might try to draw. There have been static societies by which we mean societies where there are no alterations in the size or age-composition of the population, or in tastes or customs, where there is no technical development and no change in the size or rate of capital savings. Such societies exist in our day (in Asia). In such societies people will, of course, continue to be born and to die, but that need not necessarily alter the age-composition or size of the population. See Joseph Schumpeter's *Theorie der wirtschaftlichen Entwicklung,* Leipzig, 1912, and E. Böhm-Bawerk's review, "Eine dynamische Theorie des Kapitalzinsen," in *Zeitschrift für volkswirtschaftlichen Sozialpolitik und Verwaltung,* Vol. XXII, and his *Gesammelte Schriften,* Vol. II, Vienna and Leipzig, 1926.

Professor Mises' view is that: "a static state is impossible in real life" (*Collectivist Economic Planning,* p. 109).

It might be more accurate to speak of a *stationary* society, instead of "static," and for "dynamic" to use *evolutionary.* Cf. Ragnar Frisch's "Statikk og Dynamikk i den økonomiskc Teori," *Nationaløkonomisk Tidskrift,* 1939.

1926 Dr. Rudolf Streller enumerated eight groups of definitions[3] and their number has not diminished since. As is indicated above, we understand by a dynamic society one which undergoes changes in certain directions. Now, changes and variations are also conceivable in a static society, but such are

> from their nature not real variations in time, but formal variations resulting from a comparison of different and more fully specified situations, the realization of which are considered *as alternatives*. In this sense the static law is *timeless* law.[4]

What characterizes dynamic analysis is that the situations compared are a series of successive situations.

> Any theoretic law in the formulation of which the concept of rate of growth or that of rate of reaction (as to time) is implied, is a dynamic law. All other theoretic laws are static.[5]

By choosing the dynamic form of analysis we have introduced time as a necessary factor, and this means that its significance should be taken into account in every condition discussed. The interval between the points of time chosen for the comparison of changes may totally alter the result. If the interval between the points of time of observation is shortened, the result may assume a diametrically opposite character. A month's balance can show a loss, while the year's balance for the same business shows a profit. The

---

[3] *Statik und Dynamik in der theoretischen Nationalökonomie*, Leipzig, 1926.

[4] See Ragnar Frisch, *op. cit.*, p. 322.

[5] *Op. cit.*, p. 325.

result of the first year's working of a ten-year contract can be favourable, while the final result may be unfavourable. In the same way the time fixed for carrying through a plan of production will have a decisive effect in a number of spheres both technical and economic, and, of course, on the possibility of the members of the community receiving the benefits of the results. "In the long run we are all dead."

It is extremely difficult to give the time-factor the place it deserves at each step of an economic analysis. If this form of analysis is followed, we should, when discussing any factor whatever, take into account (*a*) how it (and changes in it) affect each of the other factors in the *total* development on the basis of *different* intervals of time, and (*b*) how the factor itself is affected by each of the other factors (and changes in them) on the basis of different intervals of time.

The ever-changing reciprocal influence between each of the economic factors ought to be shown and modifications described, not only quantitatively, but also qualitatively and in reference to the rate of growth. Whether such a task is practicable or not, it at any rate lies outside the scope of this treatise. If by dynamic investigation is understood investigation of the tide of events and of the rate of growth in the different factors and of how one condition grows out of another, then one ought to try to follow the causal chain backwards, which would involve the impossible task of going back to the beginning of time.

It must suffice to point out here that in a dynamic society there exists an intricate multiplicity of changing reciprocal effects varying with the period of time, and that we shall take up for special discussion only those states of time-relation which are obviously of essential importance for our investigation. In this connection it is worth mentioning that if we examine a certain form of socialist society *disregarding* dynamic factors and find that economic calculation is not possible, it will not be made more possible by introducing new variables in the form of fresh dynamic factors.

Let us assume the following conditions: the community we are to discuss is of a certain size, say with a population of at least two millions. But even if it were only a Robinson Crusoe and his man Friday, there would still be the need for economic calculation, but survey and control would be so easy that the calculation would not raise the same problems. We further assume exchange of economic goods and services which excludes from the discussion a society composed of self-supporting family units. It is also assumed —somewhat unrealistically—that the community in question is completely sclf-supporting and has no intercourse with other communities, and, further, that the individual members of the community are different, not only as regards sex and age, but also in physique, intelligence, mentality, artistic talent, manual dexterity, energy, vitality, taste and sensibility. It is assumed that these divergences are not exclusively due to upbringing and milieu, but also to biological, hereditary factors and to glandular action, which the society in question neither can nor desires to influence in order to achieve unity of human taste and needs. This assumption—which must be accepted or rejected for reasons which lie outside economics—may appear far-fetched and superfluous, but it is not. Economic activity and with it the question of economic calculation assume a different and simpler aspect, if the society deals with entirely homogenous individuals. That one may not assume that the type of person in the socialist community will be the same as in

the capitalist society is evident from Dr. Cläre Tisch's
treatise[6] in which she writes that:

> Socialism is absolutely unthinkable with people who have the
> egoistic, individualistic idea of economy of capitalism.[7]

Actually there are a number of socialists who consider
this a *sine qua non* of the socialist order of society. This is
easily seen in the case of the so-called Utopian socialists, but
the same idea can also be found, more or less clearly expressed, among modern socialists. Dr. Eduard Heimann,
for example, says:

> True Socialism can only be based on fundamental partner-
> ship, and not on material interest.[8]

As we do not wish to discuss the ethical and psychological character of the socialist community, we shall for the
time being accept—reluctantly—the doubtful assumption
that in such a society there is no such thing as an egoistic-
individualistic disposition. However, the fact that egoistic
interests are presumed to be absent, does not mean that
differences between individuals have also ceased to exist.

Another assumption which must be discussed is that of
the aim of the community's economic activity, a question
which academic economists as a rule are disinclined to
discuss, in the same way as they are shy of expressing sympathies. This timidity comes from their desire to be objective and as such is very creditable. It is an attitude, how-

---

[6] *Wirtschaftsrechnung und Verteilung im zentralistisch organisierten sozialistischen Gemeinwesen*, Wuppertal-Elberfeld, 1932.

[7] *Op. cit.*, p. 8, footnote.

[8] See *Mehrwert und Gemeinwirtschaft*, Berlin, 1922, p. 112.

ever, which not only has its drawbacks, but is not always possible to maintain, as when, for example, there are only two alternatives and an economist in pointing out certain consequences of one of them, consequences which are generally considered disastrous, indirectly recommends the other, whether or not this was intended. One lamentable consequence of this reluctance to express sympathies is that many economists refrain from discussing ends at all. There might be little harm in this at a time when the aim of the community's activity was generally recognized, but when, as at present, this is not the case, much of economic discussion dissolves into thin air, because the aim and, consequently, the yardstick for economic activity have not yet been decided upon.

It is the aim which determines the yardstick for valuation, and, if one goes deeper, it is the aim of the community which decides what is the official and social *value*. We shall not go into all the implications of this question, but merely point out that in communities where, broadly speaking, the aim of economic activity is to satisfy the needs of the members of the community, where distribution of the community's income takes place directly in or with the production and exchange of economic goods and this production and exchange is allowed, the concept of value will appear differently than in communities where all power over economic activity is transferred to a central authority, where the production and exchange of economic goods is forbidden to individuals, and where the division of the community's goods can be made independently of and without relation to the individual's contribution to production and distribution and even independently of his subjective valuations.

The individual's subjective valuation may be, and as a rule is, different from that of the community, whether the latter is determined by free or monopolistic fixation of price or by more or less arbitrary official decrees. Differences between an individual's subjective valuations and those of the community will be found in socialist as well as in capitalist societies. If, however, the members of the community are denied facilities for giving expression to their subjective valuations and the central authority has, by definition, every opportunity to do so, for example, by abolishing markets, and reserves for itself the right to fix prices and values, it is self-evident that this may result in valuations and concepts of value different from those usually represented in economic theory.

The need for some yardstick of valuation is clearly stated by Professor Frisch in the following, which has our full agreement:

> What in the long run interests the economist is to make a *comparison* between results which have been arrived at by different processes and by different ways of arranging the factors of production in one and the same process. This is essentially a *problem of valuation,* and the condition for its solution is not only that one employs concepts and standards technically defined, but that one either explicitly or implicitly accept a definite scale of valuation, a definite principle by which the various things with a technically different nomenclature can be compared. If one starts to analyse this valuation side of the production problem, without fully realizing the necessity for fixing a *basic scale for valuation,* the whole thing degenerates into subjective fantasies.[9]

---

[9] *Tekniske og økonomiske produktivitetslover,* a mimeographed, undated pamphlet based on R. Frisch's lectures and notes.

There are two reasons why it is particularly important that the aim of the socialist community should be clearly defined. Firstly, since all initiative is relegated to the central authority, every decision taken will have far greater consequences than in a society composed of individuals who each procure their daily bread by assisting in satisfying the needs of the others; and, secondly, because the necessity and possibility of economic calculation will depend on the character of the aim. Again, the aim must be known, if we are to be able to judge whether the means employed to attain the end are being used consistently.

Anything at all can be taken as the aim of the socialist society, even the—at any rate seemingly—absurd one of creating chaos. If the latter, there will, of course, be no need for calculation and survey. An actual underlying aim might be the desire to build up a strong war machine, of impressing the rest of the world with special achievements in various spheres, or the desire of an individual person or group to gain power,[10] just as it is possible to imagine a combination of competitive aims.

The aims most often given as those of the socialist community fall into two main groups: (1) *increased* production of goods and (2) their *just* distribution. Both are indefinite and thus difficult to treat, quite apart from the fact that it is objectively impossible to determine what "just distribution" is. Disregarding the ethical problem set by the second,

---

[10] The explanation of the enthusiasms of some political economists for socialism is not, as is often assumed, conscious desire for power. In addition to sympathy for their fellow-men there undoubtedly exists an altruistically coloured conviction among them that it would be best for the common weal if leadership was placed in their hands.

and confining ourselves for the time being to the first aim, it will generally be found that by "increased production" is not meant blind production of all and sundry, but of "useful" goods. There are different ways of expressing this, such as that the goods shall be "socially" useful, or "useful to the community," and in references to the "weal of the people," "social welfare," etc.

Closer investigation reveals that underlying this there is always the idea of satisfying needs or, more accurately, of attaining "maximum satisfaction of needs." It is possible that this is merely a pretext and that the real aim is what V. Pareto calls "derivation," Karl Mannheim "ideology," and the psychologist "rationalization." However, we can neither concern ourselves here with possible underlying motives or incidental aims, nor with all conceivable conditions of economic activity in a socialist society. The discussion must be restricted to the aim as it is generally declared and even if the *nature* of the aim is merely of technical interest in such an examination as this, it may be said that economic activity which aims at satisfying the needs of the people and at raising the standard of living can hardly be characterized as absurd.

Most who have taken part in this discussion of the possibility of calculation in a socialist society have, more or less explicitly, accepted satisfaction of needs as a natural aim for the economic activity of a socialist society. This view is expressed by Dr. A. P. Lerner thus:

> As a human being and a sympathizer with socialist ends, it seems to me that maximization on such lines is completely in the spirit of all socialist ideals and particularly sympathetic to the slogan of 'scientific socialism'—'to each according to his needs'. A superior contempt for the tastes and judgment of the

'masses', and a paternal solicitude in choosing for the people what is good for them, does not seem to me to be the avoidance of an unscientific major premise about 'sacredness' (of consumers' preferences).[11]

Now, it must be admitted that the "concept of welfare" as an aim is most unpopular in theoretical economics. It has been pointed out[12] with considerable acerbity, that the moral philosophers of the nineteenth century and a few economists of the twentieth have made use of this concept, particularly in its form of "maximum welfare" and "maximum satisfaction of needs," as a political slogan in defence of the existing social order and institutions. Such an objection is quite irrelevant where "the satisfaction of needs" is given as the aim of other and different forms of society. Thus, its acceptance as a reasonable aim no more implies adherence to the view that the existing capitalist "institutions" are the expression of the highest, divine wisdom, than it does to the view, so often put forward as the opposite one, that human nature is determined first and foremost by such "institutions."

Other objections can, however, be raised against this aim, or rather against the way it is formulated. The term "maximum" or "maximalization" is not a good one, as it conjures up a possibility of summation which does not exist in reality, since the valuations of the different individuals and social groups as to what satisfies their needs, are not commensurable data. It would be much better to speak of

---

[11] "Economic Theory and Socialist Economy" in *Review of Economic Studies*, 1934–35, pp. 53–4.

[12] Some particulars of the literature on the subject are given in the footnote on p. 8.

"maximum exploitation of the factors of production with a view to satisfying the needs of the members of the society."

As the members of the society are not only recipients of the community's goods, but also represent an important factor of production, "maximalization" can imply that this factor is so intensely exploited as to go beyond satisfaction of needs. If it is maintained that disutility must also be taken into account, then "optimalization" (of needs) might be a better expression than "maximalization." On the other hand this expression has a slightly moral flavour. What is "best" for man? Not only the priest, but also the dietician has very definite opinions on this matter. This objection to maximalization may be overcome by regarding leisure as a "good" and by requiring that this need must be satisfied too.

Actually it is not so important for the purpose of our discussion to have a precise definition of this, as the main thing is to make it quite clear that the society in question has satisfaction of the individual's needs in mind. As we shall see later, there are economists who think that the problem of calculation can be solved if, and *only* if, the central authority has sovereign powers and does not have to take the expressed needs of the community into consideration. What is important for our purpose is to be clear whether the community in question aims at satisfying the needs of its members, or not. To begin with we shall base our discussion on the assumption: that the aim will be *the maximum exploitation of the community's resources with the object of satisfying the needs of its members, including that of leisure.* As this is a long and awkward formula and one to which it will often be necessary to refer, we shall reduce it to: *"maximum production for needs."*

This formula is, both in its full and contracted form, incomplete, as it omits the factor of time. The possibility of satisfying the needs of the living members of the community will be greatly influenced by whether the central authority aims at the maximum utilization of factors of production for the manufacture of consumer goods or for the production of capital goods. In other words, whether it aims at attaining the maximum in the present or in the future, to the advantage of the present or future generations. The individual in the socialist community—and this is a point to which we shall return later—in contrast to the one in a private capitalist society, will be unable to exercise any influence in this respect. All decisions regarding savings and investments will be made by the central authority. It is very difficult to know the basis on which such decisions will be made, and we must confine ourselves to assuming that the periods allotted for developing the machinery of production will not be so long as to neglect the possibility of satisfying the needs of the living generation.

Before passing to the actual discussion, the author would like to draw attention to the remarks on the price mechanism in Appendix A.

Economists well know that it is the price mechanism which in the private-economic society[13] enables the production and distribution of goods to proceed in more or less perfect order *without* a central authority and *without* pub-

---

[13] As any society, even a socialist one, after a certain degree of development uses capital in the form of implements and manufactured means of production, it is more correct to use the expression "private-economic" or "private-capitalist" instead of "capitalist," if a contrast to "socialist" is looked for. "Private-economic" is probably the best expression to use adjectively, but since "private economy" has a special meaning of its own, the best substantive to use will presumably be "private-capitalism."

lic regulation. But non-economists are not always aware of the importance of the price mechanism, and, according to Dr. R. L. Hall, this is also true of many who have formed a definite opinion as to which form of society is to be preferred:

> In the opinion of the writer, few Socialists have grasped the complexity of the modern economic structure, which functions so unobtrusively that it is easy to take for granted the inter-relations of its parts, and to assume that we shall retain our present co-ordination in a new economic order without the deliberate organization of an alternative system. It is the duty of all who advocate a change to acquaint themselves with the probable implications of that change.[14]

It is not irrelevant in such a book as this to draw attention to the existence of such a mechanism, considering that it is this mechanism which in the private-economic society provides the necessary data for calculation. An idea of it provides a better background for discussing the need and possibility of calculation in the socialist and centrally managed communities.

However, the examination must not make us prejudiced. It must be stated beforehand that that which is a necessary assumption for calculation in a capitalist society, need not necessarily be so in a socialist one. There is *a priori* nothing to prevent calculation in the socialist society from being conducted on other and better lines. In other words, our preliminary examination does not intend to set up any ideal form.

To avoid a violent break in the argument and owing to

---

[14] *The Economic System in a Socialist State,* London, 1937, p. x of the preface.

its more elementary character, this examination has been relegated to an appendix, but it is recommended that all who are in doubt as to the function and significance of the price mechanism read it at this point of the discussion. (See Appendix A.)

4

Calculation in Socialist Societies with a Natural Economy

The reader may please observe, that in the last Article for the Recovery of my Liberty, the Emperor stipulates to allow me a Quantity of Meat and Drink, sufficient for the Support of 1728 Lilliputians. Some time after, asking a Friend at Court how they came to fix on that determinate Number, he told me, that his Majesty's Mathematicians, having taken the Height of my Body by the help of a Quadrant, and finding it to exceed theirs in the Proportion of Twelve to One, they concluded from the Similarity of their Bodies, that mine must contain at least 1728 of theirs and consequently would require as much Food as was necessary to support that Number of Lilliputians. By which, the Reader may conceive an Idea of the Ingenuity of that People, as well as the prudent and exact Oeconomy of so great a Prince
—A Voyage to Lilliput.

In examining the need and possibility of economic calculation in the different forms of socialist communities, it is natural to start with a study of a socialist society which uses no money, i.e. one with a natural economy as it is sometimes called. The moneyless society is the great ideal of many socialists, and even as late as in February, 1932, the Finance Commissar of the Soviet Union said that the policy of his Finance Department aimed at preparing the day when money "could be relegated to the museums."[1]

---

[1] See Gerhard Dobbert's *Soviet Economics,* London, 1933, p. 141.

The criterion for a society with a moneyless economy is that its goods are distributed *in natura* without the use of money or of other means of payment which could serve as units for accounting. It is obvious that there must be certain difficulties in undertaking calculation in a society where neither prices nor other forms of common denominators exist. Could it be shown that economic calculation is not possible in a society with a moneyless economy owing to the difficulties it creates for calculation in the purely productive stages, this would be the end of the investigation so far as this form of society was concerned.

Nevertheless, the distribution side of the question has also to be examined, partly because the distribution of goods which have no common denominator will create the need for a different form of control, and partly because the distribution of communal goods raises special and interesting problems in a society with a moneyless economy.[2]

In this connection it should be remembered that in an economy of private enterprise production and distribution take place *uno acto,* so that distribution automatically results from the individual's contribution to the process of production, whether it takes the form of mental or physical labour, of special capability or knowledge, or of putting land or other forms of capital at the disposal of production.

In socialist communities production and distribution will be two separate operations, nor will there necessarily be any connection between contribution and remuneration, for the central authority will decide the distribution of income.

---

[2] A very thorough exposition of the relationship between a monetary and a moneyless economy will be found in Max Weber's *The Theory of Social and Economic Organisation,* London, 1947, p. 186ff.

Many economists maintain that distribution is the chief problem in any socialist society;[3] at any rate it is obviously so in one with a moneyless economy.

In discussing distribution we shall for the time being disregard the production side of the question; we shall, in other words, assume that at the moment of computation there already exists a certain quantity of consumer goods for distribution: necessaries and conveniences. By consumer goods is here understood both articles for current consumption which disappear the moment they are consumed, and such permanent and semi-permanent ones as houses, furniture, electrical and other mechanical and technical domestic appliances. "Goods" will be used as a common denominator for all these categories.

For the time being we shall only concern ourselves with those consumer goods which are available for immediate distribution and not with those which have to be held back as cover for saving, depreciation and insurance quotas. (We shall return to this question in later chapters.) Services cannot be said to exist in advance; they come into being in the moment of production, but this is a phenomenon which will be disregarded here, as it does not give rise to problems of any interest to this discussion.

The mere assumption that the goods to be distributed al-

---

[3] Professor Mises in his *Socialism* writes: "For fundamentally, Socialism is nothing but a theory of 'just' distribution; the socialist movement is nothing but an attempt to achieve this ideal. All socialist schemes start from the problem of distribution and all come back to it. For Socialism the problem of distribution is *the* economic problem" (London, 1936).

In his "The Theory of Planned Economy" in the *International Labour Review,* September, 1937, p. 393, Robert Mosse writes: "In the planned economy it (the distribution of income) becomes an independent and even a preponderant activity."

ready exist, does away with the aim of maximizing production. As to the second aim, that of a just distribution of goods, it has already been pointed out that this is a question of ethics and one which we cannot presume to judge; yet we are forced to discuss the different forms of just distribution, not so as to form an opinion as to which is most just, but because the possibility of computation varies with the method of distribution.

It may be mentioned here that this question of just distribution—with which we shall not occupy ourselves when discussing the possibilities of calculation in socialist communities with a monetary economy—is particularly *à propos* in connection with the moneyless economy, since that is supposed to be a prerequisite for just distribution.

One of the most consistent advocates of the moneyless economy, Dr. Otto Neurath, bases his recommendation of it and his criticism of the monetary economy partly on the statement that, while a monetary economy puts the rich with their money in a position to get what they want even in times of war or want, the poor are not even able to maintain the physiological minimum of existence. N. Bucharin also put justice on the side of the moneyless economy when he wrote:

> Similarly an exact registration of just distribution of these products (consumer goods) among the population is necessary. . . . The Central Statistical Department will calculate how many boots, trousers, shirts, etc., shall be produced in the course of a year. . . . The finished products will be delivered to the storehouses established for them by the community, whence they will be distributed among the comrades.[4]

---

[4] *Kommunisternes Program,* Copenhagen, 1918, p. 62.

The concept "just distribution" is obscure and there are conflicting interpretations of it. Some of the proposed definitions which are given below seem artificial and absurd, but are included because they are met with in the discussion of the socialist economy. The principles of, or rather the proposals for, distribution fall into two main groups: (1) those where distribution is to be made irrespective of the individual's contribution to production, and (2) those where distribution is to be according to contribution.

For a community with a moneyless economy there are three subdivisions of the first group:

1A.—*Equal* (per capita) distribution.
1B.—Distribution according to the *subjective value* the goods apportioned have for each individual.
1C.—Distribution according to *needs* in conformity with a scale of value determined by the State.

The second group can be subdivided into five:

2A.—Distribution according to contribution, judged by its economic value to the industry.
2B.—Distribution according to contribution, judged by the number of hours worked.
2C.—Distribution according to contribution, judged by the individual's ability and gifts.
2D.—Distribution according to contribution, judged by the individual's subjective valuation of his sacrifice.
2E.—Distribution according to *"worth,"* judged from the point of view of the community's economy.

1A. *Equal* (*per capita*) *distribution.*—By this is understood a distribution which gives each individual the same number (or quantity) of articles and goods of similar quality. A single distribution would present no difficulty in theory or practice, provided that the number of members in the community was known exactly and that the goods to be distributed could be divided by that number. One can imagine these conditions being fulfilled in a primitive society where there only are the necessities of life to be distributed, although the type of dwelling would have to be so standardized, that each received house accommodation just as large and as good in quality as everybody else.

In a moneyless economy which had reached a level where there were also conveniences to be distributed, an "equal per capita distribution" would present certain practical and theoretical difficulties. In a community of the size we have assumed, it would, practically speaking, be impossible to undertake a quantitative and qualitative equal per capita distribution of collective goods such as schools, universities, operas, theatres, libraries, picture galleries, etc. Such would presuppose that there were equally large and good educational and art establishments in each and every village, for the fact that admission was free and unrestricted would not itself be enough by reason of the geographical dispersion of the population.

If one attempts to give those living away from the cultural centres compensation in the shape of other goods, one immediately comes up against the great difficulty, typical for moneyless communities, that from their very constitution there is no common denominator in the form of prices. There will, of course, be quantitative notation in the shape of common measures for number, length, weight and time, but these cannot be added up and there is no common yardstick to determine how much the individual shall have of this or that good so as to be compensated. Nor is there any common yardstick for comparing the different conveniences with each other or with other goods.

It is obvious that 50 loaves, 4 pairs of boots and 5 theatre tickets are more than 30 loaves, 2 pairs of boots and 3 theatre tickets, but there is no comparative scale for determining whether the former are more or less than, for example, 40 loaves, 1 suit, 1 pair of skis and 10 books. (We shall return later to the question of subjective valuation and the possibility of valuing the different goods according to the cost of their production.) For the present it will be enough to say that in societies which have attained a certain cultural level distribution *in natura* will not only present difficulties in practice, but also in theory, if it is intended to give compensation for conveniences with other goods.

The assumption, not of a single distribution, but of the distribution of a stream of goods and articles to an ever-changing population, creates fresh practical difficulties, but no new theoretical ones, in so far as it can be regarded as a series of single distributions. (It is assumed here that the relationship between production of consumer goods and means of production is given. The contrary raises important and difficult questions, among them that of allowance for the factor of time.)

One objection to *per capita* distribution is that it is hardly reasonable for a child to receive the same quantity of food, drink, tobacco and conveniences as an adult. We are not concerned here with the question of how the demand for ethical justice is to be met, but the objection is important for our examination, in as far as the different proposals for meeting it alter the need and possibility of survey and computation. To attempt to meet the objection by taking account of the sex and age of the individual, increases the need for statistical survey. On the whole, the practical difficulties become greater, the more individualistic divergencies the central authority has to consider. Were this body to take the individual's height, weight, and type of work into account for the purposes of its distribution, it would need a very complicated statistical machinery. Considering that physiologists maintain that the individual's requirements of foodstuffs, vitamins and lethicins, vary even among persons of the same sex, age, height, weight and employment, there might be reason for going even further. Should the central authority do this and also take into account differences in taste (the teetotaller is not interested in rations of beer or whisky, nor the illiterate in books, nor the unmusical in concert tickets), the task becomes virtually impossible, in that the taste for such goods is continually changing. If these things *are* to be taken into account, it means that at any rate the first principle for distribution (distribution *per capital*)[5] has been abandoned and the second adopted.

1B. *Distribution according to the subjective value the goods apportioned have for each individual.*—Before this

---

[5] One obvious way of solving the difficulties created by *"per capita* distribution" is to give each individual coupons made out for amounts, so that each can *choose* the consumer goods, foodstuffs and conveniences he wishes; yet, if this is done, the assumed distribution *in natura* is abandoned.

Another obvious possibility is to allow individuals to exchange among themselves goods they don't want for those they prefer. This, however, is tantamount to the State allowing private trading. Apart from this being incompatible with the hypothesis (centralized direction of trade) it can have many consequences that would be dangerous for a socialist state. Those who put the main emphasis on the justness of distribution will be able to object that those who are cleverest in this exchanging will enjoy special advantages that will prevent the distribution conforming with the ideal of justness. Finally a general process of barter will soon produce a generally accepted means of exchange, which again conflicts with the assumption of there being a moneyless economy.

method of distribution can be practicable, there must be a quantity of goods sufficient to satisfy each individual's every subjective requirement in every detail at every time. In such a case there would be no theoretical or practical difficulties, nor would there be any need of survey or computation. However, this assumption would mean that all the goods were free, and on that basis there is no need whatever of theoretic economic discussion.

If, on the other hand, the means of satisfying requirements are scarce—as was assumed—this method of distribution breaks down, because the central authority will have no indication of how to make the distribution (rationing), if only because it will be impossible to compare the intensity of the different individuals' subjective requirements.

The measurement of requirements and utility is a large and relatively new field and one for which there is, in fact, no authorized standard like yard or kilowatt. The answer to the question, "How much do you want this?" can only be: "As much as I want it".[6] The individual has the ability —and uses it every moment—of valuing different needs. The individual is able to state what increase in his rate of consumption of one commodity will just offset a given decrease in that of another specified commodity. For this reason there is not only a certain possibility of measurement, but also of one individual being able to give *other* individuals a quantitative unit of measurement for the relative intensity of his different needs. Inasmuch as the individual can give a quantitative unit of measurement for the

---

[6] See H. Phelps-Brown's *The Framework of the Pricing System,* London, 1936.

marginal satisfaction of his various needs, it is possible to work out a schedule of substitutive functions.

However, the practical use of such a schedule is strictly limited owing to a number of special conditions which have to be taken into consideration. Whether one good is to be used as a substitute for another will in the first place depend on how large a quantity of the goods the individual concerned already possesses (he will be willing to do without more oranges in exchange for butter, if he already has many oranges and no butter, than if he has a large stock of butter). It will also depend on the extent to which the need in question has just been satisfied, on how large is the quantity of goods concerned he can *expect* to receive (measured in units of time), and, finally, on whether he will get them in the near or distant future.

It is a question not only of substitute goods, but of complementary goods. While some goods can replace each other, others—within a community with a given set of social conventions and a certain standard of living—will create the need for new goods. Thus the function of substitution will not only depend on the marginal rate of substitution between two articles, but on their relation to other articles, since alterations in the consumption of each can affect the consumers' value-judgment of the article, if marginal satisfaction is to be considered.

Again, the substitutive function applies to commodities which are divisible into homogeneous units and which are consumed with fair regularity. Goods which can only be used once and indivisibles like houses or pianos (and into this class come many luxury articles) are not consumed at any certain rate per unit of time which is variable by small increments.

We must also note that if one marginal rate of substitution is, for example, twice that of another, this does not mean that the consumer wishes the first increment to be "twice" that of the second. To quote Phelps-Brown again: "We are concerned with the oranges not as physical units but as they are valued by the consumer, and we must beware of carrying into the realm of valuation the arithmetic which applies to objects physically considered." For example, one person may say that as far as he is concerned 5 bottles of beer a week correspond to 1 lb. of tobacco a week, while for someone else it may be 10 bottles. This does not mean that beer has a greater value for the one than for the other unless one knows the value they attach to the article of comparison, in this case tobacco. One may be fond of both beer and tobacco, while the other may be a teetotaller and smoke but little.

Again it must be remembered that such a schedule only gives expression to the individual's need as experienced at a given moment, and that in all probability this will be different a few moments later, even if the relative quantities of the means of satisfying these requirements within a certain period of time remain the same, since physical and psychological factors may have affected the individual's need, the intensity of his reaction to it and so his *sensation* of need.

Finally it is important to realise that such a schedule does no more than give a picture of the relative relationship between the needs (at a given moment) of one *definite individual,* and is useless for comparing the needs (and the relationship between them) of other individuals. Even if we feel, and almost regard it as axiomatic, that two shillings give more satisfaction to a beggar than to a millionaire, yet we do not *know*—and have no means of judging —whether the beggar gets more enjoyment and a greater need satisfied with a two-shilling meal, than a millionaire with a two-shilling cigar or caviar sandwich.

Professor Ragnar Frisch has probably done most work, at any rate has got further than anybody else, in measuring the marginal utility of goods and money.[7] His investigations are particularly interesting and break fresh ground in this sphere. What is of interest for our investigation is the question of whether these methods of measurement have any practical use as a statistical and economic foundation for the policy of distribution of the central authority in a socialist society. In an article in the *Review of Economic Studies* Abraham Burk[8] has questioned the practicability of Professor Frisch's method. Yet even if Burk's objection were untenable and it were possible by this or some other method to find a quantitative measure not only for the value-judgments of the individual, but a common denominator for the subjective value-judgments of all individuals, the central authority would still be unable to use this common yardstick as a guide, since it cannot be denied that, in the world of reality and in the dynamic society we have assumed, the individual's valuations are subject to constant variation.[9]

---

[7] See, *inter alia, New Methods of Measuring Marginal Utility,* Tuebingen, 1932, dedicated to Irving Fischer, whom Frisch calls: "the pioneer of utility measurements."

[8] "Real Income, Expenditure Proportionality and Frisch's New Methods of Measuring Marginal Utility," in the *Review of Economic Studies,* October, 1936.

[9] Joan Robinson has well expressed some of the difficulties met with in investigating utility measurements: "A technique of *Gedanken Experimente* may be used to eke out the meagre equipment of behaviourist

1C. *Distribution according to needs in conformity with a scale of value determined by the State.*—The difficulties in the way of effecting a just distribution along the lines of the first two principles, together with the necessity of rationing, naturally raise the question of whether distribution can be made in accordance with a *scale of needs* laid down by the State. It may be said that such a scale of needs cannot, strictly speaking, be employed in the present case where there is a given quantity of goods to be distributed. The existing goods have to be distributed, irrespective of whether or not their composition and relative quantities correspond with the scale. The importance of such a scale is in determining production and so, future distribution. (We shall come back to this question of production in the moneyless economy.)

A scale of needs will, of course, not be fixed arbitrarily, but be constructed under reference to the supposed needs of the members of the society. It would presumably be worked out by experts on nutritive physiology as far as the first items were concerned; yet a number of goods, chiefly conveniences, will have to be scaled by the central authority according to value-judgments or on the basis of investigations and consumers' ballots. This brings us back to the

---

psychology. A series of questions may be put by the analytical economist to himself: How many bananas would I buy a week if the price were a halfpenny? How many would I buy if my income were £500 a year? How many would I buy, if oranges were seven for sixpence? How many would I buy, if I saw a poster saying 'Eat More Fruit' as I went to my office by tube? How many would I buy, if it were a hot summer? How many would I buy, if my next-door neighbour owned a Persian cat? These questions enable the economist to give a rough, imperfect, and admittedly treacherous account of his marginal utility curve for bananas."
—*Economics of Imperfect Competition,* London, 1933, p. 213.

same problems as were discussed in 1B. (It may be noted that it will be difficult to get just distribution even if the most exact measurements are made, if only because there will always be individuals whose taste and needs differ from the average. It is even conceivable that the official scale will not correspond with that of a single individual.)

It will be the task of the central authority not only to grade requirements, but, what is even more difficult, to determine the relative intensity of the different needs, so as to enable it to decide what proportion of the united means of production shall be used to satisfy each individual requirement. That, however, is not the whole of its task. Even if production is made (or there already has been produced a quantity sufficient to conform with the scale of requirements) there still remains the question of how much of each good each individual is to receive. The following might conceivably be a solution of this question: Production is solely adjusted with the purpose of completely satisfying the needs of all the members of the community for those goods, which are placed at the top of the scale of the community's needs, while production is discontinued of those goods, where there is no certainty of satisfying requirements fully. In this event, the distribution of the goods at the top of the scale will afford no theoretical difficulties (though practical ones). If, however, the scale includes requirements which cannot be completely satisfied, we are faced with the same problems and objections as were outlined in 1A.

The solution indicated implies a way of satisfying requirements, which is in sharp contrast to that normally employed. Generally man does not completely satisfy one need, before attempting to satisfy another. As a general rule when the greatest need is so far satisfied as to be felt less than those which come next, the individual starts satisfying these. That the relative intensity of needs is taken into account, is such common experience that it has even been made a "law" (Gossen's law). Actually H. H. Gossen formulated three laws, of which the following is the most important and the one which interests us:

> A person who has a free choice between several pleasures, but not sufficient time to enjoy them completely, must, however different the absolute magnitude of the individual pleasures, in order to attain the maximum pleasure, enjoy them all in part before he even completely enjoys the greatest, and *in such a way that the magnitude of each pleasure at the moment in which its enjoyment is broken off, is the same.*[10]

A more modern exposition of this law is that the individual procures sufficient of two goods "to make the marginal utility equal." Professor Ragnar Frisch has pointed out that the law can hardly be accepted in that form as the concept of marginal utility is not so defined as to be comparable for different goods. It is defined as the increase in the total utility in respect of a certain special good; that is to say, an increase of total utility obtained by a slight increase in quantity of the good concerned, measured in units of that good. Thus the degree of increase depends on the arbitrary choice of the unit of measurement. (The marginal utility of sugar is naturally measured in pounds and that of a visit to the cinema in the number of visits paid, etc.) So, in order to make Gossen's law precise, Professor Frisch brings in *prices* for the two goods and then measures the marginal utility of a good, not per technical unit per good,

---

[10] *Op. cit.*, p. 12 (italics in text).

but in units of the quantity of the good concerned which can be bought for a certain monetary unit. Thus Professor Frisch's formulation of the law is that "marginal utility shall be proportional with the prices," but this formulation will be inapplicable in the society which we are discussing, as there will be neither prices nor money.

Distribution according to contribution.—There are several reasons for the prominence given to this solution, one being the difficulties created by distribution without reference to contribution and the widespread opinion (even among socialists) that such distribution does not conform with the stipulation that the distribution should be just. Many are also inclined to fear that the members of the community would not do their best, were they all to receive the same quantity of goods irrespective of how much or how little they worked. This possibility we shall not take into account, as, for the time being, we are assuming that the egoistic-individualistic character does not exist in the socialist society.

2A. *Distribution according to contribution judged by its economic value to the industry.*—The moment we touch on the production side of the problem we come up against a question which has so far not been discussed, that of what proportion of the result is to be ascribed to man's work and what to other factors of production. Even if all the means of production are State-owned, such an allocation will—as will be shown later—be necessary if the economic principle is to be followed. Then there is the further question of whether in calculating this, account shall be taken of the fact that work varies in quality.

For the time being, however, let us disregard everything which has to do with the production side of the question and concentrate on the special problems raised by distribution in a moneyless economy. Therefore, we still assume (*a*) that there exists a given quantity of goods to be distributed, (*b*) that the individual's contribution to the result can be and has been calculated (whether or not this is possible will be discussed together with the question of production), and (*c*) that the individual's share is given in the form of a fraction of the accumulated quantity of goods produced during a certain period.

Even accepting these assumptions, it appears that this method of distribution will put difficulties in the way of computation in a society with a moneyless economy. Let us suppose that the individual's share is one millionth. It is obvious that each individual cannot demand *in natura* a millionth part of everything produced, as this will include means of production such as factories, machinery, means of transport, administrative buildings, health and cultural institutions, of which the individual cannot be given any fraction whatever. Against claiming a share of the means of production it may, however, be maintained that the individual cannot reasonably make such a claim as the means of production will later benefit him or his descendants in the shape of a large quantity of consumer goods. There are several objections to such a point of view. In the first place, not everybody has descendants and many will be more interested in the necessaries in their own hand, than in those in the bush of the future, which they do not know that they will ever live to see. In the second place, opinions may differ as to what proportion of the production shall be reserved for producing capital goods. This depends on the size of the community's saving-, depreciation- and insurance-quotas, which also raises the question of whether the amount of the community's savings is to be fixed arbitrarily by the central authority or whether it shall be determined by the individuals' subjective willingness to forgo current consumption for the benefit of the future, and whether, in such an event, this willingness (or unwillingness) can be measured. (See Chapter 7.) In the third place, these quotas can be covered not only by developing the machinery of production, but also by accumulating stocks of consumer goods. If not all the goods produced in the period in question were distributed among the members of the community, some would certainly object that the principle of distribution according to performance had been broken.

Disregarding objections of this kind and still assuming that the distribution will be made from the necessaries and conveniences remaining *after* the necessary deductions have been made, we meet the same difficulties as with the method of distribution 1A: If the goods exist in such a number or form as to be divisible by what is calculated to be the individual's share in production (in this case one millionth), then distribution will create no difficulties in theory. The difficulties will occur in the distribution of the conveniences, and this will break down over the fact that *in a society with a moneyless economy there is no common unit for computation.* This is a decisive argument against a moneyless economy in a society, which has reached a certain cultural level. The argument applies to all methods in this second group.

2B. *Distribution according to contribution judged by the number of hours worked.*—This method will make it easier to compute each individual's share and will present no difficulties in theory, provided that the number of hours each individual works is known exactly. Yet, once the share is fixed, there will be just the same difficulties and possibilities, as for the method 2A. (The possibility that distribution based exclusively on the number of hours worked, without taking into account the amount of work done, may result in a less intensive performance, is here disregarded, as we have assumed the absence of egoism.)

2C. *Distribution according to contribution judged by the individual's ability and gifts.*—In this rather artificial form of distribution computation of the individual's share will involve certain difficulties. If the share is not to be determined quite arbitrarily, exact measurements of intelligence will have to be made, as well as physical and psycho-technical tests. If it is held that man's abilities are not entirely hereditary, but can be developed or impaired, then these tests will have to be repeated at short intervals, which will create practical difficulties. There is the additional difficulty that no apparatus exists for exactly measuring certain valuable qualities such as character, charm and leadership (which includes the ability to assume responsibility and to take decisions). Finally, there is the further obstacle that both abilities which can be measured, and those which cannot, are difficult, if not impossible, to reduce to a common denominator on which the distribution can be based.

Assuming that one has found the sum of the abilities of each person engaged in production and had decided on a common denominator so that they could be proportioned to the total ability-sum of all those engaged in production during the period in question, it will be easy to work out the individual's share. Then will come the same possibilities and difficulties for distribution as those mentioned in 2A. (Whether the central authority should reward according to ability, irrespective of whether the abilities in question are utilized or not, is a problem to which we shall do no more than draw attention.)

2D. *Distribution according to contribution judged by the individual's subjective interpretation of his sacrifice.*—This form of distribution must also be called artificial. It gives rise to difficulties both in theory and in practice. Even assuming that it does not imply certain temptations for the lazy, it will at any rate bring many requests for increased wages and—according to our assumption—for cuts, too, as each individual's subjective interpretation of his labour sacrifice varies with his psychic and physical condition, which, with most people and presumably with everybody, is continually changing.[11] The chief difficulty in computing the individual's share will be that there is no common gauge for measuring the different individuals' subjective sense of sacrifice, and even if their share in the total sacrifice of all those engaged in production could be measured, there would still be the same difficulties in the way of distribution as in 2A.

2E. *Distribution according to "worth."*—Practically the only difference between this form of distribution and that according to "contribution" is that here the performance is not measured by its utility to an individual undertaking, but to the economy of the community as a whole. Whether

---

[11] Adam Smith has a different opinion of the question: "Equal quantities of labour and at all times and places may be said to be of equal value to the labourer. In his ordinary state of health, strength and spirit; in the ordinary degree of his skill and dexterity he must always lay down the same portion of his ease, his liberty and his happiness. The price which he pays must always be the same, whatever may be the quantity of goods which he receives in return for it."—*Wealth of Nations*, 4th Edn., p. 48.

the worth of the various individuals and social or professional groups is to be determined by periodical plebiscites
(in which case popular sportsmen and film stars would
presumably be voted "the most valuable") or by the central authority, there is a great danger of arbitrariness. The
decisions will in any case vary from period to period according to the ideas prevailing at the time. Once the "worth"
of the various individuals and social groups has been fixed,
there will be the same possibilities and difficulties for distribution as in 2A.

Before discussing the question of production it may be
pertinent to mention that it is the difficulties which arise in
connection with *calculation for production* which have occasioned the discussion of the possibility of economic calculation in the socialist community. The same difficulties
apply for the society with a moneyless economy as for the
other forms of society, so there is nothing to prevent their
being discussed here. There is, however, one difficulty peculiar to the society with a natural economy, which ought to
be discussed here. This is the same as that occurring in certain methods of distribution, namely, that in a society with
a moneyless economy there is no common denominator for
the various wares, goods and services. It is assumed that
prices do not exist. There is no common standard by which
to weigh the aggregate sacrifice against the aggregate output, which has been established as necessary. From this
can be concluded that *economic calculation cannot be undertaken in a socialist society with a moneyless economy.*
Any further investigation of the problem raised by calculation for production in moneyless economies is, therefore,
unnecessary.

The point of view that economic calculation is impossible

in the socialist society with a moneyless economy is not shared by everyone. Bucharin's idea (see p. 53) was taken up by A. D. Tschayanoff[12] among others. Tschayanoff realizes that even in a society with a moneyless economy one must be able to make an economic comparison of the various means of production used. Tschayanoff is an agriculturalist and points out that it is possible to measure the variations in a cow's milk-yield by variations in its fodder. Yet even in this particular case the task is not so easy, for the quantity of milk yielded is not merely a question of fodder, and once you accept the existence of other factors, you are immediately faced with the problem of how to know whether to increase the one or the other, and what to use as a means of comparison.

In Tschayanoff's opinion his system is not only practicable, but can also be used for more complicated comparisons. He takes as an example an investigation of the economic importance of growing corn, fodder, vegetables, and pasture. The only way of doing this, says Tschayanoff, is to compare the results obtained with the "socially necessary marginal norms of productivity," and this he proposes to do in the same way as with "extremity computations in agriculture." In this a theoretical ideal beast is given certain points for each part of its body, the sum of which serves as a standard by which real animals are compared. Tschayanoff proposes to give the various branches of industry "socially useful marginal norms of productivity" which the central management will determine. The following example is for computing meadow-culture:

---

[12] *Byttemarkeds og Valghandlingsteori,* a resumé of Professor Frisch's lectures, Part II, 2nd Edn., Oslo, 1935.

TO OBTAIN 1,000 UNITS OF GRAIN

	Marginal Norm of what can be used	*Actually used*	*Proportion*	
Labour	45·0	30·0	1·5	
Stock	120·0	90·0	1·3	
Land	11·0	8·5	1·3	
Freight and transport	0·6	0·6	1·0	
Buildings	15·0	25·0	0·6 ⎤ 3·3
Stores	0·5	0·4	1·2 ⎬ —
Materials	1·5	1·0	1·5 ⎦ 3
Fuel	0·03	0·03	1·0	

Thus the general communal coefficient of effectivity for the cultivation of corn is:

$$\frac{1\cdot5+1\cdot3+1\cdot3+1\cdot0+1\cdot1}{5}=1\cdot24$$

If, in the same way, one computes the economic importance of cultivating fodder and vegetables, which the central management in its plan of organization considers one quarter as important as the cultivation of corn, and of cattle-breeding, which it considers half as important, one arrives—according to Tschayanoff—at the computation for agriculture as a whole on page 73.

Thus, if the marginal norm for every branch of industry is 1, the coefficient of effectivity for agriculture is 1·23. "This system," writes Tschayanoff, "solves the same problems as the old method of calculation did in the capitalist society."

It has been objected that this system can, at best, only be used for calculation within a single branch of industry. Thus

	Coefficient of effectivity		Coefficient of importance in its branch	Total
Cultivation of meadow land	1·24	×	4	=4·96
Cultivation of fodder	1·02	×	1	=1·02
Cultivation of vegetables	0·90	×	1	=0·90
Cattle breeding	1·48	×	2	=2·96

$$9·84:8=1·23$$

different electricity plants, for instance, can compare their production of energy in calories, but not that of different kinds of energy. Dr. Cläre Tisch objects that this is conceding too much. She points to Tschayanoff's own computation according to which the marginal norm for labour is 45 while only 30 is used, and that for land is 11, of which only 8·5 is used. From this one might well suppose that there was in the community concerned a relative lack of fertile land, while labour was in comparison a relatively worthless factor. If such is the case, it is, in the opinion of Dr. Tisch, completely inadmissible to compare the two proportionals, and with this contention it is difficult to disagree.

Mere determination of the marginal norm for the individual factors of production does not solve the question of which of them shall be used and whether, for example, intensive or extensive cultivation is to be preferred. It is obvious that a system which cannot solve this problem can still less serve as a guide for the utilization of means of production in different branches of industry. Tschayanoff is, however, fully aware of this and considers that the question of comparing the profitability of the different ways of employing means of production does not arise in a society with a moneyless economy,

> for the products of these different branches are here not interchangeable, nor can they take each other's place, and can thus have no common standard for comparison.[13]

Tschayanoff cannot be criticized for not finding a common denominator when he does not consider one necessary, but it can be objected that his system neither does what he promises for it, nor takes the place of economic calculation in the capitalist society. The way in which the marginal norms and coefficients of efficiency are determined is also open to criticism, for it must from the start to a certain extent be arbitrary and will become more and more indefinite with the continual alterations in the size and tastes of the population and in the methods of production, and with the discovery of more efficient means of production, such as new fertilizers (to keep to agriculture). Tschayanoff's proposal that the central authority should determine the marginal norms and coefficients of importance also raises the question of to what extent technical considerations shall be taken into account in production and how far the worth of the finished products. And in the latter case are the valuations to be based on the choice of the consumers or on official scales of requirements? (This is a problem which has already been referred to and which will be discussed later.)

---

[13] See his article in *Archiv für Sozialwissenschaft und Sozialpolitik*, Vol. 51, 1923, p. 581.

Professor Boris Brutzkus summarily dismisses Tschayanoff's proposal for moneyless calculation and thinks that marginal norms have no real value unless they are worked out "on the basis of a common principle of value. . . . the author, however, did not succeed in doing this."[14]

In his opinion the director of agriculture will not be able to do anything with schemes for computation like Tschayanoff's.

Tschayanoff's plan has even been attacked by Marxist theorists. In *Ekonomitscheskaja Shishni*,[15] S. Strumilin[16] and E. Varga[17] repudiated Tschayanoff's methods and came to the conclusion that the socialist society must have a yardstick for value, in the same way as the capitalist society has one in money. True to their Marxist principles, Varga and Strumilin proposed that this should be labour, a solution which will be discussed in the next chapter.

One of the most persistent champions of the moneyless economy is Dr. O. Neurath.[18] As has been mentioned, his attitude is largely actuated by the desire for just distribution. Originally he was chiefly interested in distribution in time of war and his books are stamped by the World War and the period of inflation in Germany. It was originally

---

[14] *Economic Planning in Soviet Russia*, p. 14.

[15] See Brutzkus, *op. cit.*, p. 15.

[16] See Strumilin in *Ekonomitscheskaja Shishni*, Nrs. 237, 284 and 290 of 23.10.1920, 17.12.1920 and 24.12.1920 respectively. (Also Dr. O. Leichter, *op. cit.*, p. 91.)

[17] Translated in the German *Kommunismus*, Year II, Nr. 9–10, 1921.

[18] See *Durch die Kriegswirtschaft zur Naturalwirtschaft*, Munich, 1919. *Vollsozialisierung*, Part 15 of the series *Deutsche Gemeinwirtschaft*, Jena, 1920; *Gildensozialismus, Klassenkampf, Vollsozialisierung*, Dresden, 1922; *Wirtschaftsplan und Naturalrechnung*, Berlin, 1925, and in particular, "Geld und Sozialismus" in *Kampf*, XVI, Nr. 4–5.

war-economy which interested Neurath most, but he also maintains that even in peace with the help of money the rich can satisfy all his requirements, while the poor man lives in need. He further objects to the monetary system on the grounds that there is no certainty as to what quantity of goods a certain sum of money will correspond. A sum of money is a figure without any real meaning and thus, in his opinion, one ought to have a moneyless economy with "maximum satisfaction of requirements."

All the same, Dr. Neurath realizes that a society with a moneyless economy precludes the possibility of calculation and computation, and to this extent there is, strictly speaking, no necessity to occupy ourselves with his proposal here; however, his reasons for renouncing a monetary economy are of interest, if only because one often comes up against them. Dr. Neurath maintains that accurate calculation is not possible in the capitalist society either, and cites as examples the building of schools and hospitals and the maintenance of justice. It is true enough that in the case of such communal goods it is difficult or impossible to weigh the satisfaction against the input, yet the capitalist society has at least one of the links for comparison, namely, the costs. As Dr. Cläre Tisch points out, the fact that in the capitalist society there are sectors which suffer from the drawback that ideal economic balances cannot be found, is no reason to increase their number. As far as Dr. Neurath's other contentions are concerned, it must be admitted that he is right in saying that a sum of money does not represent any definite quantity of goods, *if* comparison is made at two different points of time. Yet in the capitalist society a sum of money does at one given moment represent an important unit of measurement, and as will be seen later this is not always the case in the socialist community. To determine Neurath's "maximum satisfaction of requirements" will also create difficulties, for one person attaches most importance to clothes, another to food and drink, a third to cultural goods, and a fourth to utilities which the central authority cannot provide at all, with the result that it is impossible to calculate the sum of the various individuals' requirements which have to be satisfied. (The sum of the *means* for satisfying the requirements can be calculated; but only provided that there is a common unit for calculation, which is not the case in a society with a moneyless economy.)

Even if a schedule has been accepted and it has been decided that, for instance, 500 litres of wine are preferable to 1,000 litres of beer (Mises' example), without the possibility of calculation there is nothing to guide one in determining how these goods are to be produced with the least possible expenditure. With reference to Dr. Neurath's contention that a monetary economy creates an unjust distribution, Dr. Cläre Tisch retorts that this is not due to the monetary economy as such, but that it is the unequal distribution of income which occasions the injustice which Dr. Neurath wishes to eliminate—and such an inequality can occur even in a society that does not have a monetary economy. On the other hand, it can be said in support of Dr. Neurath's point of view that money may serve as a store of value, which means that it is easier to amass a fortune in a society with a monetary, than in one with a moneyless economy.

Dr. Eduard Heimann is of the opinion that Dr. Neurath's arguments in favour of a moneyless economy are false and, further, that:[19]

---

[19] *Mehrwert und Gemeinwirtschaft*, p. 169.

A moneyless distribution directed by a central authority can, even in the case where it succeeded in getting perfect statistics of requirements, only take into consideration alterations in taste in the subsequent construction of statistics, while the price system records every slightest alteration in valuation with the accuracy of a seismograph and thus directly causes the processes of production to adapt themselves to the new situation.

Max Weber has also sharply criticized Neurath's ideas.[20] Weber has many objections to moneyless computation and much to say in favour of a monetary economy. Amongst other things he writes that:

From the purely technical point of view, money is the most 'efficient' means of economic accounting. That is, it is formally the most rational means of orienting economic activity.[21]

Karl Kautsky also realizes the necessity for a monetary economy, and he, too, attacks Neurath's ideas:[22]

Without money only two kinds of economy are possible. First, the primitive one already mentioned, and, translated into terms of modern conditions, this would mean that the whole of productive activity in the state was turned into a single factory under a central management, which would allot to each individual concern what it had to produce, receive all the products of the entire population and assign *in natura* to each business means of production and to each individual consumer his means of consumption.[23]

The ideal of such a state of affairs is the convict prison or the barracks, the inmates of which have, to all intents and purposes everything they need assigned to them *in natura*.

---

[20] *Theory of Social and Economic Organisation.*

[21] *Op. cit.,* p. 171.

[22] *Die proletarische Revolution und ihr Programm,* 2nd Edn., 1922, p. 309.

[23] *Op. cit.,* p. 314.

He further says:

It took thousands of years to create the capitalist method of production. As a standard of value and means of circulation for what is produced, it will have to persist even in a socialist society, at any rate until it enters the happy second phase of communism, and of this to-day we do not know whether it will ever be more than a pious wish, like the millennium. . . .
Whatever the organization of the socialist society, it will have to keep careful accounts, as will each of its undertakings, so that one can at any time see how much has been received and how much expended, what profit has been made or how much lost. This, however, it is quite impossible to do, if receipts and expenditure are only entered *in natura.*[24]
"If a manufacturer of machinery delivers a thrashing machine and for it is allotted, let us say, 40 pigs, 5 tons of flour, 1 ton of butter and 2,000 eggs, how can he know whether he has gained or lost on the transaction, whether he has delivered more work to the farmer than he has received, or vice versa? It is obvious that book-keeping *in natura* would soon lead to inextricable chaos.

The Marxist economist, Dr. Otto Leichter, also disassociates himself from Neurath's solution and reproaches him, amongst other things, for

the absolutely silly idea that moneyless economy is already everywhere dominant in capitalism, where money does not happen to enter into the question.[25]

and he goes on to say:

Does Neurath not know that calculation is really only possible in economic life and that it was there that the concept of rationality first originated? In music one reckons in units of

---

[24] *Ibid.,* p. 317.
[25] *Op. cit.,* p. 95.

beat, will Neurath, perhaps, call that natural computation? Thus, from whatever angle we look at Neurath's programme, we see that the moneyless economy must lead to complete economic chaos and that it makes it impossible to gain a picture of what is going on in the economy where it is used.[26]

(Dr. Leichter's own solution will be discussed in the next chapter.) Of the other economists who have defended the possibility of economic calculation in a socialist society with a moneyless economy, one may mention Dr. Carl Landauer.[27] Dr. Landauer's book is an important and restrained attack on the capitalist society, though his positive proposal is not on the same level as the rest of his book. He proposes that his society shall keep a check by means of accounts *in natura*. Professor Mises gives short shrift to this proposal and to the idea of accounting *in natura:*

> Landauer cannot understand that—and why—one is not permitted to add and subtract figures of different denominations. Such a case is, of course, beyond help.[28]

---

[26] *Ibid.,* p. 96.

[27] *Planwirtschaft und Verkehrwirtschaft,* Munich and Leipzig, 1931.

[28] *Socialism,* footnote on p. 137.

5

The Possibility of Economic Calculation in Marxist-Communist Communities

I am a communist and think that all should share, but who is to have the caviar?
—The Norwegian author, Gunnar Heiberg.

By a marxist-communist society, which from now on we will just call "communist," is meant a more "extreme" form of socialist community. This is a very indefinite term, but it is difficult to find a definition of Marxism and Communism that will be generally acceptable. One or two of the definitions most frequently put forward are purely political in character, e.g. that Communism aims at revolution, while Socialism wants to reach its goal by constitutional means. As political definitions do not touch on the problem of calculation, they will be disregarded here. The criterion that Communism means the abrogation of the right of ownership even of necessaries, is of a more economic character, but of little importance for our problem. That the Communists, in contrast to the Socialists, aim at doing away with the state,[1] *may* be of importance for the possibilities of calculation, but this, too, is not a question we shall discuss.

---

[1] See, among others, Lenin: *The State and Revolution,* London, 1917.

There has, however, been put forward a criterion for Communism which is of great significance for our investigation, namely, that in the communist community money does not function as a medium of exchange. This is presumably due to Karl Marx's assertion that monetary capital would not exist in the communist community. On the other hand, Marx admits the possibility of consumption warrants, which puts the question in quite a different light, but of these he says that they are not money, as they do not circulate:

> Monetary capital disappears when there is communal production. The community distributes the labour power and means of production among the different branches of industry. As far as I am concerned, the producers can be given paper warrants, for which they can get a quantity of the communal stores of necessaries corresponding to their labour strength. These warrants are not money. They do not circulate.[2]

Dr. Otto Leichter writes:

> Marx does not regard these paper warrants as money, because they do not circulate. If the concept of money is linked with the assumption of the circulation of goods and a general system of barter, then, of course, this labour-money cannot be money in the capitalist sense of the word, for it is, after all, not a commodity like the gold-coinage of capitalism and has no individual existence of its own.[3]

Whether or not these warrants are to be called money, is a question of definition of minor interest for our purpose. What is decisive, is whether they are to be made out for an

---

[2] *Das Kapital,* Vol. 2, Popular Edition, Berlin, 1926, p. 302.
[3] *Op. cit.,* p. 50.

amount or for *naturalia*. Lenin obviously had the latter in mind when he wrote:

> Every member of society, performing a certain part of so-cially-necessary labour, receives a certificate from society that he has done such and such a quantity of work. According to this certificate, he receives from the public stores of articles of consumption a corresponding quantity of products.[4]

If these warrants are made out for *naturalia* they can hardly be called money, but this is of subordinate interest compared with the fact that in such a case we have a socialist society with a moneyless economy, and on this assumption any further investigation of the possibility of calculation in such a communist community is unnecessary, for, as we have tried to show in the previous chapter, economic calculation cannot be undertaken in that kind of society. We shall therefore assume that our communist community has warrants made out for amounts and that in reality—whatever these claims may be called—it has adopted a monetary economy.

This transfers the whole problem of calculation to another plane, for there will now not only be a common unit of accounting, which was found to be essential in order to be able to calculate at all, but also a number of the difficulties which arise in a moneyless economy in connection with the distribution of the community's goods, will automatically disappear. Where each individual is allotted a certain sum of money or a certain quantity of warrants made out for an amount, he will *himself* be able to decide what he

---

[4] *Op. cit.*, p. 95.

shall get with them and how he shall satisfy his requirements (within the limits of the goods available and the purchasing power of the sum at his disposal). It is not only the existence of a unit of accounting, but its form, which is important for calculation; but before discussing the unit and, later, the question of money, it will be well to mention some further criteria for a communist society which are important for the problem of calculation.

Marx's "From each according to his ability. To each according to his needs," is generally taken as the chief criterion for communism. Whether, in practice, "each" will render according to his ability irrespective of how the resultant production is divided, is a question of social psychology into which we shall not enter. We still assume that those taking part in production are altruistic, but the reader is reminded that compulsory work is generally made one of the conditions of the communist social order. "The same compulsion to work for all, the establishment of industrial armies, particularly for agriculture," so reads point 8 (in the regulations for "advanced countries") in *The Communist Manifesto*[5] and Professor Laski writes: "Compulsory labour is the road to communism."[6]

"To each according to his needs" is a form of distribution of the community's goods which assumes a superfluity of all goods. It represents a desired end, an ideal state, which one can hardly expect to attain in view of the elasticity of needs and their faculty of reproduction. If this condition could be fulfilled, Lenin would be right in saying:

---

[5] *Das Kommunistische Manifest,* 10th Edn., Berlin, 1931, p. 45.
[6] *Communism,* London, 1927, p. 162.

> There will be no need for any exact calculation by society of the quantity of products to be distributed to each of their members; each will take freely. . . .[7]

However, both Marx and Lenin reckon with the possibility that during a period of transition the communist society will have to follow the individualistic and capitalist principle of rewarding according to "the work done," and it is the possibility of calculation in a communist society of this more realistic kind that we shall now investigate.

Let us assume that the central authority has at its disposal a limited, yet continually varying, quantity of resources and will employ these in such a way that the result is greater than the contribution, and will distribute the output "according to the work done." It will use a unit of accounting or a means of exchange which will also serve as a common denominator. The size and the tastes of the population, the methods of production and other factors are taken to be continually changing.

The first question to arise is what kind of common denominator is to be used. That most frequently proposed for the marxist-communist community is *hours of work*. The main theme of the marxist theory of value is that labour is the objectively decisive factor in value, a point which is also insisted upon by those marxist economists who have taken part in the discussion on economic calculation. We shall not try here to point out the defects of the marxist theory of value,[8] but shall confine ourselves to investigating the prob-

---

[7] *Op. cit.*, p. 99.

[8] See, among others, Böhm-Bawerk: *Zum Abschluss des Marxschen Systems* ("Kleinere Abhandlungen über Kapital und Zins"), Vienna and Leipzig, 1926.

lems which calculation will create for the central authority, if the unit of accounting and the yardstick are to be "hours of work."

The use of "hours of work" as a yardstick for value will produce results which are obviously absurd. It is quite possible that it will give a pound of some rare metal, like platinum or molybdenum, the same value as a pound of potatoes, because the mine worked was so rich that it required no more labour to extract a pound of metal than to cultivate a pound of potatoes. It is also possible that one set of goods will be valued higher than another set of exactly the same size and quality made in the same place at the same time, because more time was taken to make the one than the other. Or, what amounts to the same thing, it is not impossible for two sets of goods of different sizes to be given the same value, because the number of hours of work spent on them was the same.

That different results may be achieved by working a similar number of hours can be due to one group of producers working with greater intensity and being more efficient than another, or to one of them having a more competent leader and one who keeps abreast of technical developments and uses more modern machinery and methods of production. That the number of hours worked is inadequate as a yardstick of value becomes even more obvious, when it is applied to rare goods and the efforts of specially gifted individuals, like great artists and scientists. This is self-evident and Marx[9] has emphasized that "higher labour" must be reduced to terms of more ordinary labour. In his opinion this is a simple matter and one which is being done

---

[9] *Das Kapital,* Vol. 1.

daily throughout the world. He later explained this more precisely by saying that it is competition which decides the question, but, as Böhm-Bawerk points out, Marx is here really referring to supply and demand. In other words, in order that the number of hours worked should not be quite useless as a yardstick for value and as a basis for economic calculation, Marx introduced a factor which he otherwise denounces. His contention that throughout the world higher labour is daily being reduced to lower labour was hardly correct when he put it forward, and grows less and less tenable the more wages are standardized and the more general become unionized wages, "scales of wages" and the system of paying according to seniority.

At any rate, Marx's idea is of little practical importance for our central authority, considering that this is the one and only employer and that consequently there can be no real competition for labour. One solution would be for the central authority itself to determine the formulae for reducing higher labour to lower, but this would give rise to great practical difficulties (see Chapter 4) and tend to be arbitrary. Arbitrations in the judgment—and thus in the employment—of labour-power must be fraught with very grave consequences particularly in a society which has made this factor of production the only one for determining value.

Variation in the efficiency of the individual is not the only reason why the use of the number of hours worked as a yardstick for value and unit of accounting will make calculation difficult for the central authority. Even if one assumes that two groups of workers have exactly the same degree of efficiency, that they both work equally well and are equally competently led, the results of their work may still well be different, for the simple reason that one may be working under more favourable conditions than the other. One group of, let us say, agricultural labourers, may have the advantage in being given more fertile land than the other; one group of factory workers may work in a factory more favourably situated (i.e. nearer to sources of power, raw materials or customers) than the other; or the one group may be given more suitable and modern implements than the other. These examples can be multiplied without difficulty,[10] and it will suffice to say that even differences in working conditions which, owing to the greater variability of Nature, one can hardly expect to eliminate, will play their part in making a certain number of working hours give very different results in production, both as regards quality and quantity.

To persist in retaining hours of work as the only factor for determining value throughout every branch of industry, may result in the consumers being able to get 2 lb. of flour of the best quality in one shop for an amount which in another will only buy 1 lb. of medium quality flour. To put it another way, the consumers will find that the same quantity of goods of exactly similar quality will have different prices in different shops. Even the one and the same shop might on the same day have to ask different prices for goods of the same quality, if they were produced in different places where a different number of working hours was necessary to produce the same quantities. Such a result would, of course, appear most incongruous. Another probable result would be that the consumers would have to spend a large propor-

---

[10] In *Collectivist Economic Planning*, Professor N. C. Pierson gives a number of examples of how heterogeneous conditions cause value-problems in the socialist community as well.

tion of their time in finding out in which shop they could on that day buy to the best advantage.

One possible way of avoiding these consequences would be to give consumers not money, but claims to consumption (warrants) made out for quantities, but this brings us back to a moneyless economy and so must be rejected. There is, however, one possible solution (of the distribution side of the problem) and this is that the central authority should retain the number of hours worked as the unit of accounting and yardstick of value throughout every phase of production and trading *until* the last, and that the *selling prices* should be determined on another principle, for example, that of the consumers' preferences. It might possibly be maintained—and with a certain formal justification—that the principle of working hours as the factor which determines value had been preserved in as far as the final sum of all selling prices would correspond to the total sum calculated (on the basis of working hours as the unit for accounting). Actually this would only be a sham solution, as the yardstick for value would be abandoned the moment the final products were priced on a different basis. Besides, a principle would be needed for determining what was to be asked for necessaries. Consumers' preferences are not enough, as they will be influenced by what is asked for the different goods. (See Chapter 6.) Dr. Lange has discussed, though in another connection, the possibility of having two sets of prices for necessaries, but dismissed the idea on the grounds that the consumers would get to know of it and that it "would scarcely be tolerated by any civilised people."[11]

---

[11] "On the Economic Theory of Socialism," in *Review of Economic Studies*, October, 1936, p. 71.

The incongruities and difficulties which the use of working hours as the sole yardstick for value creates for the distribution of necessaries are small compared with the difficulties it will put in the way of calculation for production. In the first place, the adoption of working hours as the sole yardstick of value will *eo ipso* prevent the central authority from being able to measure the significance of other factors of production in achieving the result. For instance, it will have no data for calculating with a production factor like land, as this is not the result of any work. Against this it may be argued that, as it has been assumed that the number of hours worked is the only factor of value, there is no reason to take other factors into consideration. This objection is logically tenable, but conflicts with the factual condition (which is one of our assumptions) that there is scarcity of resources and that therefore a choice must be made between alternative uses.

It is unnecessary to advance detailed proofs to show that this last assumption is the only closest to reality. Apart from certain sources of power, such as water, sun and wind, natural resources gradually become exhausted. This is also true of soil, which becomes impaired with intensive cultivation; it is obviously the case with minerals, coal and oil, and partly so with timber. One possible objection to taking natural resources into account in economic calculation, is the allegation that in the capitalist society, too, there is indiscriminate exploitation of natural resources, for example, of coal and oil. Though this capitalist exploitation may possibly be called indiscriminate, it is a fact that these commodities are to a certain extent rationed inasmuch as the individual mining and oil companies take the scarcity of the commodity into account when fixing their prices. These are determined with reference to the length of time the mine or oil well is expected to be productive, so that scarcity is included in their calculations. Were the central authority in a communist society to do the same, it would be a breach of the principle that working hours was the only factor for determining value. Also in the case of means of production the use of working hours might lead to factors of production not being employed to the best advantage. There is a risk that the central authority will value a produced capital good so low that it will be put to so many uses that there will not be enough to go round, and that it will not be used in those places, where the result would have been greatest. Molybdenum can, as we have said, come from a mine so rich that it does not require much time to extract the metal, which means that a low price is put on it. This might result in a toy factory using molybdenum to make toy swords, with the result that there was less of this metal available for the production of hard steel. If the community in question conducts any foreign trade, there is the further risk that the central authority will export raw materials (and products made from them) which are only available in limited quantities, if, when determining prices, it only takes into account the number of working hours taken and not the scarcity of the materials in question.

There is a further objection to this method of appraising value, namely, that it will make it more difficult for the central authority to determine which piece of land is the more fertile and which factories have the most favourable situation in regard to markets and sources of power, with the result that it will not know which units of production should expand and which restrict their activity. It may perhaps be objected that the central authority has other means of making these decisions: the fertility of a piece of land can be determined by agricultural experts, and the advantages of a factory site may be decided without taking into account the size of its output *in natura*. This objection is supported by the fact that even in the private monetary economy reckoning in natural units is general. As Max Weber points out,[12] units of time are taken into account, for example, in calculating wages; factories reckon with quantities of metals, coal, lubricating oil, the humidity of the atmosphere and with the productive capacity of machinery measured in bobbins, etc. Nevertheless, these moneyless data of different denominations are insufficient for calculation. In order to calculate, one must, as we have tried to show in the previous chapter, have commensurability.

Another serious consequence of adopting the principle that working hours are the only determinant factor for value, is that the central authority will have no indication of what and how much of the various goods is to be produced, and without this it may produce things which are of little or no interest to the members of the community. It is obvious that the result of a million working hours spent in producing horse-carriages will not be of the same interest in a modern society, as if they had been devoted to the manufacture of motor cars, nor would the result of a million working hours in the clothing industry be valued as much by the public if they had been concentrated exclusively on making men's shirts, as if the production had been spread over various kinds of garments.

These objections amount in reality only to a simple demonstration of the fact that the assessment of value also de-

---

[12] *Theory of Social and Economic Organisation,* p. 188.

pends on scarcity of capital goods and the subjective value-judgment of the consumer.

Even students of Marx have admitted—more or less explicitly—that these factors do play a part. Marx himself suggested that higher labour can be reduced to more ordinary labour *via* a market where there is competition (there is no such competition in the communist community). He also admitted the importance of subjective value-judgment. Already in *Das Kapital I* he wrote:

> Finally, nothing can have value, unless it is a thing which can be used. If it is useless, then the work entailed in it is useless, does not count as work, and thus has no value.

This obviously introduced a factor which is as decisive for value as the number of hours worked. Yet this is still not a clear admission, as it can be objected that it is self-evident that articles which have no use whatsoever are worthless. However, if one starts discussing whether or not an article has any use or value at all, one must also discuss whether it has greater or less use and value. In *Das Kapital II* this is done, in as far as Marx speaks of "social necessity," and so introduces an entirely new factor in judging value. He is also using a subjective utilitarian value when he writes:

> In direct exchange of products each article is a direct means of exchange for its owner, and the same for him who is not the owner, but only in so far as it has a usable value for him.[13]

Friedrich Engels also introduces the factor of utility:

> The effective utility of the various consumption articles, compared to each other and against the amount of work nec-

---

[13] *Das Kapital I.*

essary for their production, will in the end determine the plan. Everything is very simply settled without the intermediary of the much-famed value.[14]

and in a footnote is added:

> I have already in 1844 said that this weighing up of effective utility and expenditure of labour when deciding on production, is all that remains in a communist society of the economist's concept of value.

Even Strumilin, a follower of Marx who has made a close study of the problem of economic calculation in the socialist community and who insists on the objective importance of hours of work as a basis for calculation, has been forced to admit that hours of work do *not* suffice for regulating production in the socialist community. Strumilin admits that the utility of economic goods must be taken into account: labour must be distributed in conformity with the utility of the goods, he says, and arrives at the conclusion that the utility of an economic good is reduced as its quantity is increased. Strumilin recalls Fechner's psychophysical law of the decreasing intensity of reaction with the repeated application of the stimulus. Strumilin's exposition has impelled Professor Brutzkus to express amazement that an esteemed economist like Strumilin has forgotten the doctrine of marginal utility, "which represents, after all, an application of this psychophysical law to the phenomena of economics.[15] Brutzkus reproaches Strumilin for being able to believe that the utility of economic goods can be computed *a priori* with the aid of Bernoulli's theory of so-

---

[14] *Dürings Umwälzung der Wissenschaft*, 5th Edn., Stuttgart, 1934, pp. 335–336.

[15] *Op. cit.*, p. 79.

called moral expectation and that he overlooks the fact that this formula refers to money, that is to say, to an abstract equivalent of all economic goods. Brutzkus also reminds him that the intensity of need for the various economic goods is more or less elastic, and says that the connection between the quality of such goods cannot be expressed in any simple formula. (See Chapter 4.) The chief objection to Strumilin's proposal is, as Professor Brutzkus also points out, that he has neglected to show how the utility of the various economic goods may be reduced to a unit and brought into the calculation. He talks of using "certain co-efficients," but should, in Brutzkus' opinion, have called them "uncertain."

Dr. Otto Leichter[16] has also put forward a proposal for a communist-marxist solution of the problem of calculation. It is, he himself says, based on a system of guilds. As such it does not, strictly speaking, come within the scope of a treatise on the *socialist* community. In spite of Leichter's assertion, however, his solution seems to be more suitable for a community with a central authority, and there are other things which recommend it to our attention. It is noteworthy that as early as 1923 Dr. Leichter singled out the problem of economic calculation in the socialist society for special treatment in one of his books. It is equally remarkable that he, a declared Marxist, should have chosen to discuss the conditions under which socialism can function (which, by the way, exposed him to much criticism from the Communists). Dr. Leichter's perception of the necessity for economic calculation (see the quotation on

---

[16] *Die Wirtschaftsrechnung in der Sozialistischen Gesellschaft,* Vienna, 1923.

p. 15) is also worthy of attention, and, finally, it must be mentioned that he clearly realizes the necessity for a socialist society to use money for accounting (but not for exchange). All in all, Dr. Leichter's book is a very severe criticism of everything calling itself moneyless accounting and moneyless economy (see, *inter alia,* the quotation on p. 79).

It is, however, difficult to agree with Dr. Leichter's assertion that he has proved that "a socialist economy can undertake accounting and so be rational in this sense too."[17] His own solution—as might be expected from an exponent of the marxist theory of value—is that the number of hours worked shall be the yardstick for judging value and the basis for calculation. As the above review has shown, a solution on this basis cannot be accepted. Actually, even Dr. Leichter admits this, though indirectly, in that he makes reservations which really undermine his solution, for, when it comes to the point, he wants to take other factors into account.

In the first place Dr. Leichter admits the existence of scarce goods and the necessity of calculating with ground rents and rents for mines. To defend this inconsistency he alleges that these scarce rents lose their capitalist character the moment they benefit not the individual, but the community. This point of view is as interesting as it is characteristic, and is often met with in discussing the economic theory of socialism. Whenever an argument is logically or actually weak refuge is taken behind the plea that it is the community and not the individual which benefits from the income. This, of course, is completely irrelevant. The point

---

[17] *Ibid.,* p. 107.

is, has Dr. Leichter, by admitting and taking into account the existence of scarce goods and the necessity of calculating with ground and mine rents, abandoned the principle of labour being the yardstick for value? This is obviously the case. Who is to receive the income and how is it to be distributed, are questions without significance in this connection. Instead of introducing the factor of distribution, Dr. Leichter should have gone closer into the decisive and central question of how such ground and mine rents are to be fixed in the socialist society. That is the problem to be solved.

In this connection it may be opportune to draw attention to a misunderstanding for which Dr. Leichter is responsible. He says that Professor Maurice Bourguin in the second chapter of his *Les Systèmes Socialistes* gives a solution of the problem which corresponds "in every detail" with his own.[18] It is natural that Dr. Leichter finds points of similarity between that chapter and his own solution, considering that it is there that Professor Bourguin describes the marxist theory of value. Dr. Leichter must have overlooked the fact that Professor Bourguin ends his chapter with the following statement:

> Will value based on labour be able in the collectivist world to fill the dual rôle played by price, that of equilibrium-factor and factor of progress? If not, what forces will be able to take its place? The whole problem of collectivism is contained in these two questions of equilibrium and progress.[19]

Dr. Leichter must also have overlooked the fact that a few pages further on Professor Bourguin writes:

---

[18] *Op. cit.*, p. 74.
[19] *Op. cit.* (Third Edition, Paris, 1933), p. 23.

> In default of a value which freely follows supply and de-
> mand, in the absence of a price giving quantitatively com-
> parable expression to the various collective needs, it seems
> that even with the best statistics at its disposal, the manage-
> ment will have to act blindly.[20]

In a footnote Bourguin criticizes Rodbertus for not seizing
on this difficulty and, instead, of suppressing the problem
by maintaining that human needs are the same, *"en sup-
posant cette serie connue."* Finally Dr. Leichter seems to
have overlooked the fact that in his profound and comprehensive book Professor Bourguin makes many analogous
statements on the importance of price mechanism, and that
consequently he can *not* quote him in his own support, but
should rather give him the name he so often uses: "market-
fetishist."

The second point in which Dr. Leichter departs from
the principle of labour being the yardstick of value is that
he does not entirely succeed in disregarding the value-judgments of the consumers. To be sure he mocks long and often
at the "market-fetishists" and expressly says that the socialist society is absolutely capable of doing without price
fluctuations as "warning signals" for regulating production.[21] Yet, when it comes to the point, these are to be taken
into account to a certain extent. No increase in price may
take place (not even in the case of scarce goods), but "it
is difficult with decreases in price occasioned by small demand."[22] Here, presumably, the market, the tastes of the
consumer and demand are to make themselves felt.

---

[20] *Op. cit.,* p. 49.
[21] *Op. cit.,* p. 83.
[22] *Ibid.,* p. 83.

Professor Mises[23] and Dr. Tisch,[24] both of whom have criticized Dr. Leichter's solution—though on other premises—take him to task for not knowing the subjective doctrine of value. Actually, he knows it well, for not only does he criticize it in so many words, but he seems unable to get away from it. Thus he writes:

> A business will be particularly productive, if it produces a great quantity of goods of high value with the least possible expenditure, that is, as cheaply as possible.[25]

Here it obviously must be subjective value he is thinking of (whether based on the consumers' or the central authority's value-judgment), for if the value is to be judged exclusively by the number of working hours, the products can hardly be both "cheap" and "of high value" at the same time.

In support of the use of the number of working hours as a yardstick for judging value Dr. Leichter alleges, *inter alia,* that producers in a capitalist society make use of economic calculation, and from this he draws the astounding conclusion that the costs of production are the decisive ones and that supply and demand have no influence. If this were not so, calculation would, in his opinion, be pure humbug.[26] After such an argument one can—in spite of everything— understand that Dr. Leichter's acquaintance with the subjective theory of value may be questioned, for, as is well

---

[23] See "Neue Beiträge zum Problem der sozialistischen Wirtschaftsrechnung," in *Archiv für Sozialwissenschaft und Socialpolitik,* 1926, especially pp. 497–500.

[24] *Op. cit.,* pp. 142, 158.

[25] *Ibid.,* p. 106.

[26] *Ibid.,* p. 22.

known, calculation and a knowledge of the costs do not mean that the costs alone decide the price. (It is worth nothing that, like Max Weber, Dr. Leichter is already making use of the concepts of an ante- and post-calculation.)

To justify the use of scarce rents Dr. Leichter alleges that such goods are few and that "most goods" are not scarce, which has led Professor Mises[27] to ask him to name an economic good, where economizing is unnecessary—and that is, indeed, all that needs to be said.

All this leads up to the conclusion that the marxist-communist principle of working hours does not give a sufficient foundation for calculation to enable "the economic principle" to be followed. Consequently it is, for our purpose, unnecessary to occupy ourselves further with solutions which presuppose such a yardstick for judging value as is assumed in these societies.

---

[27] *Op. cit.,* p. 500.

6

Money and the Formation of Prices of Consumer Goods in a Socialist Society with Free Choice of Goods and Occupation[1]

W hat is to be understood by money has been the subject of much argument in economic theory. We shall not enter into that discussion here. When comparing money in capitalist and socialist communities the most important thing to settle is what its functions in the respective societies are to be. Without pretending to give any definition, one is presumably justified in saying that the chief function of money in a capitalist society is that of a medium of exchange, a medium of fulfilling payment (legal discharging of debts), a medium of storing value, and a measure of value (at a given moment and in anticipation of future values). In the capitalist community the monetary expression of value is price. From another point of view price is the expression of exchange-relationship.[2] There is no

---

[1] A monetary economy was also assumed in the previous chapter, so its implications might have been discussed there, but it was natural to concentrate in that chapter on the consequences of the communist-marxist principles.

[2] As we shall see later (cf., *inter alia*, Chapter 14), an attempt is made in this discussion to extend the concept of price and to let prices represent something more and something else than an expression of exchange-relationships.

contradiction in these two dicta. On the contrary, in economics there is a growing tendency to put an equals-sign between value and the result of exchange-relationships.[3]

This is to give the theory of value a much more modest rôle than it had before. Reference to price says even less than reference to "supply and demand." Attention is confined to the result of the conflict between the various factors, disregarding the forces behind them, such as (for supply): number of hours worked and scarcity of resources, and (for demand): subjective valuations of needs and sacrifices—to name the most important ones. One is admittedly on safer ground, when sticking to prices with their special faculty of synthesizing a variety of heterogeneous factors. In a barter market prices can be expressed by their relative barter-relationship to other goods, but the machinery of exchange is simplified and improved by the use of a generally accepted means of exchange which makes it possible to express every price in terms of one good or one unit of value. Thus monetary economy represents a perfection of barter economy.

In Chapter 2 it was said that we had no right to assume the existence of either value-relationships, markets or prices in a socialist society. However, further examination[4] has shown that a monetary economy is a necessity, since a moneyless one does not provide that common denominator which is essential for calculation; and that claims to consumption (warrants) made out for an amount are better than ones made out for a specific quantity of goods *in*

---

[3] Cf. L. M. Fraser: *Economic Thought and Language,* London, 1937, p. 351.
[4] Cf. Chapters 4 and 5.

natura and give their possessor a better opportunity of choosing what needs he will satisfy and to what extent (within the scope of the goods offered and of the purchasing power at his disposal). Finally, the conclusion has been reached that if the central authority is to avoid producing goods in which no one has any interest, it will have to take account of the utility of its products. If not, the goods produced might be said to have a value according to the yardstick used, for example, hours of work, but not necessarily to have one in the eyes of the consumer.

Does acceptance of these conclusions imply that our socialist society is to have a monetary economy similar to that in a capitalist society? Not necessarily. There are essential differences. Seeing that the State is the one and only employer and the sole owner of all goods which may be sold and bought, the socialist society can manage with a giro- or clearing arrangement. In theory it has particularly favourable facilities for carrying this through. Theoretically all payments (whether for raw materials, power, transport or semi-finished products at every stage of production, for wages and consumer goods), can be made by means of cross book-entries. The common unit of reckoning used may be anything one likes, from hours of work to motor-headlights or tillers, as long as it is used consistently. No sort of cover is necessary and one can imagine that the socialist community can manage with money of an entirely different kind to that used in the capitalist society.

In this connection it may be mentioned that money-of-account, of the kind possible in a socialist community, has come to occupy a dominant place in certain central treatises on monetary theory. Professor J. M. Keynes begins his treatise on money as follows:

> Money-of-Account, namely, that in which Debts and Prices and General Purchasing Power are *expressed,* is the primary concept of a Theory of Money.[5]

In his *Currency and Credit,*[6] R. G. Hawtrey takes as his starting point a civilized society which makes use of credit (money-of-account), but not of circulating money. The object of this abstract experiment is to determine the specific function of money, and Hawtrey arrives at the conclusion that it is that of settling debts (which may be performed by "money-of-account").

Even if the facilities for using money-of-account and clearing arrangements are especially favourable in a socialist society and even if it is theoretically possible to use them, there exist great practical difficulties. It is, of course, out of the question that the buyer and seller should meet in person to adjust debits and credits. Drafts or cheques would have to be used. With a cheque- or a clearing-arrangement misuse would be possible by overdrawing accounts. Even if one assumes that fraud is unthinkable in a socialist society, it will nevertheless be possible for accounts to be overdrawn through forgetfulness, failure to make note of expenditure, or faulty bookkeeping. If the person receiving the cheque was obliged to see that there was cover, the practical usefulness of such a clearing system would, of course, be further curtailed. The chief objection, however, is that such an arrangement would be most unwieldy. One has only to think how troublesome it would be to write out a cheque every time one wanted to disburse some small account, such as a tip or bus fare. The amount of book-

---

[5] *A Treatise on Money,* London, 1930, I, pp. 3–4.

[6] *Currency and Credit,* 3rd Edn., London, 1928, Chapter I.

keeping necessary to write up all the milliards of transactions would be enormous. Sooner or later people would start demanding circulation-money as well.[7]

Whether this circulation-money is to be called money or not, is a question of definition and of subordinate interest to this discussion. If one accepts the extreme definition that everything which is accepted as a means of payment is money, then such circulation-money will be money. Also if the central authority only allows communal goods to be distributed against these warrants and forbids any private barter, the members of the community would be forced to accept and use them as money.

It is, however, necessary to point out that this circulation money in a socialist state differs in various respects from money in the capitalist society. One difference is that in a socialist society its circulation will be considerably restricted in that the members of the community, *qua* consumers, can only use it to make purchases in the State's shops and will not be in a position to employ it for buying means of production, raw materials or semi-manufactured goods, or for barter transactions among themselves. This means that the process of circulation will be much shorter than in the capitalist society. In the socialist community the money will go *from the State* (or one of its organs) *to* the consumer and *from* him back *to* the State (or one of its organs). Thus circulation-money is really rather a mislead-

---

[7] Dr. Tisch has gone thoroughly into the question of how far the consumption-warrants, on which her proposed solution of the problem of calculation is based, are money or not. In this connection she gives a full and interesting summary of the rather mixed discussion of money in marxist literature. After a thorough discussion Dr. Tisch comes to the conclusion that money-of-account and clearing alone are impracticable.

ing term and it might be better to call them claims-to-consumption (warrants), keeping in mind, however, that they are made out for amounts and *not* for naturalia.

The fact that the process of circulation is short in distance does not necessarily mean that it will be so in time, for even these claims to consumption can serve as a means of storing value, as a means of hoarding. It seems doubtful that hoarding is such a decisive factor for trade and employment in capitalist societies as Professor Keynes makes out (in his *"General Theory of Employment, Interest, and Money"*), but, in any case, the consequences of hoarding are not necessarily the same in a socialist community, considering that the volume of production of capital goods as well as of consumers' goods is entirely in the hands of the central authority. Whether or not this is compatible with the aim of maximum production for satisfying needs will be discussed in Chapter 14. For the time being we shall assume that it is so and that the central authority has sovereign powers for fixing the kind and volume of production, and that it keeps labour employed, even to the extent of starting an undertaking *solely* for the sake of employment. In this case the only result of hoarding[8] in a socialist community would be that a proportion of the consumer goods put at the disposal of the members during the period in question would remain unsold.

If the aim is continuous turn-over and accumulation of goods is considered undesirable, there are various solutions imaginable. One would be to reduce prices so far that it

---

[8] That the concept of hoarding has been variously interpreted in modern literature, is not relevant in this connection. (See "The Concept of Hoarding," by Joan Robinson, in *Economic Journal,* June, 1938.)

would be more tempting to buy than to hoard. (We shall return shortly to this alternative and the question of fixing prices for consumer goods.) Another way would be to give the money a restricted term of validity, so that the members of the community would either have to use them within a certain period or get nothing for them. Seeing that money in a socialist community has a very restricted use, such limitation of the period of validity is more natural than the "stamping" proposed, e.g., by Silvio Gesell. On the other hand the use of money with a restricted period of validity may have unfortunate secondary effects. (See Chapter 8.)

A third solution would be to make an extra distribution of purchasing power in the shape of higher wages or a social dividend.[9] Such an extra distribution may create certain difficulties. If the unsold goods were of such a kind or quality that nobody wanted them, then the consumers will merely hoard the extra money as well in the hope of being able later to buy goods more suitable to their desires and needs. If such goods did come on the market later the central authority would run the risk of more money being suddenly used (or more warrants presented) than there were goods to meet. Such a situation would arise from other causes, too, for instance, from fear of a rise in prices, or simply because the desire to buy had increased owing to a change of season, which can call forth both unconscious physiological reactions and a desire to provide oneself with clothes and other articles suitable to the time of year.

To eliminate the factor of uncertainty inherent in the

---

[9] For the form of distribution of "social dividends," see the discussion between Dr. Lerner and Dr. Lange in *Review of Economic Studies,* October, 1936, and February, 1937.

hoarding of warrants, it has been suggested that the central authority should tempt the people to invest in bonds, so that it at any time has full control over all outstanding purchasing power. To achieve this, the bonds must be long-term or, preferably, unredeemable. To admit of conversion, redemption or sale would give the savers the opportunity of making that sudden use of their money which it is desired to avoid. If the hoarding should be the result of a desire to keep the money for later purchases of goods, investment in long-term bonds would not appear a very attractive alternative. In order to attract purchases the rate of interest would have to be high. If people were allowed to invest in presumably safe State bonds, bearing a high rate of interest, it would be possible for the parsimonious eventually to live a rentier existence, and this many socialists consider incompatible with the socialist society.

Between money in a capitalist society and money in a socialist one (money being used in the widest sense of the word, including means-of-accounting and claims-to-consumption) there is also the large and essential difference, that money-of-account does not necessarily need to have the same denomination as claims-to-consumption or bear any relation to them in respect of value. This is due to the fact that the State is the sole owner of the means of production and the one and only employer. Production and distribution do not take place *uno acto,* as they do in a capitalist society in which distribution occurs directly out of the production of the economic goods and their exchange, and as its ultimate result. The socialist state on the other hand can allow distribution to be quite independent of the process of production (within the scope of the goods available for distribution). As long as the central authority has the only say in the distribution of communal goods, it can employ one unit of reckoning for production and another for distribution.

The matter, however, takes on a different complexion if it is admitted that the central authority should take into account the utility of the goods produced. This introduces a new factor and necessitates a yardstick to which the central authority must refer. Now, what is useful will depend on the end. That which is useful in a community aiming at rapidly building up its war-machine, is not necessarily so in one which looks to satisfy the needs of its members.

Taking maximum satisfaction of needs as a reasonable working hypothesis, an important question arises: who is to decide what can best serve as means of satisfying the needs of the members of the community, and *what* is useful for them? Here there are two possibilities: either that the members of the community themselves determine the nature and intensity of their needs, or that others, e.g. the central authority, do it for them. To those that believe that people differ not least in their tastes and needs, it will appear unreasonable that the central authority should determine how the individual is to satisfy his needs, or that production should be based on scales of needs fixed by that authority. There are, however, some who think that the State, whether in a socialist or capitalist community, best knows what is good for the members of the community to consume.[10]

---

[10] The different individuals' ideas about this matter seem to depend on their attitude to their fellow men and surroundings in general. People seem—irrespective of "race" and in every phase of civilization—to be divided into two different types: the one demands, as a matter of course,

Both alternatives have been put forward in the discussion of economic calculation in socialist communities. Most of the participants assume, as a matter of course, that there must be free choice of goods and occupation. Some have even made this a pre-condition in their proposed solution of the problem. There are, however, others who think that the problem of calculation can only be solved if these facilities are abolished. Whether one should accept the one or the other alternative is not for the theoretical economist to decide. Both will be discussed here. First, let us assume that the members of the community have a free choice of goods and occupation.[11]

---

respect for the individual's personal character and tastes, while the other prefers common rules for all, feels himself attracted by the mass and thinks that others, too, should merge and incorporate themselves in the mass. It would take too long to discuss here what lies at the back of these two attitudes, or to analyse the attempts to rationalize the state of mind that seems to be derived from instinct. Analogous and equally divergent views are to be found among the Realists and Nominalists of the Middle Ages.

[11] As has been mentioned the majority of those who have taken part in the discussion of the possibility of calculation in the socialist community think that this solution is the natural one. Dr. A. P. Lerner wrote in "Economic Theory" in the *Review of Economic Studies,* 1934–5, that scales of consumption worked out by the bureaucrats of the central authority would be undemocratic and incompatible with socialist ideals. Dr. Oskar Lange concurred in this in his article "On the Economic Theory of Socialism" in the same journal for 1936–7. Dr. Lerner, for his part, makes the reservation that he speaks as a "human being and a sympathizer with socialist ends."

Seeing that Dr. Lerner and Dr. Lange have embarked on a value-judgment in using such a yardstick as "democratic or undemocratic" one would seem entitled to ask whether it were not undemocratic that the socialist state should (1) forbid the members of the community to produce goods they and their fellow-men need, (2) forbid them to engage people for this end, and (3) forbid them to have other employers than the State.

Free choice of goods may mean two things. Either that the consumers can freely choose between the goods available, but that they have no chance of directing the course of production. In that case the preference scale chosen by the central authority is the only deciding factor. Or it may mean that the consumers are able to influence production, which is changed according to their preferences as shown by their effective demand. This latter is the usual interpretation given to free consumer choice and the one which will be used here.

It has been mentioned that a socialist community might under certain conditions have different denominations for money-of-account and consumption-warrants. If we assume that the members of the community shall themselves determine their needs and the trend of production, this contention becomes untenable. In that case it would be more natural to have the same denomination for the prices of necessaries and of means of production (that is to say, to have the same monetary unit for money-of-account and claims-to-consumption), so that the prices of consumer goods can be used for direct calculation and exercise their influence on the prices of means of production—and *vice versa*. This does not imply that one common denomination for money-of-account and claims-to-consumption makes prices in a socialist community serviceable as data for calculation; that point will be gone into later. First, we must quite briefly discuss certain consequences of the assumption that there is a free choice of occupation.

Free choice of occupation can mean both free choice of profession and of the positions for which one may be qualified. Where there is no free choice of occupation the members of the community—either on the basis of intelligence and physio-psychological tests or arbitrarily—will have assigned to them the profession they must choose, and they will have to take the situation assigned to them by the central authority or its agents. Here again, the economist as such is not able to say which alternative should be chosen, even though it is probable that the amount performed will be greater where the work is voluntary, than if compulsory. Should this assumption be correct, as it is generally supposed to be, there will be economic consequences attendant on the choice, which will thus influence the possibility of attaining the end of maximum production to satisfy needs. Here, too, we shall discuss both suppositions, but, for the time being, we assume that there is a free choice of both profession and occupation, keeping in mind, however, that the choice will necessarily be restricted, when there is *ex-definitione* only one employer. Even if the choice of occupation is free in theory, those looking for work may, in practice, have to take what is offered them.

The assumption of free choice of occupation does not greatly affect the question of the possibility of calculation, but it will put certain difficulties in the way of achieving optimal distribution and optimal use of the community's man-power. As this is of a certain theoretical interest, it will be discussed briefly here, even though it does lie somewhat outside the scope of a discussion on calculation.

The natural result of a free choice of occupation will be a rush for the professions and situations which are considered the most attractive. If the State is not able to order people to take up the various types of work, it will have to employ a graded wage-scale if it is to obtain optimal distribution of man-power. This creates a difficulty for those who think that a graduated scale of wages is incompatible with the principle of just and equal distribution. Dr. Oskar Lange[12] has taken up the question and found certain difficulties, for he is not one of those who assume that egoistic-individualistic behavior will disappear under socialism.

Dr. Lange realizes that differentiation of incomes is required in order to obtain optimal distribution of labour, but he tries to show that no real differentiation is necessary. It is important for him to prove this, as he wants to have both free choice of occupation and goods *and* a distribution of income which will maximize "the total welfare of the community".

In his opinion this can only be achieved if the following two conditions are satisfied: (1) that the distribution is such that the same demand-price offered by the different consumers represents an equal urgency of needs, as is obtained if the marginal utility of income is the same for all consumers, and (2) that the distribution leads to such apportionment of the services of labour between the different occupations as to make the difference of the value of the marginal product of labour in the different occupations equal to the differences in the marginal disutility involved in their pursuit.

In Dr. Lange's opinion the first condition is satisfied, when all consumers have the same income, "assuming the marginal utility curves of income to be the same for all individuals." This assumption is wholly unrealistic. It is inadmissible to assume that similar incomes give the same marginal utility curves (see Chapter 4). As Mrs. Joan Robinson puts it, "It is not really justifiable to talk about

---

[12] "On the Economic Theory of Socialism, II," in the *Review of Economic Studies,* February, 1937.

maximum satisfaction to a whole population," for the reason that "to a strictly logical mind any discussion of utility to more than one individual is repugnant."[13]

Dr. Lange is aware that the assumption does not correspond to reality, but holds that "such differences (of 'sensitiveness') would disappear in the relatively homogeneous social stratification of a socialist society and all differences as to 'sensitiveness' would be of a purely individual character." This new assumption, that the citizens of the socialist state will grow into unsensitive automata is doubtful, but very revealing, and so is his disregard of individual characteristics.

Dr. Lange admits (*a*) that optimal distribution of labour necessitates differentiated income, and (*b*) that this may seem to be in contradiction with condition (1). Now he says that this is not really so. By putting leisure, safety, agreeableness of work, etc., into the utility-scales of the individuals, "the disutility of any occupation can be represented as opportunity-cost."

Thus, in Dr. Lange's opinion, the choice of an occupation offering a lower money income, but also a smaller disutility, may be interpreted as *purchase* of leisure, safety, agreeableness of work, etc. He also hints at the possibility of the central authority paying the same money income to any citizen, and charging *a price* for the pursuit of each occupation. He goes on to draw the conclusion that not only is there no contradiction between the two conditions, but that condition (2) is necessary in order to satisfy condition (1).

There are several reasons for not accepting Dr. Lange's

---

[13] *Economics of Imperfect Competition,* London, 1933, p. 318.

subtle argument (which seems, by the way, to be based on arguments advanced by Adam Smith). In the first place, he is arguing in a circle, or, rather, is contradicting himself: he starts by requiring differentiated income, but arrives at the conclusion that the incomes are in reality the same, seeing that from the higher incomes must be subtracted the disutility, which makes it carry a higher salary, and to the lower must be added the advantages (in the shape of leisure, safety, etc.) which make them low. One cannot have at one time differentiated and equal wages. One must either stick to nominal wages, expressed in amounts, *or* to real wages, where advantages and disadvantages are taken into account.

In the second place, optimal distribution of labour does not merely mean geographical distribution (as to places and industries) and a distribution of manual labour, but optimal exploitation of efficiency, professional knowledge, capabilities and readiness to assume responsibility. An employer—in this case the central authority—cannot, when fixing wages, merely take into consideration whether the position in question represents greater or less amenity in his own or the opinion of the applicant. Such criteria cannot be used for grading wages.

The chief thing and the real criterion must be the importance of the performance for the production-result. Unless one believes that all individuals are possessed of the same efficiency, professional knowledge, capabilities and readiness to assume responsibility, the application of this criterion will create differentiated wages in conflict with Dr. Lange's conditions.

We now revert to the question of how the central authority is to procure reliable data for regulating production.

Incorrect data regarding preferences will make itself felt throughout the whole system and distort production in all stages. Wrong production resulting from incorrect data means a loss of utility for the community.

The question of how correct data about consumers' preferences is to be obtained in the socialist society has not been gone into very deeply in the discussion on the possibilities of calculation, even by those who postulate production of needs and free choice of goods (and occupation). Dr. Herbert Zassenhaus has expressed the opinion[14] that the sceptics have been too much occupied with distribution in the socialist community. This is a surprising assertion. To the sceptics belongs the honour of having started the discussion, but to the advocates belongs the honour of having most discussed how satisfaction of needs should be determined, presumably from a feeling that certain difficulties were involved. But even after their treatment, there exist greater problems than have hitherto been pointed out.

Ballots (e.g. together with mannequin parades) have been suggested for obtaining data for determining consumers' preferences. Such an expedient does not solve the difficulties. It is quite impossible for consumers to give a scale of preferences for all consumer goods through such ballots and still less so to indicate the nuances in their desires or the relative strength of their different needs. Further, the final calculation would be enormously difficult, quite apart from the fact that the consumers would have to keep continuously balloting, as the number of consumers, their needs and the relative strength of their needs, are constantly

---

[14] See "Neuere Planwirtschaftsliteratur und die Theorie der Planwirtschaft," in *Zeitschrift für Nationalökonomie,* 1936.

changing. Besides, such an artificial form of voting is entirely superfluous if claims-to-consumption, made out for amounts (money) are used. In his purchases the consumer then has an opportunity, as simple as it is effective, of showing his preferences for the goods available. He is (within the range of goods offered) able to maximize the utility of the purchasing power at his disposal, so that the marginal utility of each unity of income (unit of reckoning) becomes the same for all goods.

It might appear that this solves the problem: the demand will show whether an article is preferred or not; if at the end of the period of reckoning there is a shortage of one article, this would show that more ought to be produced. Unsold goods would be an indication that less should be produced (at the prices fixed).

However, it is not as easy as that. Only under certain definite conditions will a surplus or shortage of goods be an indication of preference on the part of the consumer. In the first place, an opportunity of choice must really exist, not only from among different kinds of goods, but from among goods of the same kind, at different prices and of different quality.

Another and equally important condition is that there shall not be issued more claims-to-consumption than there are consumer goods. If that should be done (or if the same kind of money is used for consumer goods as for the payment of raw materials and semi-manufactured goods, and a part of this latter is used to buy consumer goods), there will be a shortage of these goods. In such a case there will be no indication of how much shall be produced of the different goods and qualities. Just as in tennis a score of 6–0, 6–0 gives no indication of how much better the winner is, so stocks of unsold goods do not reveal how strongly the different goods are desired. Even in the event of the central authority issuing the exact number of claims-to-consumption to absorb the necessaries produced—a postulate often put forward in the discussion of socialism—there will still be no serviceable data for determining what the consumers really want.

If periodic shortages occur, the central authority will not only lack data for these periods, but the whole foundation for determining consumers' preferences may be destroyed, for the consumers will soon learn from experience and use their claims-to-consumption to buy any goods obtainable, so as to get *something* in exchange. The same thing will happen, if the consumers should for one reason or another come to mistrust the value of the money. Such a mistrust would also be a strong stimulant to substitute real values for money, even though the need for the articles in question were not great at the time. Fear of possible inflation would, therefore, likewise contribute to destroy the value of sales-statistics as indications for production.

Whether the demand for consumer goods will give reliable data, will also depend on other factors such as the length of the period of accounting and observation and the facilities for buying on credit and by instalments. Of still greater importance is the question whether the central authority uses fixed prices or prices varying with the demand for the different articles (of different qualities) during the period of accounting. The central authority has supreme power in fixing prices, inasmuch as it has a complete monopoly both as producer and distributor. Here we come up against a problem of calculation of a special kind. Even if we assume for the moment that the problem of calculating production is solved and that there are sufficient goods of every kind to give full facilities for choice, there still remains the problem of how selling prices are to be determined. If fixed prices are maintained and there is not enough of a certain article at the price fixed, the result will be that the central authority receives no indication of how strong the demand for the article in question has been, as there will be queues of would-be consumers, and, presumably, forced rationing. On the other hand, if prices are graded for the different goods according to demand, the central authority gets a stimulated sale of goods for which there has been little demand and a retarded sale of those which have been in greater demand. This last procedure also represents a form of "rationing," but a rationing more in harmony with the aim we have assumed in this chapter, namely, that the members of the community shall themselves be able to determine the scale of preference of their needs and to what extent they wish each of them to be satisfied. If the prices of articles are increased as demands increase and stocks diminish, the number of consumers asking for them will be restricted and the result will be that the goods go to those who feel the need for them so strongly that they are willing to make the corresponding higher sacrifice, that is, to pay the higher price (and *can* pay it).

It is obvious from what has just been said that varying prices will give the best indication of the demand and of the strength of the demand, but the adoption of this solution raises the question of whether the central authority is to increase and lower prices equally along the whole line, or take into account the fact that not only does the elasticity of demand vary for the different articles and qualities, but it also varies as between different villages and districts, and also at different periods and seasons. In other words, is the central authority to regard its retail shops as monopolistic selling branches (what they really are) or as independent units possessing full freedom in their price policies? It is obvious that this latter alternative will give the members of the community the best opportunity to grade the satisfaction of their needs. It also represents the greatest degree of free competition in the last link in the process of production. Whether such competition and such an independent price policy is compatible with socialist ideas, is a question to which we shall revert later. (See Chapter 13.) If competition and independent price policy are adopted, it is evident that one of the principles, from which the champions of socialism expect so much, is broken, viz. centralized planning and centralized initiative-taking.

Even if this objection were passed over, the alternative of varying prices will not solve all the difficulties for the central authority: the demand for an individual article is not only a function of its price, but of the prices of all articles offered for sale. In addition, it depends on the existence of substitute goods, complementary goods and their prices. (See Chapter 4.) The data the central authority can hope to get from the different shops will scarcely prove a sound basis for planning production. If it is possible at all to work out curves of demand on the basis of such data (as has been asserted), these will vary not only because of possible differences in the demand in the town or country district concerned, but also because the shops in the district in question have altered the prices of other goods. In theory the problem is not insoluble, but it will put enormous practical difficulties in the way of calculation.

In addition it must be pointed out that the way the central

authority fixes prices will have a strong influence on the consumers' purchases. The height of a price will influence not only the consumers' demand for these individual articles, but also the use made of their total purchasing power. One must also remember that the retail shops can obviously not be left to fix their prices without regard to what they themselves have to pay for the articles. Their power of fixing their prices according to the demand has its natural limits in the production costs (including selling costs).

How and to what extent the central authority should take into account the cost of production (which depends on the value of the means of production for which there are no markets) and to what extent it shall take into account data of demand, and how these data are to be collated, is merely one of the problems of calculation the socialist community has to face. If the aim "maximum production for satisfaction of needs" is accepted, it is self-evident that the consumers' readiness to pay rising prices for an article should in the last resort lead to more of it being produced, which would mean that more labour power and more capital (means of production and land) should be employed. The task before the central authority is to assure an automatic increase in supply when demand rises.

If it is agreed that a policy of autonomous pricing for the individual shop is compatible with socialism, it is natural to ask why the demand for consumer goods in a socialist society should be less suitable a guide to production than in a private-capitalist one. The explanation is that the basis is entirely different. In a private capitalist society there usually exist alongside the competing autonomous retailers several autonomous, more or less, competing wholesalers, all of whom have established data of costs on which to work. They aim first and foremost at obtaining a maximum profit and do not consciously endeavour to contribute to the maximum satisfaction of the needs of the buying public, which, in a socialist society, is the declared aim. Further, there is only one monopolistic seller and no markets which automatically provide data for calculation. In a private-capitalistic society even the monopolies have certain cost-data at their disposal. If nothing else, there will usually exist prices of goods which may substitute the monopoly's raw materials as well as finished products. Even assuming that the monopoly was absolute and there was no basis of comparison or calculation for either raw materials or the finished product, the task would still be infinitely much easier for a monopolistic concern in a private capitalist society than for the central authority, because the monopoly only concerns itself with obtaining maximum profit.

It is natural to ask whether the central authority could not likewise aim at maximum profit[15] and thus facilitate its task. It might, of course, but having absolute monopolistic power both as producer and as distributor, there is no limit to its ability to maximize profits. Our discussion is based on the assumption that it is maximum production for needs which is the end. In that case the task is entirely different, viz. in the first place to obtain data to determine the changing needs of the members of the community, and, secondly, to incorporate these data in the system of calculation so that they give an indication of how the limited resources

---

[15] As we shall see later (Appendix C) the concept of profit will not be foreign to the socialist community.

can best be employed in alternative uses to achieve this end.

One can imagine various intermediate forms between fixed and variable prices. The most obvious is to maintain fixed low prices (or to have special shops with fixed low prices) for necessaries and a free market with variable prices for luxuries and other articles. This, however, would give the central authority the *least* reliable guide to production. Whether one assumes that there is a certain system in the distribution of claims-to-consumption (a certain connection between the claims distributed and the total price of the goods offered) or mere arbitrariness, the result will be that there will be a "run" on the goods with particularly low prices (or to the shops which sell them). They will always be sold out, from which there will be no other conclusion to be drawn than that at these low prices a larger quantity might have been sold. In the free market, on the other hand, prices will be forced up, because only a small part of the claims can be used in the shops with the cheaper goods. There will be more left for the purchase of free articles, and the central authority will have no indication whatever of the extent to which needs have been satisfied in respect of the cheap and the free articles.

The problems and difficulties connected with fixing prices for necessaries in a socialist society have, as mentioned, scarcely been touched on by those taking part in this discussion, although many of them are aware that to have correct data regarding consumers' preferences is a necessary condition for obtaining that valuation of the means of production which is indispensable to achieve the given end.

The question has been taken up by the first Englishman

who took part in the discussion, H. D. Dickinson.[16] On the subject of calculation of necessaries, he writes:

> The selling agency will sell on the basis of what the market will bear, raising the price when stocks fall short and lowering it when they accumulate.

Mr. Dickinson realizes that "construction of demand schedules" is a very difficult task, since the demand for an article is not merely a function of its price, but the prices of all other articles. (On this point he refers to Cassels' *Theory of Social Economy,* new edition, pp. 139–147.)

There are many objections to Mr. Dickinson's solution, or rather, different suggestions for a solution (see also Chapter 10), but here we shall consider only his proposal to solve the problem of calculating necessaries. Dr. A. P. Lerner, who likewise believes in the possibility of calculation in the socialist society, says of Mr. Dickinson's solution.[17]

> . . . where the concepts have not been sufficiently refined, where a complex thing appears simple, there will be transferred from the capitalist to the socialist society institutions and organizations which find themselves in conflict with their environment. This kind of error is seen in Mr. Dickinson's use of statistically determined demand curves. In the capitalist society it is perhaps possible to get some estimate of a demand curve upon the assumption in each case that other prices are constant. Mr. Dickinson transfers curves drawn up in this way to be added together, thus contradicting the assumption in each case that prices are constant.

---

[16] See "Price Formation in a Socialist Community" in *Economic Journal,* June, 1953.

[17] See "Economic Theory and Socialist Economy" in *Review of Economic Studies,* 1934–5, p. 52.

On one point Dr. Lerner's criticism seems to be built on faulty premises, and that is where he upbraids Dickinson for assuming that price is a function of only one variable. Dickinson specifically draws attention to the theoretical difficulties arising out of the demand for an article being a function of the price of all other articles. However, there are objections to others of Dickinson's proposals, *inter alia* to that that the prices of necessities shall be put as high as "the market will bear." If the state trebles the price of food-stuffs from one week to the other, the market will "bear" it, for people must have foodstuffs and these, in accordance with the assumptions, can only be obtained from the state's shops. Thus a price-policy which aimed at fully exploiting the state's monopolistic position, would not throw much light on consumer's preferences.

The people who ought to be particularly interested in the reliability of the data expressing consumers' preferences, are those who propose "the trial and error method." We shall return to these solutions (see Chapter 11), and here discuss only the fixation of prices for necessaries. What the advocates of the "trial and error method" really mean is, that it is of no consequence what prices are originally fixed. In their opinion the fixing of prices—and the problem of economic calculation in the socialist community in general—can be solved if the central authority takes any surplus or shortage of necessaries as an indication of whether more or less of the article in question is to be produced.

The first to propose this trial and error method was Enrico Barone,[18] but its most ardent champion has been

---

[18] "Über die Ökonomische Theorie der Planwirtschaft" in *Zeitschrift für Nationalökonomie*, Vol. V, Vienna, 1934.

Professor Fred M. Taylor. (See his paper *The Guidance of Production in a Socialist State,* with which he opened the meeting of the American Economic Association in Chicago on 27th December, 1928.[19]) For Professor Taylor the problem is simple. He wants the central authority to fix temporary prices for all goods, including means of production, and goes on to say:

> If, in regulating productive processes, the authorities were actually using for any particular factor a valuation which was too high or too low, that fact would soon disclose itself in unmistakable ways . . . too high a valuation of any factor would cause the stock of that factor to show a surplus at the end of the productive period.[20]

In the same way too low a valuation would lead to a shortage of the article or factor of production in question. Thus, after various attempts, one would be able to fix the correct accountancy prices for the factors of production. In his treatise *On the Economic Theory of Socialism*[21] Dr. Oskar Lange strongly supports Professor Taylor's solution. He mentions that it is the historically given prices which will be the basis for "the process of successive trials," but says that one can just as well start with a set of fortuitous prices, e.g., by drawing numbers out of an urn.[22]

As we have tried to demonstrate in this chapter, the question is far from simple. The extent to which a surplus or shortage of goods will serve as data for consumers' preferences will depend on many factors, *inter alia* on the stability

---

[19] See *American Economic Review*, 1929, p. 1 (also referred to on p. 4).

[20] *Op. cit.,* p. 7.

[21] See *Review of Economic Studies,* October, 1936.

[22] Dr. Lange is referring to Walras: *Element d'économie politique pure.*

of the value of money, on the greater or smaller selection
of goods, on whether the prices are variable or fixed, and,
in the latter case, on whether the central authority's valuation coincides with that of the consumers. It must further
be mentioned that the advocates of the "trial and error
method" obviously assume that the community will be
static, and expect that conditions will remain unaltered,
while the "trial" is being made. On this assumption it is
possible that the method suggested would one day lead
to a satisfactory result, but the problem before us is to get
a satisfactory result in a community where there is continuous variation. We shall come back to the other aspects
of this attempted solution in Chapter 11.

The "trial and error method" has also been proposed by
W. Crosby Roper Jr.[23] who thinks that a shortage of necessaries will be a "clear indication"[24] of what the central authority has to do. At the same time he is, however, fully
aware of the difficulties and is strongly sceptical of being
able to obtain reliable data:

> This description of the process makes it seem rather simple
> and easily accomplished. It is a question, apparently, of ad-
> justing a few mistakes at the beginning and then sitting down
> to watch the system work. But again we ignore the almost in-
> credible complication of the economic process. . . . At the
> establishment of a price system with perhaps only one or two
> considerable errors (an almost unbelievable assumption), those
> one or two errors would involve changes extending through the
> whole structure. If the number of serious mistakes were greater,
> it would take a considerable time and a great deal of careful
> calculation to reach a position of equilibrium, where factors

---

[23] See *The Problem of Pricing in a Socialist State*, Cambridge, Mass.,
1931.
[24] *Op. cit.*, p. 58.

would be priced exactly according to marginal productivity, where these prices would be equal for factors of equal efficiency, and where the whole theoretical system of stable equilibrium was realised. As a matter of fact, this equilibrium could be reached only in a static economy which can never exist.[25]

Mr. Roper well expresses the fact that the indications are after all not so clear and that the consequences of incorrect data will be serious and far-reaching.

---

[25] *Op. cit.*, pp. 58–59.

7

Reserves, Profit and Risk in the Socialist State

We now come to the calculation of means of production, in Professor von Mises' opinion Socialism's greatest problem. In the socialist state there is, by definition, no right of private ownership of means of production and hence neither markets nor prices for them. Consequently, Professor von Mises asserts, economic calculation, and with it economic activity, is impossible in a socialist community,[1] and for that reason he maintains that any form of socialism is impossible. We shall not express an opinion about this till we have discussed the various objections to it and the attempts that have been made to solve the problem Mises has pointed out. First, however, we shall discuss some factors of calculation which any socialist state will have to take into account if it is to follow "the economic principle" and wishes to aim at economic progress. These are interest, rent, risk- and depreciation-quotas.

It is natural to ask why these quotas should necessarily be included in the calculation of production and why the socialist state cannot cover them by taxation, as do the

---

[1] Cf. *Socialism,* p. 119, and *Collectivist Economic Planning,* p. 92.

capitalist societies with their expenditure for social and cultural ends. They can, of course, but as in the socialist community the state is the only employer, it would merely mean that the state would have to reimburse the taxpayer by paying him correspondingly higher wages or in some other way. Such a method of procedure does not absolve the central authority from having to determine the size of the quota. Both in order to save themselves the trouble and expense entailed in collecting extra taxes, and to spare the members of the community the annoyance of paying taxes, it would be simpler for the central authority to withhold sufficient of the production to cover these quotas and to distribute to the members of the community only what was sufficient for their consumption.

In early socialist literature it is maintained that the workers in the socialist state will be paid "the whole output of production." It has even been advanced that the workers should be allowed freely to dispose of the whole product of the mine or factory in which they work. The absurdity of this interpretation is obvious. Even if only work were recognized as a factor of production, the workers in a factory producing finished goods would at any rate have to give a part of the product to the workers who produce the raw materials, semi-manufactured goods or machinery, or in other ways took part in the earlier stages of production. Even for workers engaged at the same stage of production, the result would be nonsensical. The workers in a rich mine would receive higher rewards than those in a poor one, those in a molybdenum mine higher than those in an iron-ore mine, and those in the best situated vineyards much more than the workers in the potato fields. (See also Chapter 5.)

If the entire result of the community's economic activity were shared among all the workers, the result would be less nonsensical, but not even that can be done in practice, if the community in question aims at economic and cultural progress. If that is its aim, the central authority will have to withhold part of the product and set aside certain amounts for various ends. The matter is quite clear in regard to cultural and social ends. Provided the socialist state wishes to maintain or to create a certain cultural and social level, reserves will have to be set aside. This amount will be determined more or less arbitrarily. This is also the case in capitalist societies, but nevertheless there is one great difference. The capitalist state has certain cost data on which to base its calculations. Its public authorities can invite tenders and learn in advance, for example, what a hospital of such and such a size, with such and such equipment, erected in such and such a locality, will cost in comparison with a library of a certain size and with a certain stock in a given locality. In the socialist community there will be no such data expressing the relative scarcity of the resources existing at any given time and to what degree these resources are in demand for various other ends.

Arbitrary as is the method in the capitalist state for determining cultural quotas, it will be considerably more so in the socialist state, unless it can find some other method of procuring similar cost data. To set aside a certain percentage of the community's income will lead nowhere. In order to make comparisons as indicated above, absolute figures are needed.

While most people will admit that there is justification for setting aside funds for cultural and social purposes, few socialists will admit the necessity of profit in a socialist state.

Such a claim may admittedly *prima facie* appear surprising. It is obvious that the state, having absolute monopoly both as producer, dealer and employer, can secure a profit. But does it *need* to, as long as its aim is the satisfaction of the needs of the members of the community? The answer depends on how profit is defined.

Profit is one of the more difficult and obstinate concepts in the doctrine of value and distribution. It can be a *kind* of income, a *part* of an income or a *way* of regarding an income. Profit-income is a residual income which falls to the owner of the business as the owner of that business. He does not need to be sole owner of the individual means of production. They can be borrowed or mortgaged, but the means of production and the *combination* of them are his and the surplus which may remain after the costs of production and the reward for his own work (not merely wages for work contributed, but for professional knowledge and for his contribution as co-ordinating factor) are paid, falls to him as owner with all the advantages—and risks—this may entail.

One characteristic of profit is that it results from buying at a lower price than that at which the article is sold (after all costs are covered). This characteristic makes one think of middlemen and professional speculators, and as neither they nor the owners of private business undertakings have any place in the socialist state, one might well believe that there would therefore be no question of profit. Nevertheless, if the central authority allows the retail shops independently to raise the prices of necessaries in strong demand (as mentioned in the previous chapter), it thereby gives the shops an opportunity to make an income, for which there is no other suitable name than profit. The case

would be the same, even if the central authority itself ordered the increase in price and appropriated the additional
income. Further, it is obvious that there must be question
of profit, if the central authority allows free competition
among business units, as some of those taking part in the
discussion have advocated. (See Chapter 13.)

Profit is, however, something else and something more
than a difference in price or a trading surplus resulting from
efficient conduct and organizing ability. It can also be regarded—and in fact represents—a risk premium. As risk-
quota the socialist community cannot neglect to take profit
into consideration in its calculations (or, if you like) that
element in profit which is made up of the factor of risk).

There are two reasons why the calculation of profit in the
form of a risk-factor is indispensable. If no account is taken
of risk in the socialist community, it will in the first place
appear quite natural to employ resources in any branch of
production whatever, even where there is infinitely little
chance of there being a demand for the product.[2] In the
second place the risk factor of profit is necessary to stimulate activity intended for the future and which is thus *ipso
facto* risky.

H. D. Dickinson thinks that a socialist society can eliminate many risks, among them those due to "simultaneous
action of a number of entrepreneurs ignorant of each others'
decisions,"[3] but he admits that in a community where there
is a free choice of occupation and goods, there will occur an
element of risk which must be taken into account.

---

[2] Cf. "Price Formation in a Socialist Community" by H. D. Dickinson in
Economic Journal, 1933.

[3] *Op. cit.,* p. 245.

It is, however, not the opportunity of free choice which is the decisive factor or the only one to create risk. Whether or not there is free choice of occupation and goods the central authority must, in a dynamic community aiming at economic progress, undertake investments to which there are risks attached. The exploitation of new inventions and new methods necessitates investments and reconstructions which are time-consuming and therefore include an element of risk.

In the capitalist community this risk is borne partly by those engaged in regular productive activity, who are afraid of being left out if they do not use the latest methods, and partly by speculators who own, or can borrow, the necessary capital and who think they can make a profit.[4] As the socialist state has monopolized all business activity, the central authority must itself undertake this risk. This involves

---

[4] It is immaterial what those who carry the risk are called. If one says that the chief characteristic of a speculator is that he acts on the basis of a comparison between present and future values, anyone engaged in long-term economic activity may be called a speculator. If speculators are not merely investors, but what the Americans call "promoters," those who bring together the representatives of technique (inventors), capital, commercial instinct and legal knowledge and get them to work together, they are making a contribution, the importance of which laymen often undervalue.

Experts in the sphere of risk-taking recognize, however, the importance of the promoter. Professor A. S. Dewing concluded a long description of the special attributes promoters must have, with the following words:

"It is this prophetic imagination of the promoter that blazes the paths of industrial progress. Through the economic changes that follow in the march he leads, civilization moves." (Cf. *The Financial Policy of Corporation,* New York, 1919, p. 166.) On the previous page he quotes from Professor E. F. Mead, who wrote *Corporation Finance,* 1915:

"The promoter performs an indispensable function in the community by discovering, formulating and assembling the business propositions by whose development the wealth of society is increased."

difficulties of various kinds. The first consists in the fact that in a socialist state there will by definition be no individual able to engage in productive activity which will bring him either profit or loss.

The discussion on socialism has largely turned on how far the individual can be expected to work his best, when he cannot enjoy the fruits of his labour. This is a question of psychology, which we shall not discuss in all its implications here. We are still using the (unrealistic) assumption that egoistic individualism has no place in the socialist community, and that the individual will give of his best, even if the surplus goes to others. We are here not discussing the capacity and will of employers, but the changed conditions resulting from altered institutions. Even if we assume that sabotage is out of the question in a socialist state and that each will pull his weight according to his capabilities, it seems most unlikely that individuals who have no interests of ownership will reach exactly the same decisions as those that have. One may be for or against private ownership, for or against its consequences, but presumably everyone will admit that elimination of private ownership must have an effect on decisions taken in regard to investments to which an element of risk is attached.

Actually, the way in which chances and possibilities are weighed against each other in the capitalist economy is quite peculiar. On the one hand there is a possibility of profit which—at any rate in part—falls to the person who takes the risk, while on the other hand, he is penalized with the loss of his own property if things go wrong. It is difficult to judge the full implication of this dual incentive to activity and caution. It can certainly not be measured quantitatively, if only for the reason that the result does not necessarily take the form of action. A decision to turn down a project may be just as far-reaching.

Many people will regard it as an advantage that the estimation of risk is left to those who themselves carry the loss if their judgment should prove wrong, and who harvest the advantages when their judgment is right. One should remember in this connection that correct estimation of risk means correct estimation of needs which will be backed by the means to satisfy them (effective demand) by a future distribution of income, which (if the accepted end is satisfaction of needs) will involve a rational employment of resources (with this distribution of income given).

Others will take the opposite point of view, and pointing to the recurrent periods of depression and the permanent state of misery in many quarters, maintain that the system has condemned itself. It is true that there does not seem to be any simultaneous inclination for activity and caution. A business cycle is, in the main, characterized either by optimism, or by pessimism. Those who are concerned with economic activity, whether private or public, seem to be strongly inclined to act alike. The reasons for this—in other words the problem of the trade cycle—will not be discussed here. But this much can be said for the capitalist economy: even if faith in the future, and so the volume of activity, are subject to great variations, the private entrepreneur will, even in optimistic periods, know that it is his own means which are lost if things go wrong, and he will, even in the most pessimistic periods, be on the look-out for possibilities which appear profitable.

No matter which argument one finds the most convincing, it is obvious that the socialist economy will have to find another way of judging risk than that of the capitalist economy. The task is clearly one to be assumed by the central authority. To leave the decision to atomistic business-leaders would imply a competition incompatible with socialism, but it is worth noticing that it would seem to entail less risk-taking and slower economic progress, irrespective of whether the leaders of the socialist undertakings are assumed to be egoistic or altruistic. If egoistic they have no inducement to take steps involving risk, as they have no prospect of making a profit for themselves. If they are assumed to be altruistic, the result is likely to be the same. Correct estimation of risks will give the concern in question an advantage over its competitors, which could cause them unpleasantness and possibly even endanger their position. Thus, an altruistic manager, out of consideration for his colleagues, will be chary of taking any risk which might put him ahead of them.

Risk will have to be estimated by the central authority, and this will create difficulties of various kinds. There are no sure criteria of how far a community should go in taking risks. The risks taken will partly depend on the factor of time, that is to say, on the speed with which it is hoped to attain a certain desired standard of living. A high level of industrial research will give, if not the certainty, at least the hope, of speedier technical development. One danger will be that too many risks are taken, with the result that the losses, which must follow when risks are taken over a longer period, grow so large that the possibility of satisfying the needs of the contemporary generation is "unreasonably" reduced. There is also a possibility of too few risks being taken, which would mean that the community does not achieve so rapid a development in technique and in regard to new possibilities for satisfying needs, as would otherwise have been possible.

In this connection it must be kept in mind that with the given end—production for needs—the risk will be determined by the degree in which the final products are accepted by the members of the community. Should they not want the products which are the final result of an investment on which a risk was taken, it will have been a bad investment. The risk will be less in a community with an undeveloped industry and large resources, than in one with relatively few natural resources and in an advanced stage of technical development. In the former, the central authority can embark on new ventures in practically every field with the certainty of satisfying needs and no great risk of going wrong. In the latter community this risk will be very great.

The extent of the risk will also depend on the degree to which there are alternative uses for the resources employed, should the first use of them prove unfortunate. There is less risk in building factories and producing machinery which can be used for several purposes, than if they can only be used for a single purpose and have to be scrapped if there is no demand for the goods they produce.

There are even difficulties in the way of a purely technical fixation of the risk-quota. Actually, it is misleading to use an expression like risk-quota, as this can give the impression that the problem is solved once the size of the quota has been fixed, e.g. as a percentage of the community's income. This is not the case. There are still many problems to be faced, both technical and of calculation. Dickinson says that the task is difficult, because the risk has to be computed for "each transaction and type of transaction."[5] He hopes that the socialist community "should in time evolve a statistical treatment of risk based on the frequency distribution of sales and price changes."[6]

This is to underestimate the difficulties. The risk-quota cannot be fixed for one "type" of transaction any more than it can be determined in advance, but it must be fixed—as Dickinson says to begin with—for each individual case. Even if it is a question of exactly the same object (e.g. a clutch on a machine which can be used exclusively for the production of a certain article of a certain quality) the costs of research for improvement will vary from time to time, not only with the extent of the experiments made, but because the price of the same quantity of material and labour can fluctuate, either because of the community's monetary policy or with the technical developments and the size and age-composition of the population.

The central authority can put aside a certain sum for scientific research and for laboratories for applied science. That part is simple. The difficulties occur when one has to decide, whether a proposal from one of these laboratories, or an idea of some inventor, is to be experimented with and developed or not. Such a step may involve new methods, new factories, new machines and new goods; there is no past experience to go by and no certainty that the result will correspond to the effort involved.

When it is a question of new methods entailing a saving, one would think that it was easy to determine the quota. To decide whether it would pay to make alterations which would entail, for example, a saving of 25 percent, one must

---

[5] *Op. cit.*, p. 245.

[6] *Ibid.*, p. 245.

nevertheless know what the alterations will cost, and here
one comes up against the old difficulty that there are no
prices for means of production (prices to show whether the
materials could have been better used for other purposes).
Even if we make the (unrealistic) assumption, that the extent of the experiments and all data as to cost are known in
advance, this would merely help the central authority to
decide its attitude to inventions for the improvement of
methods of production. When it is a question of activity,
which in the last resource aims at necessaries, there will still
remain one large and incalculable factor, viz. the reaction
of the members of the community.[7]

---

[7] The difficulty of estimating in advance the rentability of an invention
is illustrated by an enquiry made some years ago in America, which
showed that of the money invested in inventions over a certain period
93.5 per cent. had been lost. The special difficulties in the way of judging
public taste in advance can be seen from what Professor A. S. Dewing
says:

"After all has been said one must conclude that the exploitation of a
new invention, intended to meet a general demand—like a new collar
button, a new hairpin, or even a new camera—is at best a mere gamble.
The psychology of the 'people' is so complex that the value they will place
on a new article is absolutely unpredictable."

Op. cit., p. 157.

That in spite of these obvious risks it is still possible to get new inventions financed in a capitalist society, is due partly to the fact that an
invention which really takes on, can bring in an enormous return and
partly to the fact that there is a number of people who seem to be ir-
resistibly attracted by risky investments of this kind. This attraction may
be due to the hope of large profits. In the case of small savers it is often
due to the belief that money which has been earned with toil and saved
by self-denial deserves a larger return than the banks offer. It may also be
due to a more ideal desire to let humanity benefit by new ideas and new
inventions.

Quite apart from the motive, it is an interesting psychological phenomenon that people of this type will time and again invest their savings in
inventions, even though such earlier investments have only brought them

There are wider implications to the acceptance (1) of "maximum production for needs" as the aim and (2) of the reaction of the public as the yardstick. It implies that technical perfection is not the decisive factor, for, on the assumptions made, a technically outstanding invention or method should not be used unless the requisite labour, time, energy, machinery and materials would satisfy more of the needs of the citizens than they would if used in any other way or in any other combination.[8] If the central authority's calculators are to be able to draw up such a balance, they must have data which will give them a picture of the relative scarcity of resources existing at any one time, and also fresh and reliable data as to the consumers' preferences for the different articles and qualities.

An anticipatory estimate of a risk for a non-instantaneous transaction will be difficult and uncertain in any society whatever. To this extent the capitalist and socialist com-

---

loss. This type of person will also be found in the socialist community, but it will not be possible to make use of their peculiar attributes and self-sacrifice, as the socialist community does not allow commercial activity on one's own account.

[8] Anyone who has studied or occupied himself with the exploitation of inventions, will know how there usually occurs a clash between the inventor, striving for technical perfection, and the financier, who attaches most importance to cost and rentability. The present trend in the world from price-economy to a "planned" economy gives the "engineer mentality" more and more scope. In communities—like the socialist—where it is sought to eliminate completely considerations of "profit" and "rentability," there is a danger of unilateral importance being attached to the technical side. A product which is technically perfect is *ex hypothesi* ideal for its purpose from the technical point of view: it gives joy to the engineers and technical experts and can even give laymen aesthetic pleasure, but it must be insisted that the production of a technically perfect article is economically irrational and an economic misuse of labour and material, if these would have satisfied more needs had they been used for another purpose.

munities are alike. The markets of the former, however, do give data which make it possible to calculate what a transaction or experiment will cost. Even though there is no knowing whether a new product will bring in an income large enough to cover the expenditure, one does at any rate know what the expenditure is going to be. Even future costs, at any rate for a period of six to twelve months, will be known in the capitalist society, because of its forward markets where prices are quoted for future delivery. This means that one is able to eliminate part of that risk which is always attendant on the future. There are various factors which determine forward prices (as for instance the price of the goods for immediate delivery and various costs connected with warehousing, *inter alia* interest), but it is worth noting that forward markets presuppose the existence of private traders and speculators who are willing to bear the risk of the future. It is also worth remembering that (1) the cost-data with which one calculates in a capitalist society take the form of a more or less complete result of the conflict between an offer, which registers the scarcity of existing resources, and a demand, registering the strength of various needs, and (2) that a socialist community with free choice of goods also needs such data for calculating the risk-quota.

8

Interest in the Socialist Society

Whether one accepts the possibility of interest in the socialist community or not is mainly a question of definition not only of interest, but also of such concepts as capital, saving, investment and hoarding. The very fact that these concepts are so differently defined by the various economists—even differently by the one and the same economist at different times—shows how intricate the question is. Here there is room for nothing but a very cursory survey.

It can be said at once that *payment* of interest is not a necessity in a socialist society where by definition the state is the only entrepreneur and the sole owner of the means of production, but that does not mean that it is unnecessary to include interest as a cost item in the *calculations* of the central authority. Whether one regards interest as a necessary item of calculation depends on what theory of interest one accepts.

Those who accept the productivity theory and the utility theory will have to admit that the use of produced means of production is a factor of cost which has to be taken into calculation. If, however, interest is regarded, as in the abstinence theory, as a premium for individual saving, it is unnecessary to include it in the calculation, since the state has no need to appeal to the willingness to save of the members of the community, as it can arbitrarily decide how much shall be set aside from current consumption for the various purposes. If the Marxist doctrine of interest is accepted, according to which interest is the result of capitalist exploitation, then naturally there will be no such thing as interest, since private capital has been abolished.[1]

According to Böhm-Bawerk's theory of interest which is based on the view that interest is an agio of present goods against future goods, it will also exist in socialist communities. As a matter of fact, he expressly says so in the chapter on "*Das Zins in Sozialistenstaat.*[2]

There will also be interest in the socialist community, if Professor Cassel is right in his theory that interest is the result of scarcity of capital. Cassel devotes a special chapter to demonstrating this.[3]

According to Schumpeter's dynamic theory of interest,[4] interest arises because entrepreneurs without capital obtain control of means of production, for which under existing conditions of ownership they have to pay by handing over

---

[1] This theory of interest is discussed and criticized in Eugen von Böhm-Bawerk's "Capital und Capitalzins II," *Geschichte und Kritik des Capitalzinstheoriens,* Innsbruck, 1900.

[2] See "Capital und Capitalzins I," *Positive Theorie des Capitals,* p. 338–396. Böhm-Bawerk's theory of interest is criticized in Gustav Cassel's *Teoretisk Socialökonomi,* Stockholm, 1934, p. 202; and in Emil Sax's *Der Kapitalzins,* Berlin, 1916; and his view on the "perspective of future goods" in O. Morgenstern's article "Das Zeitmoment in der Wertlehre" in *Zeitschrift für Nationalökonomie,* 1934.

[3] *Op. cit.,* p. 258.

[4] See *Theorie der wirtschaftlichen Entwicklung,* Leipzig, 1912.

to the owners part of the profits from their enterprise. If this theory, which Emil Lederer calls the most flexible and the most explicit of them all,[5] is correct, there will be no interest in the socialist community, because it does not allow of either entrepreneurs or private ownership of means of production. Schumpeter himself points out that in the communist society[6] there is no such thing as interest as a *"selbstständige Werterscheinung."*

More recently, J. M. Keynes has defined interest as the

> *price* of hoards in the sense that it measures the pecuniary sacrifice which the holder of a hoard thinks it worth while to suffer in preferring it to other claims and assets having an equal present value.[7]

---

[5] See "Developments in Economic Theory" in *American Economic Review*, 1936, Supp., p. 156. For a criticism of Schumpeter's theory, see Böhm-Bawerk's "Eine dynamische Theorie des Kapitalzinsen" in *Zeitschrift für Volkswirtschaftlichen Sozialpolitik*, Vol. XXII and *Gesammelte Schriften*, Vol II, Vienna and Leipzig, 1926.

[6] *Op. cit.*, p. 348.

[7] See "Alternative Theories of the Rate of Interest" in *Economic Journal*, June, 1937, p. 251. It is better to stick to this article, rather than to refer to *The General Theory of Employment, Interest and Money*, 1936, both because it is clearer and a later interpretation. In his *General Theory* Keynes wrote at one point that "the rate of interest is a purely monetary phenomenon" (pp. 355–356), and at another that interest "sets a standard to which the marginal efficiency of a capital-asset must attain if it is to be newly produced," (p. 222); and referring to the significance of interest rates for investment, he wrote the following, which can hardly be said to make for clarity: "Our conclusion can be stated in the most general form (taking the propensity to consume as given) as follows. No further increase in the rate of investment is possible when the greatest amongst the own-rates of own-interest of all available assets is equal to the greatest amongst the marginal efficiencies of all assets, measured in terms of the asset whose own-rate of own-interest is greatest" (p. 236).

This is amplified on the preceding page:

> The function of the rate of interest is to modify the money-prices of other capital assets in such a way as to equalize the attraction of holding them and holding cash. This has nothing whatever to do with current saving or new investment.

Now, how are those who accept Keynes' definition to answer the question of whether or not there will be such a thing as interest in the socialist community? Keynes did not himself go into this question, even though he called his book *General Theory*. As was said in Chapter 6 there is nothing to prevent money claims-to-consumption being saved even in the socialist community, and one can even imagine the central authority accepting loans so as to reduce the number of hoarded claims-to-consumption and to prevent them from being suddenly presented *en masse*. It is, therefore, very possible to have interest in the socialist community. It is another question, whether such interest can be called a price, seeing that the central authority can arbitrarily regulate not only the distribution of the claims-to-consumption, but also the possibility of there being any alternative use for them at all (by reducing the supply of consumer goods). According to Keynes' definition you *can* have interest in the socialist community, even *payment* of interest, but this interest is such that the central authority does not necessarily have to take it into account in its calculations for production, since it has nothing whatever to do with current saving or new investment."[8]

---

[8] In his "Alternative Theories of the Rate of Interest" in *Economic Journal*, September, 1937, D. H. Robertson wrote that acceptance of Keynes' definition did not preclude one from regarding interest as the price of the use of a loan (p. 429) nor as the reward for marginal inconvenience

In the *Economic Journal* of December, 1932, there is an article by Professor Bertil Ohlin in which, as spokesman of the Stockholm School, he criticises Professor Keynes' *General Theory* with reference to the theory of interest. He draws attention, however, to the fact that this has been but little analysed by the Stockholm School. Professor Ohlin answers the question of how the level of interest is determined, thus:

> The answer is that the rate of interest is simply the price of credit, and that it is therefore governed by the supply of and demand for credit.[9]

This means that interest must not only be payment for keeping cash, but for investment in other "claims," which includes shares and other securities. According to Ohlin's definition one could have interest in a socialist community in so far as one can imagine there being bonds. On the other hand, if this is so, it brings us back to the question of whether "price" is a suitable term for bond interest, which is essentially fixed by the state in its capacity of monopolistic or, to borrow Mrs. Robinson's terms, monopsonistic buyer of labour and issuer of loans.

Ohlin's definition has this advantage that it is more comprehensive than Keynes', but all the same it is not comprehensive enough. In the first place, it is not much use refer-

---

or abstaining from consumption (p. 431). One must agree with this view that interest has several functions, but Keynes has expressly stated that according to his definition interest can have nothing to do "with current saving and new investment" (see above) and that is a point of the greatest interest in a discussion of economic calculation in the socialist society.

[9] See "Some Notes on the Stockholm Theory of Saving and Investment III" in *Economic Journal* June, 1937, p. 224.

ring to "supply and demand" without knowing what creates them, which is just what we want to know.

There seems no other way of discussing the place of interest in the socialist economy (and its place in the economic calculation of that economy) than by reviewing the place it occupies in the capitalist economy. Though there is much to be said against such a review in a book like this (*inter alia* that the question is an intricate one and that a short survey of it can easily be superficial and defective) it is natural to go more closely into the question, if only because it has been asserted that the impossibility of calculating interest in the socialist economy is one of the most serious objections that can be made against socialism (of which more later). It must be emphasized that the object of this review is merely to put forward individual aspects of the mutual interdependence between interest, savings and investment.

Professor Ohlin's definition of interest is suitable as a starting point. Savings can be defined in various ways. The general one is that they are income minus consumption, but there is a somewhat wider definition, or rather, interpretation, which is that savings represent the accumulation of resources through the restriction of immediate consumption. By investment is understood the conversion of the saved resources into a relatively, or completely, non-liquid form.[10]

---

[10] It must be stressed that this interpretation of saving and investment does not agree with that used in the present discussion of interest. There is no essential distinction between the latter and that of L. M. Fraser in his book *Economic Thought and Language,* London, 1937, but most today make "saving" *ex definitione* equal to "investment," among them Keynes and also Ohlin on behalf of the Stockholm School. (See *Economic Journal,* June, 1937.) Our interpretation is that saving is equiv-

Before we begin this review it is well to remember that we wanted to base the discussion on the assumption that conditions were dynamic. This is particularly desirable when discussing concepts like saving and investment in capitalist communities. In a dynamic community saving is influenced by the constantly changing distribution of income,[11] and investment means, by definition, an increase in the community's capital (assuming that the final products are accepted according to the yardstick adopted in that community). On the other hand, the factors which have now to be treated are so intimately interrelated that, taking it all in all, they can only be discussed here on the assumption that *ceteris paribus,* conditions are static.

To begin with savings: it is evident that in a capitalist

---

alent to investment, where a firm spends current income for new investment or where a farmer builds a new outhouse in his spare time, but there *is* a difference—and an interval of time—when in a monetary economy saved means are (1) hoarded or (2) put in a bank which does not want to lend them out or cannot find acceptable borrowers.

[11] There are two main forms of alteration in the distribution of income. Generally one thinks of displacements between the various social groups. One forgets that in private capitalist societies the individual person's and family's income is continually altering. This can happen without any change in the income of the group or in the relationship between the incomes of the various groups. In societies with reasonably free competition without *fideikommis* or privileges (allodial rights, etc.) it is seldom that large incomes or fortunes are maintained for many generations. This is not only due to fluctuations in economic activity, wars, unstable currency conditions, heavy taxation, and the decline in the respect for contracts, but to the simple fact that in a society with private capitalist economy and competition, the individual person or family is constantly exposed to the risk of having his income or fortune reduced, unless it renders services or produces products which the other members of the society demand and which they—with the given, though constantly changing distribution of income—are able to acquire. This is true, whether the services are intellectual, artistic, manual labour or the provision of capital.

community there are individuals who are willing to re-
nounce present goods for the sake of future goods. People
in the temperate zones have always been forced by the great
disparity between summer and winter to accumulate a certain amount of stores from season to season. Even in these
days of specialization, when the task of supplying natural
foodstuffs has been taken over by definite groups, such individuals are still to be found. In the use they make of their
resources and their income they take into account not only
the satisfaction of their immediate needs, but also the needs
which their experience tells them will arise over the whole
income period. One can say that such an arrangement is
evidence of common-sense and foresight, but one cannot
overlook the possibility of an individual's willingness to save
being to a large extent the result of physiological processes
and childhood experiences, as some psychologists maintain.

There is no basis for judging what proportion of saving is
made with the object of getting an increased future income.
Increased income is obviously the aim of direct saving in
non-monetary form which occurs as well in a monetary
economy (draining of land, clearing fresh ground, gather-
ing stones, building houses and fences, increasing the number of plants and animals by not consuming or selling
them).

Increased income is also the aim of direct, but monetary
saving, which takes place when corporations instead of distributing their income in the form of dividends use it to
expand their productive equipment. The motives the state
may have when it saves by using taxes for investment purposes (see definition on p. 148) or for the repayment of
debts, are so manifold that we cannot enter into them here.

The tendency is at present towards public and corporate

saving, but individual monetary saving still remains an important factor. To what extent this is determined by the possibility of increasing income, it is difficult to say, as conditions change from one phase of the business cycle to another. The general view is that high and rising rates of interest stimulate saving, but on the other hand it has been suggested—and not without reason—that a low rate of interest forces those who aim at some definite level of future income from investments to save *more*.

If it is true, as is always being contended and seems to be borne out empirically,[12] that the extent and rate of saving is determined by those with large incomes, the obvious conclusion is that interest only plays a small part in determining the volume of savings. People with large incomes will normally make their standard of living, which is fixed by custom and social convention, the constant factor, and let their amount of saving be variable. If that is the way things are, the state of the business cycle will be a more important factor than interest in determining the savings of active capitalists. For passive capitalists a higher rate of interest will mean a higher rate of saving, but only for new savings, since they cannot enjoy the higher rate for what they have already invested (unless they have "invested" in cash or convertible securities).

If it is correct that the standard of living is the primary concern, then it follows that the volume of saving will also be influenced by changes in the level of prices, since higher or lower prices will require a larger or smaller outlay to

---

[12] See *America's Capacity to Consume*, Brookings Institution, Washington, 1934, and *Kapitalbildung* by J. Marschak and W. Lederer, London, 1936, etc.

maintain that standard. It is possible, even probable, that this larger or smaller outlay will—for the individual—be neutralized by a larger or smaller income resulting from the rise or fall in the level of prices, but there is no certainty that a rising or falling price level means rising or falling incomes (or changes in the distribution of the national income).[13]

If, on the other hand, it is the willingness to save which is the constant factor with most individuals, whether this be due to instinct, childhood experiences, custom or common sense, this still means that the rate of interest is a subordinate factor in determining the extent of saving.[14]

Now these considerations are only tenable so long as the rate of interest keeps within certain limits. If there were an opportunity to invest in long-term, gilt-edged securities at 25 per cent per annum, presumably many would find such an interest rate worth considerable sacrifice in the form of saving.

If one goes to the other extreme and considers interest rates of 2, 1 and 0 per cent, the matter becomes uncertain. It is more than probable that 0 per cent interest would have a restrictive effect on savings, but it is not impossible that large sections of the population would continue to save —to ensure their old age or their family's future—even if

---

[13] Reservations of this kind, especially with reference to fluctuations of prices, can be made in respect of most statements in this, necessarily short, survey of the relationship between interest, saving and investment in the capitalist society.

[14] That an alteration in the interest-rate or in the level of economic activity may cause dislocation of already invested means (what Johan Akerman calls an alteration in the "quality of the saving quota") does not affect the point discussed here, which is the extent of the savings and the relationship between savings and investment.

they did not receive any interest. It is even conceivable that people with a deep-rooted instinct to save would accept a negative interest rate (-1 or -2 per cent), especially if this gave them absolute certainty that the principal would be paid back.

If one accepts the definition of interest as the price of credit, it must be emphasized that this price occurs in a market where price-formation is most imperfect and which is influenced by a number of factors other than saving and investment.

The various types of loans have their own markets, but we shall take as our common index the official[15] discount rate which influences most loans. (The exceptions are relatively few. The interest on loans which entail a large risk[16] or which are bound up with a lot of labour as, for example, pawnbroking, are usually little affected by alterations in the official discount rate. The same is true, at any rate periodically, of interest on certain long-term loans.)

The discount rate is fixed by the directors of the central bank and the politicians, not, of course, arbitrarily, for it depends on many things, of which the liquidity of the central bank is presumably the most important. This liquidity again depends on a number of factors, chief of which is the position of the private banks. Practically speaking all lending activity is reflected, even though in many cases only

---

[15] In this connection it is of minor importance that offcial discount rates are not always the same as the effective rates, since banks of issue in some countries (e.g. Sweden) give private banks a rebate on re-discounts.

[16] The imperfection of price formation in the loan markets is also expressed in the fact that respectable financial institutions are content to accept or reject requests for loans and do not as a rule offer a loan at higher rates. (We cannot indulge in further discussion of the risk factor implied in interest rates.)

indirectly, in the position of the private banks. Any change in their position, any shifting in the relation between loans and deposits, is a factor to which great weight is generally given in fixing the discount rate, even in cases where the position of the private banks is so liquid, that they are not borrowers at the central bank.

Nevertheless, it is of special interest to our discussion to see that there are a number of *other* factors than savings, which influence discount policy. If the view is accepted, that the interest rate is an important factor affecting the level of economic activity (and it is a view that can be accepted only with strong reservations and with due reference to the phase of the business cycle), the rate of discount will be altered for reasons of *business cycle policy*. These reasons differ in different phases of the business cycle, from country to country, and even from time to time during the same phase and in the same country; they may have regard to a variety of indices such as the wholesale price level, or the cost of living, or the index of production, or stock exchange speculation, or movements in exchange rates, or a combination of these or other factors. The legal cover is a variable factor in that it can be altered, but as a general rule it may be said that the discount rate is altered when the central bank's reserves are approaching the minimum level in force at the time.

This means that in countries on the gold standard or which use gold as an exchange standard, *gold or currency holdings,* or rather the movements in them, play a definite part. These movements are determined by the balance of payments, among other things. This, in turn, is determined *inter alia,* by the extent of capital exports and imports (which again are influenced by political factors both at home and abroad) and by the difference in value between the total quantity of goods and services the community in question buys and sells. This difference in value is influenced both by changes in prices in the various groups of goods and services within the country and by changes in the price-levels of the different countries.

We cannot follow the causal chain any further, and shall only mention one more factor: devaluation and revaluation of currencies. This makes it possible for the central bank concerned to write up or down its holdings of metal or foreign currencies, and consequently to contract or expand the credit basis of the central bank and community in question, which can and usually does influence the central bank's interest policy and rate of discount. It may be remarked here that a higher or lower price for gold means higher or lower profits for its producers and so—assuming that costs do not rise or fall correspondingly—a greater or smaller output. As long as gold serves directly or indirectly as a basis for credit, the writing up or down of gold values will also indirectly influence the level of the interest rate.

Psychological considerations may play their part to the extent that an increase in the rate of discount which the rules might demand, is not made because the financial authorities are afraid that it will be regarded as a sign of weakness and defeat its own purpose.

These considerations show that savings are not the only factor which affect the height of the interest rate. In this connection it must be repeated that there are also savings which lie outside the loan market, namely those which involve no money transaction (see p. 150) and those which businesses make by expanding, modernizing or making new purchases directly out of current income without having recourse to a loan. Both these forms of investing occur *uno acto* with saving.

The effect on the interest rate of the saving which takes the form of hoarding[17] will depend on the form and intensity of the hoarding. If hoarding is more or less constant, that is both in form and extent, the effect will be small or nil. An increasing tendency to hoard can have a hardening effect on the rate of interest if the money is tucked away in cupboard drawers and money boxes, as this *ceteris paribus* means that the cash reserves of the private banks will decrease. A decrease in hoarding will have the opposite effect.

As hoarding and liquidity preference have been thrust very much into the forefront in contemporary discussion of interest and the business cycle, it may not be out of place to mention that this liquidity preference is partly involuntary, at any rate as far as active business is concerned. It is first and foremost lack of sales (or fear of such a lack in the future) which creates liquidity preference. Liquidity preference is not an end in itself; it is a regrettable choice which is made merely because there is no alternative and, given the scale of values reigning at the moment, no attractive opportunities for using or investing one's money.

The relationship between investment and the interest rate is also a very complicated phenomenon. The demand for credit is likewise influenced in many ways and is subject to sudden fluctuations. Investment made *uno acto* with saving has no direct influence on the interest market, any more than has saving of the same kind. However, it should

---

[17] Hoarding is not necessarily a consequence of saving. An individual can spend all his income in a given period and yet increase his cash holdings through sale of capital assets.

be noted—and this is very important—that saving, even if it takes place *uno acto* with investment, creates several credit objects which means greater possibilities (credit basis) for later loan activities (which, besides, vary greatly with the movement of the business cycle and so with the optimism or pessimism of business-men and bankers). On the assumption that both the velocity of circulation of cash and deposits, and the tendency to hoard remain constant, an increase in borrowing and lending will mean increased deposits.[18]

This brings us to the question of what is the significance of variations in the amount of money (and credit) for saving and investment. About this there are a variety of opinions, which as a rule can be traced back to different ways of looking at the quantity theory and the "banking" and "currency" theories. Here we shall merely mention one elementary, but very important feature, namely that increased lending activity may have repercussions on the price level.

As regards investment not made *uno acto* with saving, the investment will—*ceteris paribus*—tend to tighten interest rates. Unless it is financed out of hoards, it either means that loans are increased, which means—other things being equal—smaller cash reserves, or it means the withdrawal of deposits which likewise means smaller cash reserves. Here

---

[18] This, of course, does not mean that an individual bank can increase its loans so as to achieve increased deposits. Where the cash reserve requirements remain constant (whether they are based on law or custom) the bank concerned will run the risk of deposits going to other banks and of its own liquidity being reduced. That the deposits may return in a different form, e.g. as demand deposits instead of time deposits, which imply higher cash reserves, is a further objection, but not relevant when, as has been assumed, the propensity to hoarding is constant.

again we come up against the velocity of circulation of cash and deposits—a very important and incalculable factor.

Having said that both saving and investment affect interest rates *via* the cash reserves of the private banks, it is time to mention that these are determined, apart from the legal regulations, by what the banks and the public regard as a reasonable cash reserve for deposits.

In this connection one must mention another important factor—particularly important in the present day loan market—namely *open market operations,* by which is understood purchases and sales by the central bank in the home market (usually of gold, foreign exchange and bills) intended to influence the private banks' cash reserves and so their ability to lend, which means that they affect the loan and interest markets.

One of the most interesting problems in the theory of money and practical monetary policy, is that of determining how far a central bank can increase investment (or at any rate the opportunities for lending) by open market operations without having regard to the movements of deposits, and what consequences and repercussions this may have.

The answer depends on many factors. First one has to find out whether a broadening of the credit basis also leads to increased lending activity. There is no *a priori* certainty of that. In a capitalist economy the initiative behind lending activity rests with the business-men and they can not be forced to take up loans. If they do not wish to borrow, the result of the central bank's buying is that the liquidity of the private banks increases and, presumably, also that the interest rates fall, but it cannot lead of itself to an increase in investment.

If the increased quantity of money and credit is not used

for investment, but for consumption, there is danger of inflation (by which is here meant a rise in prices caused by an increase in the media of exchange in relation to the objects of exchange). Here again the velocity of circulation of money comes in as an important variable. Whether active open market operations will have an inflationary effect or not, will also depend on the amount of investment made in the same or the previous period outside the money and loan markets.

This, again, will depend on whether the results of the investments, both of those made outside and of those made *via* financial institutions, have been accepted by the public and can exercise an influence on the price of goods. If the results (the consumer goods) are not accepted, with the result that means of production have been produced which are not wanted,[19] then purchasing power has been put in circulation which does not find a counterpart in the form of saleable goods, and this, other things being equal, signifies inflation (but this effect may be counter-acted by a lower velocity of circulation for cash and deposits *or* by hoarding).

Whether an increase in the amount of money, whether rising prices and an increase in loans will affect savings, will also depend on whether the savers are engaged in branches of industry which benefit *immediately* from the increased prices through increased incomes (both nominal and real) or whether they are in other branches where higher prices

---

[19] Professor Mises writes in *Socialism,* p. 203: "The fact that consumption is restricted for the sake of constructing big plants of different kinds is not evidence that new capital is created. These plants will have to prove in the future whether they will contribute to the better supply of commodities wanted for the improvement of the economic situation of the country."

merely lead to an increase in their expenditure without giving them higher incomes.

There is not much point in going closer into this question, as its significance for judging conditions in a socialist society is merely subsidiary. In one respect, however, the conditions are the same: if the result of an investment is not "approved" by the public, there is a waste of the community's resources. That means there is less chance of satisfying needs, in other words a faulty investment for a society which aims at "maximum production for needs."

As regards the effect of interest rates on investment—and on the demand for credit—one can speak with greater certainty. It is obvious that interest is more important as a factor influencing investment than it is as a factor influencing saving. As a matter of course, the rate of interest will be of considerable importance for projects which depend on large loans (in relation to their entrepreneurs' own capital) and long-term loans (e.g. in buying property and house building). The determining factor in making a new investment with borrowed capital is, nevertheless, profitability, and profit accrues only *after* all costs, including interest, have been calculated.

As it is a question of the production of future goods, it really is the *expectation* of profit which is the determining factor. Expectations are as a rule so complicated that we shall not go closer into the question here (see Appendix A), but they are most largely influenced by the course of the business cycle. If expectations are such that a business man can count on a net profit of 15-20-30 per cent and on being able to pay the loan back quickly, even the possibility of having to pay a very high rate of interest does not have any restrictive effect. But if, on the other hand, the business man is convinced that prices are going to fall, even a zero interest rate may not tempt him.

The experience of the 1930's shows—what could have been predicted—that low interest rates do not automatically stimulate investment. Low and falling interest rates still seem to have less significance than the retarding influence of high rates of interest. The direction in which interest rates are moving seems to play a larger part than their absolute height. Likewise the rate at which they move, plays its part. Small alterations, each of which is relatively insignificant and which are made at such long intervals that the public accustoms itself to them, may not have any influence at all. Here one has to take account of factors such as the public's psychological attitude during the period in question and how much faith it has in the desire of the financial authorities to influence the level of economic activity and in the effectiveness of discount policy for this purpose.

The influence of the interest rate on investment will also depend on the size of the "social sector" in the community in question (see Appendix A) as this sector is "indifferent to profitability."[20]

The above analysis has touched on the mutual interdependence between interest on the one hand and saving and investment on the other, but not on that between saving and investment. Here there are large and difficult problems. It is characteristic of the prevailing uncertainty that while Professor Spiethoff thinks that the change from good to bad times in trade is due to investment being too large in relation to saving, Professor Keynes thinks it is because saving is

---

[20] The phrase is taken from *Kapitalbildung* where the question is gone into more closely in the first "Theoretischer Teil."

too large in relation to investment, while Professor Hayek is of the opinion that there can be no disparity between saving and investment so long as inflation does not take place.[21]

We have said that investment presupposes saving. For this statement to have any value, we must go into it a little more deeply. It does *not* mean that a sufficiently large store of consumer goods and raw materials has to be saved to cover the investment period. Nor, obviously, does it mean that there will be any conformity either in quantity or in value between saving and investment. As regards the value aspect, the future valuation will always be an unknown quantity, while, as far as the quantity aspect is concerned, investment implies (by definition) the transformation of the saved resources into a relatively non-liquid form.

This raises the far-reaching question of how far savings may occur *before* investment, or whether they can be made *simultaneously* or even *after* investment.

To judge the importance of savings for investment, one must take into account what has been saved previously and the stage of technological development of the community in question. Also, as has been mentioned, movements in the general level of economic activity are an important factor.

In regard to the other relationship, that concerning the importance of investment for the level of economic activity, it is clear that, if the level of employment is treated as the main criterion of the level of economic activity, the end of

---

[21] For a more detailed discussion, see "The Theory of Saving" II, by C. Bresciani-Torroni in *Economica,* May, 1936. See also the chapters "The Over-investment Theories" and "The Underconsumption Theories" in Gottfried von Haberler's *Prosperity and Depression,* Geneva, 1937.

a wave of investment (whether of new or re-investment) will bring with it a shift in economic activity, in that it may mean transference of labour.

In this connection attention must be drawn to three factors which are of importance in analysing both the course of the business cycle and the relationship between the interest rate and investment: (1) There is an intimate connection between the trade cycle and activity in the capital goods industries. (2) Firms in the later stages of production have usually a larger burden of interest than those in the earlier stages. (3) Activity in firms in the later stages of production (or, if you like, concerns on the outer circuit of the roundabout process of production) in capitalist societies presupposes confidence in the future.

From (1) and (2) we can infer that the interest rate is also a very important factor influencing the level of economic activity. This, however, is in the author's opinion largely counterbalanced by (3), since the fact that these firms are in the later stages (on the outer circuit) means that their *expectations of the future* are of decisive importance. A factor which points in the same direction is that one can wait to order and renew means of production, which is not always the case with consumption goods and the products of firms in the earlier stages.

Before we leave this question of "interest in the capitalist society" it must be pointed out that interest, quite apart from its significance for saving and investment and *vice versa,* is of importance as an *element of cost, as a factor in calculations.* If a concern or an entrepreneur is working with borrowed funds, the interest is entered as expenditure on the debit side of the profit and loss account. Even if the concern works exclusively with its own capital, interest is taken into consideration; in business analyses and comparisons "interest on own capital" is entered as a separate item. In practice it will be possible to find individual concerns where this is not done. One reason for this is that such an entry has little bearing on tax liabilities, in so far as the expense item "interest on own capital" is counterbalanced by a corresponding income from interest. But that it does not appear among the expense items, does not mean that it has not to be taken into account in judging whether a concern is fit to survive or not. When it has to be decided whether a business shall be established—or wound up—consideration is taken of what interest those providing the capital can get, with as much (or little) risk, by employing their capital elsewhere. Tradition or consideration for his employees may perhaps induce the owner of a business, which is not earning enough to cover its interest on the capital invested, to carry on, but it will be clear both to himself and to his competitors that the business is being continued for philanthropic motives and not for economic reasons.

In this cursory review of individual aspects of the problem of interest in the capitalist economy questions have been discussed some of which may appear simple, but which are —and this must be emphasized—very controversial. However, most people will probably accept the following conclusions: (1) In a capitalist society some individuals have a propensity to save. (2) There exist facilities for individual saving and so for satisfying this propensity. (3) Savings are a necessary prerequisite and basis for investment. (4) In the capitalist economy there are data in the shape of rates of interest for various classes of loans and deposits. (5) The rate of interest is determined not only by saving and investment, but also by other factors. (6) Interest figures among the costs that are taken into account when judging whether a business justifies its existence or not.

The question now to be answered is whether and to what extent conditions will be analogous in a socialist society, whether it is necessary to save and invest in such a community, and in that event, how the necessary data for calculation are to be obtained, when the aim is the satisfaction of the needs of the members of the community.

(1) One may presume that there will still be people with the urge to save even in the socialist society. The central authority may say that it is irrational and contrary to reason for the members of their community to wish to secure themselves and their dependents, since the socialist society will look after all in the event of sickness, unemployment and old age. The central authority may think that urges to save due to childhood experiences will be eliminated by a different type of childhood experience. It may say that the inclination to save is due to a human instinct and that human instincts will be altered under socialism. Irrespective of what point of view it takes, it cannot get away from the fact that if there is this urge to save, it will have to satisfy it so long as it aims at "the satisfaction of the needs of the members of the community."

(2) It is comparatively simple to provide the members of the community with facilities for individual saving. In the first place there will always be an opportunity for saving through the purchase of durable consumer goods and non-perishable foodstuffs and luxury goods. This way of saving will, however, scarcely satisfy those individuals who like to hold titles, not to buy. Nor will it satisfy those who desire the greatest degree of liquidity, i.e. monetary claims.

Saving in the form of monetary claims can create difficulties for the distribution of consumer goods, as they may lead to mass presentation of claims-to-consumption and an uneven rate of sale for goods (see p. 106). To avoid such an eventuality, i.e. in order to eliminate the possibility of hoarding, the use of money with a limited period of validity has been suggested. What is wanted here, however, is the opposite, viz: an arrangement to make hoarding possible. It is obvious that if the central authority finds the disadvantages of a possible mass presentation of claims to consumption smaller than the advantages of giving the members of the community facilities for individual saving, it cannot limit the period of validity. On the contrary, in this case the members of the community should be allowed to expect that their money will have a fixed value.

Another way of making money saving possible is the issue of bonds. One presumable objection to this is that they make inequality in the distribution of wealth possible, which is just what most friends of socialism say the socialist society will eliminate. However, inequality in the distribution of wealth is a logical consequence of facilities for saving. The payment of interest in itself implies the possibility of unequal distribution of income. However, the interest on bonds whose one and only object is to provide an outlet for people's urge to save can be low. If, on the other hand, the central authority issues bonds with the object of preventing hoarding, the interest rate will have to be made high and the bonds irredeemable (see Chapter 6, p. 108).

The fact that the central authority may give the members of the community facilities for satisfying their urge to save does not mean that it is they who determine what the volume of savings is to be. By being the one and only entrepreneur, the state will be alone in deciding whether there is to be real saving and, if so, how much. It will not be necessary for the members of the community to do the actual real saving. The central authority can decide the production of future goods, hold back supplies and by this or other means make the volume of saving it thinks fit without asking anyone. Thus what the community saves will be little or no indication of the individuals' will to save, since their saving to all intents and purposes will be regulated by the central authority, which in its capacity as the one and only employer determines prices and thus the level of real wages, and as the only borrower, or practically so, the rate of interest.

(3) In judging the need for saving and investment in the socialist society, let us first consider one or two simple facts that characterize production of capital goods, whether the form of the community be socialist or private-capitalist.

The first is this, that in modern, industrialized societies production involves the use of produced means of production (tools, machinery, factories and means of transport etc.), since their use saves time and effort. The second is that all production, including that of the means of production, requires time in any kind of community. The third, that the roundabout process of production which results from producing and using the produced means of production demands (*a*) labour, power and raw materials, not only to make the means of production, but also to produce the intermediate products at the various stages of production, and (*b*) a store, or a continual supply, of consumers' goods (food and luxuries) for the workers engaged in this roundabout process of production.

This relationship may be obscured in the capitalist society since the savings are not always made by the same individuals who make the investments. In the socialist society it would be clearer, since the central authority will have sovereign power to regulate the extent of both savings and investment. Thus, in the socialist society, it will be obvious that an increase in the production of means of production will imply that the members of the community are relatively less able to satisfy their immediate needs.

As the accepted aim is production for needs, this will involve making a choice. What do the members of the community prefer? More goods to-day and fewer in the future, or fewer to-day and more in the future, or a combination of the two and, in that case, which? The answer will depend on how many more goods they will get and on the interval of time, that is to say, on how long it will be before they get them. Though some individuals rate the thought of future enjoyment higher than present enjoyment and the possession itself, most people consider a bird in the hand worth two in the bush, and prefer the certain to the uncertain. Thus the central authority will presumably be justified in considering that waiting is a sacrifice and, also, in assuming that the magnitude of this sacrifice will depend on the time it takes to achieve the increased quantity of goods.

If the period of waiting is to be so long that it becomes possible that an individual may never get any enjoyment of these future goods because of old age or of his having died in the meantime, he must be expected to prefer immediate goods, though, of course, he might be willing to make the sacrifice to benefit his descendants. This same argument will allow the central authority to maintain that in determining the volume of the savings quota, it must not only take the present generation into consideration, but also the following ones. The central authority may also claim that it is paying prior regard to future generations. This, in theory, provides a justification for expanding the apparatus of production to such an extent as to entail shortages so great that part of the existing population starves to death. This, however, would conflict with our hypothesis that it is the needs of the present members of the community which the central authority must satisfy. This means that in considering each expansion of the apparatus of production the central authority must take into consideration the amount of time the process will require.[22] The value of the future goods will have to be discounted somehow to give their present value and so provide a basis for comparison with the goods "invested." To do this, there must in the first place be what we may call a "coefficient of discount."[23] The determination of this factor, which is only part of the task, creates many and considerable difficulties.

---

[22] This bears no reference to the time-factor's significance for interest in the capitalist society. That a calculation is made per unit of time does not necessarily mean that time is the decisive factor. It seems to the author unjustifiable to judge the question of interest without taking account of the *productivity* and *scarcity* of the *capital*. One is probably entitled to say that all the main theories of interest are built up on the productivity: Böhm-Bawerk writes of the advantages of "round-about production," Schumpeter of "economic development," and Cassel of "the result of the economic activity." With reference to the time factor, see, among others: C. A. J. v. Gadolin's "Bermerkungen zur Diskussion über die Zeitkonzeption des Kapitals" in *Zeitschrift für Nationalökonomie,* and P. N. Rosenstein-Rodan's "The Role of Time in Economic Theory" in *Economica,* 1934, where the various problems connected with the time-factor are discussed.

[23] That interest is used as such a discount-coefficient in the capitalist society does not entitle us to call a possible discount-coefficient in the socialist society interest. In the capitalist society interest has more functions than just that of discount-coefficient.

The coefficient of discount we are looking for is an expression of the community's valuation of present goods in relation to a greater quantity of future goods (greater, because an increase in the quantity of goods and/or a reduction in working hours and effort is indirect production's *raison d'être*) and it must cover the entire economy and not just be marginal. How can this discount factor be found?

To take one simple example: the central authority is in a position to increase the production of bread by employing mechanical baking. The manufacture of the machinery and the erection of the factories will take a certain time and involve certain costs. We assume that these can be expressed in terms of bread. The point of departure is that an increase in the bread ration of the future will entail a reduction of the bread ration during the period of construction. In a socialist society the prices of the means of production and hence the cost data do not exist. For the time being, we will disregard the factor of sacrifice and stick to the first part of the task, that is to compare a certain greater quantity of bread in the future with the quantity which the consumers receive in the present. This gives us a clearer illustration of the difficulties entailed in determining a discount-factor of this kind.

The data required are (1) the size of the increase in quantity, (2) the length of time required before the increased quantity is available, (3) the people's valuation of the present good, and (4) their valuation of the future good.

(1) It is assumed that the extent by which the quantity is to be increased has been decided on as an end. This Datum is thus given.

(2) On the face of it, it would appear simple to deter-

mine the interval of time. If, for example, the production of bread is to be doubled, so and so many factories must be built to produce the machinery the bakeries need; there must be built so and so many bakeries, so and so many new railways and lorries for the carriage of the grain and bread, etc. and the engineers will be able to say that this should take such and such a length of time. Let us assume that all the technical data have been correct and that all the factories are finished on the date given, so that spasmodic increases in the satisfaction of the future requirements of bread are eliminated. Nevertheless difficulties will occur by reason of the fact that the interval depends on *which* means of production are used and in *what* combination.

This is not merely a technical question. For an industrialized society it is in fact not only one good that is produced, but many, and not only one particular means of production is used, but several, which to a greater or lesser extent can be substituted for each other. What has to be ascertained is not simply the combination of the factors of production that is technically the best, but whether or not these factors could have been put to a better use in the same or another combination for another end.

Though the object is the "maximum production for needs," the central authority will in practice have to treat each individual capital good as if it were a production factor of its own and test it out in every conceivable combination in which it might be used. These experiments must be made simultaneously, so as to avoid the various kinds of change that the passage of time introduces. Once the best combination has been found, that is to say, best not merely from the technical point of view but also in relation to the scarcity of the capital good concerned, and to the extent and intensity of the demand for the final product, then, but only then, can the interval of time be determined.

(3) To obtain accurate data for judging the people's valuation of the present good, certain hypotheses must be satisfied, which will raise many difficulties in a socialist community. (See Chapter 5.)

(4) The attempt to determine the "value" of the future good will meet with even greater difficulties. If the central authority puts its own price on the future good, as it can do in its capacity as the one and only employer and producer in the same way as it does with the present consumer's good, the whole thing becomes arbitrary and there is no point in our investigating it, since it is the people's valuation of the future good in relation to the present good, that we are looking for.

Nor is it possible to calculate the value of the future good on the basis of the materials and means of production used. The usual difficulties are met with here: in the socialist community there are, by definition, no markets and therefore no market prices for means of production. It wouldn't even help, if there were. What we are searching for are future prices and, unless forward markets exist, these must be determined on the basis of present prices with interest added. To attempt to make this addition brings us back to where we started, as it is just a rate of interest, or, rather, a discount factor, at which we are trying to arrive.

In view of these difficulties the central authority will have to look for other ways of finding a discount factor that will make the "maximum production for needs" possible over a longer period of time. One can imagine it trying to obtain the necessary material by means of the "interview method" and asking individuals what their attitude would be to a permanent increase in the bread-ration entailing a temporary reduction in it. The size of the increase is determined by the central authority and so is given, as in the previous case. Here, too, the same difficulties will be encountered as in the previous case in regard to (2) the interval, and (3) the future price.

In one respect, however, the interview-method can yield better results than general calculations. Assuming that the central authority has found the interval and the future price of one individual article (the increase in production being given) the individual person will be able to say which he prefers: the large quantity of goods in the future or the present goods (see p. 221, Chapter 11). He will be able to make a direct comparison between the larger quantity of goods in the future[24] (larger than the present quantity) that will result from the change-over to mechanical baking. In other words, he can make a direct comparison between the reward and the sacrifice.

Actually, the sacrifice is already indicated, in as much as we have assumed a future price different from the present price. To make a comparison it is presumably easier to assume the price unchanged and let the sacrifice simply be a smaller ration during the period of construction. The most accurate result will be reached, if those interviewed are presented with varying data (increase in production and sacrifice). We shall return later to some difficulties implied in measuring the sacrifice.

---

[24] It is really inaccurate to use the term "quantity." As we are concerned with a *flow* of consumer goods, the time factor ought to be taken into consideration here as well. To avoid making the style too involved we have not used the expression "quantity per unit of time," which would have been the correct one to use.

The individual person's valuation of future goods against present goods will be influenced by a complex of factors. It will vary not only with his intelligence and emotional make-up, but also with the present level of his income, his expected income and its purchasing power, his present and expected needs and his expectation of life. All the same, after a certain amount of pondering the normal individual will be able to give a direct answer, whether or not he considers an increase of so-and-so many per cent in the bread ration after a certain interval worth a reduction of so many per cent during that interval.

Such an answer, however, will not get the central authority very far. It will, of course, give a certain individual's discount factor at a given moment for a certain article (see p. 59), but this will be of no use to the central authority in its production policy, for the simple reason that people's tastes and valuations change almost incessantly.

There is the additional fact that one and the same individual's coefficient of discount will vary for different commodities according to the elasticity of need for the commodity concerned. If an average coefficient of discount were to be calculated for each person, use would have to be made of "weighted coefficients." This would create new problems, quite apart from the fact that such coefficients cannot be added, since they are really incommensurable magnitudes. Account must also be taken of the fact that the individual person's coefficient of discount for a certain good will change with an alteration in the supply of future goods, not only because his valuation is influenced by the total quantity, but because certain goods are complementary and substitutional.

That is not the end of the difficulties. What is wanted is a coefficient of discount that will be valid for all members of the community, and not for individual persons only. Even if a coefficient of discount were found for each individual person, it could not give any common coefficient valid for them all, as they cannot be added.

It must be pointed out that difficulties in getting a discount factor are in fact much greater than we have portrayed them here, where we have only gone into the question of the comparison of consumer goods. If roundabout production was exclusively concerned with the construction of factories, machinery, warehouses and means of transport, which can be used to produce a certain consumer good, such an assumption would have been permissible. In reality, however, roundabout production consists to a large extent in the manufacture of means of production that can be used for the production of *different* consumer goods and also different *capital* goods (machines, tools, means of transport, power stations are typical examples). It is impossible to fix a coefficient of discount for capital goods on the basis of people's individual subjective valuation of their present and future utility.

As so far we have given little attention to the factor of sacrifice, it must be emphasized that the prerequisite for an increased quantity of goods in the future is a reduction in the flow of present goods. The question of sacrifice raises new difficulties. If it should appear that a quantity of future goods after being discounted down to their present value is worth less than the smaller quantity of present goods, either by reason of the length of the interval of time or of Gossen's laws,[25] the matter will be clear and the central au-

---

[25] See p. 41.

thority will have a valuable indication that it would be uneconomic to begin production of the good concerned. If,
however, it should appear that the discounted value of the
future good was greater than that of the present good, the
question of sacrifice would have to be gone into. In the
first example given, the discount factor—provided it could
be calculated at all—merely made it possible to compare
people's subjective valuation of future goods with present
goods, which gave the central authority no indication of
how much of the present goods (or of other present goods
of the same "value") people would sacrifice in order to acquire a greater quantity of future goods.

This sacrifice is in an analogous position with utility:
each individual's assessment of the sacrifice will change with
time. Then, too, the sacrifice (reluctance to have the flow
of present goods reduced) will increase the more production is switched over to future production. The matter
would be a comparatively simple one, if it were merely a
question of restricting the current consumption of bread
or shoes, so as to get more bread or shoes (in the future),
but the sacrifice will increase progressively and become
more and more difficult to assess, as more such sacrifices
are demanded. The sacrifice curve is no more proportional
and rectilinear than is that of the satisfaction of needs.
There is also the fact that each individual's readiness to
accept sacrifices and his sacrifice curve will vary over time,
and that it is impossible to add together possible data for
arriving at the sacrifices of individual goods he is prepared
to make. This means that the central authority will be left
without any indication of how much of all forms of present
goods the members of the community are ready to sacrifice
in the aggregate, in other words, that it cannot get any

picture of the total saving the community is prepared to make.

(4) Even in the socialist society it is desirable that there should be data in the shape of interest rates, but in such a community these interest rates will reflect the relationship between saving and investment even less than in the capitalist society, partly because they do not figure in any market where the lender and borrower compete, and partly because the central authority can arbitrarily determine both the extent of saving permissible to the members of the community and the price that shall be paid for loans.

(5) and (6) In the socialist society not only interest rates, but also saving and investment, will have to be determined arbitrarily by the central authority.

(7) For this reason the interest rate will not have any real significance. The central authority will have no data it can use as a costing factor in judging a concern's right to exist.

There will be two results of the absence of interest rates with which to calculate. The first is what has just been mentioned, that the central authority will lack a measure of the productivity and value of the different concerns. The amount of capital used will vary from one branch of industry to another and from one concern to another. If it does not charge to annual expenses an allowance for the values which these capital goods represent, the central authority will never know whether the greater or lesser output per labour-hour is due to a greater or lesser employment of capital, greater or lesser efficiency (on the part of the management and workers), or to other factors. The principle remains the same, whatever you reckon as capital. If the original factors of production are put in a class of their own, their use must be counted as a cost factor of its own, as a rent. (For reasons which will transpire in the next chapter, this method of procedure is adopted here.) Thus the capital with which the concern will have to be debited, will consist of manufactured means of production: factories, machinery, tools, semi-manufactured goods and raw materials with which they have been supplied. In both cases there will arise the difficulty in calculation, that in the socialist community there are no known prices for means of production. "Interest" expressed as a percentage is of no use as a factor of calculation, where interest must be expressed as a price or an amount commensurate with the other costing factors.

The second and more important consequence of there being no interest rates with which to calculate, is that the central authority's calculations do not automatically include *time* as an economic factor in the form of annual debiting of interest. Its aim of maximum production for needs cannot be achieved, when in making its decisions it takes no account of the time it takes to open mines, build factories, produce machinery, plant forests, drain land, etc. If a greater quantity of the society's resources is used for *future* ends than its members are prepared to sacrifice for those ends, this means reduced welfare for the community.

In a socialist society the people will no longer be able to influence the relationship between production of future goods and of present goods. In a capitalist society the people at any rate have some means of influencing the level of interest rates (and thus of investment) through their monetary savings, and also by their ability to make non-monetary savings, and also by their ability to make non-monetary investments *in natura* simultaneously with their savings. Neither of these possibilities will exist in the socialist community, since the state is by definition the one and only producer and the only trader, since it does not allow private individuals to produce or exchange means of production for their own account, nor in any other way permits any private initiative in investment matters. Without an interest rate the central authority will be deprived of a necessary costing factor and datum for calculation.

To conclude this chapter on interest we shall quote various economists' opinions on interest in the socialist society. As has been mentioned, this has been the subject of special discussion by many economists (Böhm-Bawerk, Marx, Cassel and Schumpeter, among others), and their opinion as to whether interest may or may not exist, depended on the presence, or absence, of the factor they have stressed as most important in explaining interest on capital.

V. Pareto says[26] that, since loans are forbidden, there really won't exist *"d'intérêt (loyer net de l'épargne)"* in the socialist society, but all the same there will be something that represents the sacrifice entailed by foregoing the consumption of economic goods.[27] The example he takes is that of the socialist government sharing out 100 kg. of artichokes for the removal of the stones from a patch of ground, which will make an increase of 5 kgs. in the crop of artichokes possible. These 5 kg. are called *"une prime pour le retard de la jouissance de la consommation,"* but fundamentally it is just *"l'intérêt."* He says: *"Le gouvernement socialiste devra, pour obtenir le maximum d'ophélimité, distribuer la partie des marchandises qu'il prélève sur*

---

[26] *Cours d'Economie Politique, II,* Lausanne, 1897.
[27] *Op. cit.,* p. 369.

le produit total, entre les différents usages qu'on en peut faire, de sorte que la prime pour le retard de la jouissance soit égale pour chacun de ces usages."[28]

The question of interest has also been treated, or, at least, touched upon, by many of those who took part in the discussion of the possibility of calculation in the socialist community. Beginning with those who believe in such a possibility, there is Mrs. Wootton, who says that:

> Interest is . . . payment for a real cost: namely, that of waiting for a deferred result or making the (in all probability, normally painful) effort of saving.[29] . . . No planned enterprise, can . . . be said to cover its costs unless its proceeds provide in full for interest as well as for wages and materials. But here we come up against the unanswerable question: What is 'full interest' in a socialized economy.[30]

She writes that in the absence of a capital market "the true cost of abstinence cannot be tested out."[31] Mrs. Wootton has a greater respect for the importance of pricing of interest in the capitalist society than has the author of this treatise, but there is no discrepancy between Mrs. Wootton's conclusion and his, when she says:

> Where capital goods are collectively owned and their creation made a matter of collective determination, interest remains a real economic cost indeed; but that its measurement in quantitative terms becomes so difficult that current rates of interest cease to be any use as guides to practical policy.[32]

---

[28] *Ibid.*, p. 370.
[29] *Plan or No Plan*, p. 96.
[30] *Op. cit.*, p. 98.
[31] *Ibid.*, p. 98.
[32] *Ibid.*, p. 100.

H. D. Dickinson's conception of the socialist society assumes, as has been mentioned, the continuance of many of the capitalist society's forms of organization, among others autonomous concerns "similar to limited liability companies in a capitalist corporation."[33] Dickinson is of the opinion that every entrepreneur can submit different alternative plans for his business, assuming interest rates of 6, 5, 4, 3, etc. per cent and that, on the basis of these plans, it will be possible to construct an aggregate demand schedule for capital.[34]

Here it must be objected, in the first place, that demand schedules cannot be simply added together, and, secondly, that there must be a market to provide them with a common denominator. Further, no attention is given to the utility factor, since it is assumed, as Dickinson does in so many words, that there are free markets. He obviously also, by implication, assumes a *given* amount of capital, for he takes no account of the sacrifice involved in continued saving. The volume of saving in a socialist community must and will be determined arbitrarily by the central authority. (See also Mrs. Wootton's objection to Dickinson's argument.)[35]

Dickinson uses "years' purchase" to express interest rates, which is an interesting suggestion. One example he uses is that of a railway, which is to cross a piece of high ground, where the choice is between a tunnel, implying large non-recurrent costs and small running costs, and building it over the top, when the non-recurrent costs will be less and the running costs large. Dickinson is of the

---

[33] "Price Formation in a Socialist Community" in *Economic Journal,* 1933.
[34] *Ibid.,* p. 243.
[35] *Op. cit.,* p. 99, footnote.

opinion that the works proposed can be classified according to the "years' purchase" they involve and that a balance can be arrived at by continuing investment in all branches of production up to the same number of "years' purchase." Even if we accept Dickinson's assumption—strange as it is for the socialist society—that there is a free market for means of production (and consequently prices to calculate with), his proposal does not get us any further. His yardstick can only by used when it is a question of comparing the costs of installation with an annual saving in running expenses; it cannot be used for means of production for the manufacture of *new* consumers' goods, where the utility factor comes in, nor for means of production that can be used for a variety of purposes (e.g. a tool factory).

Examples often quoted in discussing interest in the socialist society are those of drainage schemes, clearing of ground, etc. where the costs are expressed in the same unit as the resulting product (grain, artichokes, etc.). The use of 100 tons of corn for paying the labourers is assumed to give an increase in production of, e.g. five tons, and the question is then raised whether or not the draining shall be undertaken. It may not be out of place to recall that in modern industrialized communities interest calculations cannot be made *in natura*. The whole problem appears comparatively simple when the resulting product is of the same kind as that which is used to produce it, but in the world of reality the final product is the result of several production factors. If corn or another commodity is to be taken as the unit of measurement, it must be explained on what principle the value of the various *other* factors has been judged.

Dr. Cläre Tisch has devoted considerable attention to

this discussion on interest.[36] In her opinion interest will occur as a *"Rechnungsgrösse"* (since present goods have an agio against future goods) but she doesn't indicate in what manner or at what height this *"Rechnungsgrösse"* is to be fixed.

Dr. Oscar Lange assumes without further discussion that the members of the community can have no influence on interest or on the extent and rate of increase of savings in a socialist community. He writes that: "a rate of accumulation which does not reflect the preferences of the consumers as to the timeshape of the flow of income may be regarded as a diminution of social welfare."[37] He is, however, of the opinion, that this deficiency is outweighed by the many advantages of socialism.

Dr. A. P. Lerner asserts that interest represents the marginal productivity of waiting, which itself depends on saving and investment.[38] Overlooking the fact that interest is determined by other factors than these, this does little to explain what takes place in reality.

H. Zassenhaus[39] says that there cannot be such a thing as interest on capital in a socialist society, since the entrepreneurs' remuneration goes to the benefit of the consumer. Later, he says that not even a socialist society can indulge in roundabout production without simultaneously lessening the production of consumer goods. He also points out that

---

[36] *Op. cit.*, pp. 38–46; 75–84.

[37] "On the Economic Theory and Socialist Economy, II" in *Review of Economic Studies*, February, 1937, p. 127.

[38] See "Economic Theory and Socialist Economy" in *Review of Economic Studies*, 1934–35, p. 56.

[39] See "Über die ökonomische Theorie der Planwirtschaft" in *Zeitschrift fur Nationalökonomie*, 1934, pp. 521–522.

if the ministry of production wishes to make use of individual savings, there could be a prize for saving, which would be similar to interest on capital, but he also points out that the ministry could make this prize larger or smaller at the time of distribution, and that the influence this "interest" could have on the apportionment of new investments in the different branches of production would be quite insignificant.

Here it must be mentioned that Zassenhaus fails to point out that the central authority must have a discount factor (and prices for capital goods), if it wishes to make economic calculations. The fact that in a socialist society interest on capital will not exist as a payment for services does not mean that it can be eliminated as a factor of calculation.

Dr. Eduard Heimann has often discussed this question of interest and the frequency with which he has changed his opinion gives a good idea of how tricky the problem is. Originally Dr. Heimann maintained that Professor Cassel was wrong when he wrote in *Theoretische Sozialökonomie* that the laws which governed interest rates in the capitalist society would also hold good in the socialist one. Dr. Heimann objected that the circumstances would be different since "the formation of a price assumes the existence of a market divided into separate parts."[40]

This opinion is very interesting both in this and in another connection, for it constitutes a very important argument against the attempt made by Dr. Heimann and many other economists to solve the problem of calculation by advocating competition in the socialist society. (We shall revert to this question in Chapter 13.) In this connection,

---

[40] *Mehrwert und Gemeinwirtschaft,* Berlin, 1922, p. 68.

too, Dr. Heimann has said that interest will not be "an eternal category in economics . . . but is peculiar to private economy."[41] He further mentions the necessity of "absolute interest on scarcity," a question that will be discussed in the next chapter. Later, however, he comes to the conclusion that interest is an eternal category, and in his "Zur Kritik des Kapitalismus und der Nationalökonomie"[42] he says that it is "right to say, that, for example, interest is an eternal category of all types of economic systems, since a certain value must always be imputed to capital for the part its plays in the production of goods."[43] This is correct, but hardly consistent with his previous views.

Some of those who are sceptical of the possibility of economic calculation in socialist societies maintain that interest should figure in the calculations of even a socialist society, but that this is impossible because of the lack of a market for capital. For Professor Mises, who has devoted some attention to the question, the chief point is that there won't be any prices on the means of production.

That this question of interest will continue to have practical significance in the socialist society is shown by a theoretical example constructed by Professor Brutzkus.[44] He assumes that the world consisted of nothing but socialist societies and that Russian workers had asked their English colleagues to lend them locomotives, machinery and tools to enable them to develop their production apparatus more quickly. Brutzkus says that, if the English were not able to

---

[41] *Op. cit.*, p. 69.

[42] *Blätter für den religiösen Sozialismus*, 1926.

[43] *Op. cit.*, p. 17.

[44] *Op. cit.*, p. 56.

ask for interest, it would be quite reasonable for them to
reply that they needed these means of production themselves, pointing out that they were aiming at better hous-
ing and, in any case, must first attain the level of their
American brethren, practically all of whom had their own
cars. It would be quite different, if the English workers
were to receive interest to compensate them for such an outlay. The payment of interest in such circumstances (Brutzkus ironically calls it "a consequence of exploitation")
would be natural and, no doubt, practised.

Professor Pierson[45] has also used the transfer of capital
between different countries to illustrate the continued existence of the problem of interest (and exchange) in socialist societies.

Professor Georg Halm has concerned himself more than
most with this question of interest, to which he attaches
great importance. He writes:

> Now it is unfortunate that this allowance for interest, the
> need for which is urgently dictated by economic conditions,
> cannot be adopted in the socialist economy. Perhaps this is the
> most serious objection that can be maintained against so-
> cialism.[46]

Professor Halm bases his contention that the fixing of
interest rates is impossible on the same argument as that
used by the socialists to show that the calculation of interest is unnecessary in the socialist society, namely, that
the society owns all capital goods. This means that the
capital is not owned by many individuals and so there
cannot be a market with supply and demand, such as is

---

[45] *Collectivist Economic Planning,* p. 66.
[46] *Collectivist Economic Planning,* p. 161.

necessary for arriving at a price. Halm builds on Mises' point, which he calls "pioneering," but the most serious point for him is apparently not that the lack of market prices precludes economic calculation and the economic use of capital goods, but that it makes it impossible to calculate interest, since interest is a price that has to be calculated as a certain fraction of a value expressed in money.

One must agree with many of Professor Halm's points, but it is not easy to follow him when he goes so far as to maintain that "allowance for interest . . . cannot be adopted" and that this "is the most serious objection that can be maintained against socialism." As far as the use of interest is concerned, it is not inconceivable that the central authority may choose an arbitrary rate of interest so as to have a discount-factor to prevent present values and future values being calculated alike, irrespective of the interval of time. Professor Halm is perfectly right in saying that such an interest rate will give no indication of the scarcity of capital;[47] right too, when he says that it is merely circular reasoning to use a fictitious rate of interest to find the value of a capital good, which has to be assumed before the rate of interest can be determined.[48] However, it is unlikely that any catastrophe would happen to the socialist society if its central authority, for the sake of easy comparison of the amount of capital issued to the various con-

---

[47] He is reckoning with concrete capital goods and not with the demand for capital, for which he has been rebuked by Dr. Cläre Tisch among others. As far as it can be understood, this is a matter of subordinate interest for this discussion. Besides, it can be rightly maintained that there will be no demand for capital in socialist societies, since in them money is a warrant for consumer goods and does permit the purchase of capital goods.

[48] *Op. cit.* See footnote on p. 256.

cerns, should take an arbitrary rate of interest. After all, interest rates have not fluctuated so violently in industrialized societies during the last hundred years. And Professor Halm will undoubtedly agree that the central authority will be better served with a fictitious rate of interest, than with none, and it was he who showed how economic calculation is impossible without a factor of discount.

It should be recalled that in market economies, too, interest is influenced by factors that have little or nothing to do with the scarcity of capital, saving or investment, and that not even in such a society is interest the only factor influencing the volume of saving and investment.[49]

In any event one cannot agree with the second part of Professor Halm's contention: that the absence of interest is the main objection to socialism. The lack of prices for the means of production will occur far more often and lead to far more dangerous miscalculations than any lack of interest rates. But it is admittedly an objection against the socialist society that it cannot possibly allow the community's willingness—or unwillingness—to restrict current consumption to have any effect on investment, as the savings quota can only be determined arbitrarily by the central authority.

---

[49] On the other hand it can justifiably be maintained that in the years after the outbreak of the First World War savings and investment had markedly little influence on interest rates, and *vice versa*.

The development, both monetary, political and cultural, of many European countries might well have taken a different course, if the state and its financial authorities had allowed interest more latitude to express the relationship between savings and the lack of savings on the one hand and investment and the destruction of capital on the other. We have not yet seen the consequences of the expanded credit basis and of the controlled fixation of interest which are typical features of the monetary policy of many countries in the last decades.

9

Rent in the Socialist Society

From a business point of view, rent on land and interest on capital in the private capitalist society tend to merge. This is partly because both are expressed in money (in purchasing power) and partly because rent on land does not figure as such either in the recipient's or in the payer's accounts. It is entered under different names such as farm-rent and interest-on-capital, and partly because income from rent can be exchanged for income from capital and *vice versa* (assuming that in the society in question the regulations regarding concessions and alodial possession are not too strict). Legally, technically, emotionally and in respect of liquidity it may make considerable difference to an individual whether he receives rent from land or draws interest from capital. This difference will to a certain extent depend on the conditions of his ownership, but in practice and from the economic point of view the difference need not be great.

When a company, for example, takes over the rights to a waterfall from two landowners, there is no difference economically between the one who accepts payment in the form of some of the company's bonds and the other who, wishing to retain his rights of ownership, merely grants the company a perpetual lease for a rent corresponding to the interest on the bonds. In this connection it is worth remembering that the German word for "interest," *Zins,* comes from the Latin *census,* which in Roman and Germanic countries was the word used to describe public valuation of a citizen's fortune (consisting in earlier days mostly of land) to determine his right to vote and eligibility. According to Gustav Cassel[1] it was dealing in fixed rents from land (which thus became fixed interest on capital) which made canon law alter its attitude to the question of interest and so contributed to the church's removal of its ban on usury.

While for the individual rent on land has all the appearances of income derived from capital, in theory and for the economist it falls within various categories. Rent on land and interest on capital in reality belong to different categories.[2] What the theoretical economist understands by rent on land or, rather, what economic theory understands by the payment of rent on land (what Keilhau calls *ground-tribute*) comprises in the capitalist society several distinct factors. To discuss these[3] in a book on the socialist society would take us too far from our subject, nor is it necessary. It will be sufficient to point out that in certain respects the problem appears more simple in the socialist society, where the dividing-line between interest on capital and rent on land will be much sharper owing to the absence of trade in fixed property and capital goods. As the state owns all

---

[1] *Teoretisk Socialökonomi,* p. 193.

[2] See Wilhelm Keilhau: *Grundrentelaeren,* Christiania, 1916, and L. M. Fraser: *Economic Thought and Language.*

[3] See also Keilhau and Fraser, L. V. Birch: *Denokonomiske Virksomhed, II,* Copenhagen, 1928.

capital goods, there will be no rents in the sense of payment (ground-tribute) for the use of land (soil, forests,
mines, waterfalls and building-plots). Nevertheless, there
is no denying that, whether in the socialist or in the private-
capitalist society, different areas of land have a more or a
less fortunate situation, a higher or a lower quality, and
are more or less suitable for various purposes; that forests
differ in their rate of growth, are more or less suitable for
development, and are better or worse situated; that mines
are more or less rich, more or less well situated; that waterfalls can be more or less conveniently situated and have a
greater or a lesser volume and height of fall; that building
sites are better or worse situated and so of greater or lesser
importance. For arable land and pasture, mines, waterfalls
and factories, a good situation means being in the proximity
of means of transport and markets. Except in the case of
pasture and waterfalls it also means proximity to sources of
power. What is considered a good situation for a dwelling
house will vary according to more subjective conceptions.

Whatever the type of land there will always be the risk
of the central authority putting it to a less desirable use (according to the ends stated), if it does not take differences
in situation and suitability into account. Thus economic
calculation will require a rent, or, if you like, a differential
rent, which will express the difference in output in relation
to the input (or the difference in costs per unit of output)
arising out of the greater or lesser suitability of the land
and its better or worse location. A differential rent of this
kind is also necessary to give the central authority a basis
for estimating the importance of other factors of production which have to be employed (see Chapter 5). If rent is
left out of its calculations, the central authority will have

no means of knowing whether a difference in results is due to human factors, to the use of a greater or smaller amount of capital, or to the nature and position of the land.

How can this difference in suitability and situation be determined? Here one comes up against the usual difficulty that in the socialist society there are no markets for the means of production and, hence, no prices for land, or for the yield from land. Certain natural data can be procured: the rate of growth of the timber in a wood, the horsepower of a waterfall that has been developed, and modern geophysical instruments can determine the presence of various metals. An area's greater or lesser suitability for various purposes can also be determined in terms of the product concerned. Such data, however, cannot be used for calculation, for which a common denominator is required. It is of little use to know that a certain area can yield so and so many tons per acre of a certain variety of grain after the use of so and so many pounds of fertilizer and so and so many working hours. Nor does it bring us any further to know that a waterfall will supply so and so many horsepower after the expenditure of so and so many hours' work and such and such quantities of such and such materials, if there are no prices attached to these materials which would enable us to ascertain whether or not they might be used to better advantage elsewhere.

It is in respect of building land that it is particularly obvious that calculations *in natura* lead nowhere. The nature of the land can be determined by geological investigation which will show how large a structure can be erected, but it will not help to determine whether the land should be used for dwelling houses, public buildings or factories and what kind of factories. The socialist society cannot make an economic calculation without a price or a differential rent to express both the scarcity value of the land and its most desirable use in relation to the end.

In a capitalist society land and the "power of the soil" are objects of exchange or at any rate of supply and demand. A better position and/or possible higher quality is expressed in its changing hands at a higher price or in a higher rent being set upon it. (If the land is bought with borrowed funds, the interest will be higher, and if it is purchased outright for cash the rent is in reality paid for in the income the purchaser might have had from his money had he invested it elsewhere where the risk was equivalent.) We shall not concern ourselves here with the many types of "external" and "internal" conditions capable of altering the value of land and hence the rent. We shall merely point out that in the capitalist society fresh values are constantly being put on land as it changes hands and as offers for it are made by those who consider that it could be put to more profitable uses.

There can be no such automatic change in land valuations and rents in the socialist society, where the state owns both the land and the different concerns. One can imagine periodical valuations being undertaken, which would take both the present use of the land and possible alternative uses into consideration, the purpose of which would be to obtain the calculation factors which we have tried to show to be necessary and which rents represent. This is not the place to discuss whether such periodical, official valuations could, in a dynamic society, take the place of a market with many contracting parties. To this most important point in our argument we shall return later (see Chapter 14 and the appendices). Here we may recall that in arguing against Professor Cassel's opinion that there would be price-fixing for rents in the socialist society, Dr. Heimann originally maintained that price-fixing for rents pre-supposed the existence of individual competitors in the market, which would not be the case in the socialist society (see p. 184). As Dr. Heimann writes in this connection of the necessity for scarcity rents, it may be mentioned that in reality it is, of course, not only the scarcity of the land and natural sources of power that must be included as calculation factors, but the scarcity of all factors of production.

To calculate these scarcity factors Dr. Heimann proposed imputation as well as computation. Of imputation he writes that there exists "an elastic band" between consumer goods and production factors and that the valuation of consumer goods "radiates back to the valuation of the factors of production."

> As soon as real competition prevails in the market for consumer goods, the resulting price-level is reproduced automatically in all stages of production, in so far as only the price-law is duly employed, independently of the disposition of the parties in the market for producer's goods.[4]

There is no contesting the existence of a connection and interdependence between the value of the final product and the factors of production. This, however, does not mean that the values put on the factors of production can be "imputed," or determined exclusively from the values put on the final products. This could only be done if the factors of production were always used in fixed proportions and they were only used to produce a single product. This, of course, is not the case in the world of reality and especially not in a dynamic society. In the first place the question of

---

[4] See *Mehrwert und Gemeinwirtschaft,* p. 188–89.

alternative uses of production factors for the production of various goods, and in the second place the question of different combinations of production factors, depend, *inter alia,* on their own changing prices (see also p. 171).

We mentioned above public settlement of the value of land and it is of interest to note that Dr. Heimann originally spoke of "prices" in connection with demand for consumer goods, but of "Bedeutungsgrössen" in connection with factors of production.[5] Later,[6] in answering a criticism made by Professor Halm, he said that his "Bedeutungsgrössen" were synonymous with prices. This introduces the very important question of what is to be understood by price: is it to be merely a numerical denomination, fixed more or less arbitrarily, or is it to be a synthesizing index which simultaneously expresses a number of different factors, among them the assumed scarcity of resources? To this question, as we have said, we shall return and in Chapter 13 we shall also discuss the question of whether it is possible with the help of competition to create prices that can be used as calculation factors in the socialist society.

The most important thing to lay down in concluding this chapter is that without calculating a rent that expresses the relative scarcity of the land and of its derivative products and of their importance for various purposes, the central authority will have no opportunity of following the economic principle of comparing cost with result, or, in this case, of achieving the goal it has set itself: maximum production for needs.

[5] See "Zur Kritik des Kapitalismus und Nationalökonomie" in *Blätter für religiösen Sozialismus,* 1926.
[6] *Soziale Theorie des Kapitalismus. Theorie der Sozialpolitik,* Tübingen, 1929.

10

Depreciation in the Socialist Society

In any community whatsoever the value of means of production will alter with time. A large demand for the products and services provided by a factor of production can cause its value to rise temporarily, but all in all its value will decrease in the course of time owing to depreciation (age, wear, etc.). Even when Nature is the factor of production, its value and productive capacity will fall through use. Soil that is continually used for one and the same purpose becomes impoverished, a forest where too much is felled loses in value, and mines and oil-wells can become exhausted.

Any business or community wishing to follow "the economic principle" must take this depreciation into account. If it is not offset by a corresponding saving or appropriation, it will mean that the business or community in question is living on its capital. Let us, for the sake of simplicity, disregard "natural" factors of production and the rarer cases of appreciation of their value, and confine ourselves to depreciation caused by (1) age and wear and tear, (2) new methods of production and the invention of new equipment that can produce at lower cost, or (3) decreased demand for the goods and services provided by a given kind of capital equipment.

Calling the corresponding writing-down of these capital items "depreciation",[1] the question arises of how the socialist society is to determine the size of its quota for depreciation. Here we come up against the usual difficulty that in such a community there exist neither markets nor market prices for either new or second-hand capital equipment. The technician can indicate a percentage for wear and tear, but if a quota for wear and tear is to be used in calculations, it must not be expressed only as a percentage, but as a price of value. Nor will the central authority be able to determine by reference to a framework of prices, whether inventions in the shape of new machinery ought to increase the depreciation allowance or not. This brings us back to the fact that the use of resources ought to be decided by economic and not by technical considerations of their utility (see p. 141). An illustration of the conflict between these two considerations would be the following: in a capitalist society a machine with a life of twenty years is scrapped after, say, two years, because of a new invention or an improvement in the method of production that accelerated or increased production beyond that of which the scrapped machine was capable. It can also be seen when the opposite happens and an old factory with old machinery forces a technically perfect factory to cease production or reorganize or adopt another method of writing-down its capital because the older one can be run at lower costs.

A community that neglects to take depreciation quotas—

---

[1] See, *inter alia,* W. M. Cole: *Accounts, their Construction and Interpretation,* Cambridge, Mass., 1915.

economically determined—into its calculations will not necessarily be retrograde, but it will run the risk of depriving itself of the opportunity of benefiting from possible technical developments otherwise possible and thus of not achieving for its members that maximization of production for consumer needs, which it has set up as its goal. Again, there will be a danger of greater attention being paid to the technical side of a matter than to the economic, and this can also prevent it achieving its end.

The fixing of depreciation quotas by economic criteria presupposes the existence of a price for capital resources of all kinds, which on the "supply" side will express the scarcity of these capital resources, and on the "demand" side the use of them which the community values highest. In the socialist society it is difficult to obtain reliable data to express variations in demand for final products (see Chapter 6, p. 116) and *ex definitione* there are no prices to express the scarcity of capital resources.

Depreciation is discussed by Professor Hayek, one of the few to have done so, in his final paper in *Collectivist Economic Planning*. He attaches great weight to the difficulties in calculating depreciation quotas in the socialist society. He discusses depreciation and the extent to which the problem of calculation can be solved by reference to marginal costs of production in the individual concern, and here there is no doubt that the question of depreciation is of the greatest importance. Generally speaking, however, it is not so certain that failure to calculate depreciation quotas need have grave consequences, provided the depreciation takes other forms, as it may.

Depreciation can be and is being calculated in the capitalist society in more or less rough and ready forms, either

(1) by debiting the profit-and-loss account with a depreciation quota corresponding to the loss in value, or (2) by trying to maintain the machinery at its original value by repairing it, or, as this is difficult, (3) by a combination of writing-off and maintenance-expenditure. A rougher form is (4) that the concern does not attempt to repair the factory or machinery in question, but simply lets it decay and gets new capital equipment corresponding to the supposed decreased value; or, again, (5) it merely waits till the equipment in question is completely worn out, and then replaces it. This latter method of procedure is not unusual in public or semi-public concerns, where new purchases depend on political factors. Computations for such a concern, where purchases are made periodically or spasmodically, naturally give a completely false picture of the situation during the intermediate periods and such a system would naturally be useless as a basis for anyone wanting to overcome the difficulties of calculation by recourse to "marginal costs." One can, however, well imagine that the socialist society may have recourse to this method of calculating depreciation, which really amounts to a complete periodic repurchase of machinery and represents a kind of forced depreciation. It is no ideal economic calculation, but it would over a longer period tend to maintain the machinery of production physically and technically.

This opinion (that neglect to calculate with depreciation quotas will scarcely be of decisive importance for the future of the socialist society) is also based on the fact that in the capitalist society depreciation is determined, except in the best conducted businesses, comparatively arbitrarily and differs widely not only with the actual wear and tear, age or modernity of the plant, but with the incidence of taxation, the phase of the trade cycle, and with the extent of the surplus or deficit in the accounts, and with existing expectations as to the possibility of the appearance of more modern equipment and other factors of the same kind. The very difference in the views of the various Inland Revenue Authorities as to what can be written off shows that in the capitalist society depreciation is assessed rather arbitrarily. Though it can be said that Professor Hayek attaches too much importance to depreciation in the socialist community, Dr. Lerner for his part goes too far when, in refuting Professor Hayek's opinion (that "the hiring of the instrument involves a cost which appears as an objective item to be considered by the hirer") he says that:

> there is a catch in this. The objective cost of hiring the instrument depends upon the estimated value of the future use that is sacrificed to the present when the instrument is hired, since this governs the hiring fee charged. The question is then the sociological one, whether the Socialist Trust is able to estimate the future value more accurately or less accurately than the competitive owner of the hired instrument, and here we leave pure economic theory.[2]

Dr. Lerner goes on to say:

> It is not strictly accurate to say, as Dr. Hayek does, that the cost of using the instrument depends upon the price of the product itself, and thereby to suggest that the derivation of a supply price from the cost would involve circular reasoning.
>
> The cost depends not on the present price, but on the _expected future price;_ and this must be true whatever the form of the economy.

---

[2] See "Statics and Dynamics in Socialist Economics" in _Economic Journal,_ June, 1937, p. 269.

The correctness of Dr. Lerner's argument depends on whether the current product-price determines the hiring fee of the factor. Surely not, for the current value of the product is only a co-determinant without dominance. There will always be many other factors in determining the hiring price. For example, lower prices of machinery will mean lower hiring prices. What is more important is that in the capitalist society the depreciation quota is determined on existing data. If, in such a society, the owner of a given type of equipment is offered a machine with a similar output capacity to that he already has, but which is considerably cheaper, he has no need of conjecture as to the value of the final product to know that the value of his own machine must be written-down. Nor does he base his action on expectation, but on knowledge, when he writes down the value of his capital equipment after having been undersold by a competitor who has got superior equipment, whether in the form of a cheaper machine, a more modernly equipped factory, or a better situated warehouse.

Another question is that the amount to be written-off can be determined by other factors and that the economically correct depreciation can be frustrated by the Revenue authorities. The most interesting thing in this connection, however, is whether and how the manager of the Socialist Trust is to be able to get similar data for determining his depreciation quota. Dr. Lerner does not go into that question; if he did he would find that the possibilities for economic depreciation in the socialist community are almost nil, by reason of the lack of market data, and this will mean reduced possibilities for attaining the optimum economic utilization of existing resources in relation to the ends stated.

11

Mises' Theory. Proposed Solutions: Mathematical Solutions and the "Experimental Method"

The three previous chapters have been concerned with various factors which the central authority in the socialist society must include in its calculations and accounting if "the economic principle" is to be followed. These factors all had one thing in common; they were either difficult, or impossible, to determine without prices for the means of production.

If it should be impossible in the socialist society to put prices on means of production, this will entail other and far more serious consequences than that these factors can not be measured. Unless there are prices for the means of production the economic activity of any modern, industrialized community will be haphazard. Without such prices the central authority will lack the necessary data to determine how and in what combination the various means of production can be put to the optimum economic use. Nor will it be able to follow the fundamental law that should govern all economic activity, namely that the result varies according to the different combinations of production factors.[1]

---

[1] This view may cause surprise, since the increasing and diminishing

Without prices to indicate their scarcity, those means of production which exist only in limited numbers and quantity (in the society or place concerned) could be used for purposes that are without importance in relation to the given end, with the result that more important aims could not be achieved. Without prices for means of production the central authority will have no data for determining whether the contribution and the sacrifice are greater or smaller than the result. Without them calculation is impossible, and without calculation there can be no rational conduct, nor any rational use of the community's resources. On the whole, all who have taken part in this discussion are agreed that prices for means of production are necessary for calculation and that calculation is a necessary prerequisite of rational economic activity.

Now Professor Mises' assertion is that it is impossible to arrive at prices for means of production in the socialist society. His argument is that in the socialist society the state, by definition, owns the means of production, hence there will be no markets or prices for them. From this follows, in Mises' opinion, that economic calculation will be impossible and socialism unfeasible.[2] The first statement follows from the definition, and as such is unassailable. The

yields resulting from such attempted combinations are, in theoretic discussion, generally measured *in natura* and expressed in units of quantity of one of the production factors or of the final product. Economic calculation, however, demands prices, prices that are commensurable and express the relative scarcity of the means of production in relation to its various possible uses and the different combinations. See also Professor Ragnar Frisch's *Inledning til produksjonsteorien* (Stencil), Oslo, 1937, and Professor George M. Peterson's *Diminishing Return and Planned Economy,* New York, 1937.

[2] For references, see footnote on p. 82.

correctness of the second will depend on what is understood by markets, prices and calculation. We shall repeatedly revert to this question when discussing the solutions proposed by Mises' opponents.

Mises' opponents naturally have this in common: they all agree that his point of view is false. The solutions they have put forward, however, differ greatly, and some have even raised strong and serious objections to the others' proposals.

The solutions proposed fall mainly into two groups: one insisting that prices can be put on means of production and agreeing to—and in certain cases assuming—the existence of free choice of goods and occupation, while the second and smaller group holds that this free choice cannot be sustained in the socialist society. The solutions of this latter group will be dealt with separately at the end. We still assume free choice of goods and services, and (2) free choice of occupation and place of work.

The solutions of the first group coincide to a certain extent. In many cases one and the same person has put forward several solutions. As the assumptions on which they base their argument are not always indicated precisely, it is difficult to classify them exactly, but roughly they fall into the following groups: (1) Solutions that aim at a moneyless economy. (2) Those that are based on the original Marxian theory of value, and in which the input of labour is regarded as the only factor determining value. (3) "Mathematical solutions" and those which recommend the "experimental method." (4) Those that recommend marginal costing, and (5) those that aim at introducing competition. A relatively comprehensive survey of them all can be found in *Collectivist Economic Planning,* in which special attention should be given to Professor Hayek's concluding chapter "The Present State of the Debate." Cläre Tisch's contribution gives a good general picture of what had appeared in German up to that time.

We are not here concerned with those solutions that are based on a moneyless economy or on the theory of labour-values, since it has already been demonstrated that economic calculation cannot be made on that basis,[3] a view generally accepted by those now partaking in the discussion (with the exception of Drs. G. Dobbert and C. Landauer among others).[4]

Most of the solutions proposed are allied to group 3, called "mathematical solutions." That of Dr. Cläre Tisch is mentioned first, because her solution is expressively put forward as a counter to Mises. She contests Mises' point that in the socialist community there will be no exchange between two contracting parties. There will, rightly enough, be no markets, but there will be a choice and that, in her opinion, is sufficient to create the exchange-relationship Mises demands. Here she is in the strong position of being able to quote Mises himself as saying that the economic transactions of the management of an isolated economy can "in one sense" be called exchange (*Theorie des Geldes,* p. 10). Now, Mises added that not even the greatest genius

---

[3] See Chapters 4 and 5.

[4] In "L'Economia Programmatica nella URSS" in *L'Economia Programmatica* by L. Brocard, C. Landauer, I. A. Hobson, L. L. Lorwin, G. Dobbert and U. Spirito, Florence, 1933; and in "L'Economia Russa" in *Nuovo Esperienze Economiche* by E. v. Beckerath, G. D. H. Cole, L. L. Lorwin, G. Dobbert, J. B. Condliffe, S. Nagao and U. Spirito, Florence, 1935, according to Herbert Zassenhaus in *Zeitschrift für Nationalökonomie,* 1936. See also p. 51.

can perceive "the importance" of one of innumerable goods of a higher order. To this Dr. Tisch rightly says that this is a practical and not a theoretical objection. But then, however, she seems to be underestimating the importance of the practical difficulties when she writes:

> Naturally an enormous statistical apparatus will be needed to deal with production and the technical coefficients, but this can all be worked out by subordinates and need not burden the 'mind' of the Director of Industry.[5]

Besides, Dr. Tisch agrees with Mises that a monetary system is a prerequisite for calculation and that a moneyless economy leads nowhere. However, she maintains that the claims-to-consumption in a socialist community are money and that the existence of money makes it possible to price the means of production. Dr. Tisch builds up her solution on Professor Cassel's *Theoretische Sozialökonomie* and maintains that mathematical economics have given us exact methods for determining the equivalent prices of means of production without markets:

> when only certain data are known to one, and one takes into consideration the prerequisites of equilibrium (price and cost, supply and demand).

She refers us to statements by Walras, Pareto, Schumpeter and, especially, Barone,[6] but she herself builds on Cas-

---

[5] *Op. cit.*, pp. 66–67.

[6] Respectively, *Element d'économie politique pure*, Lausanne, 1829; *Cours d'Économie politique, II*, Lausanne, 1897 (in which Pareto refers to Irving Fisher's *Mathematical Investigations in the Theory of Value and Prices*); *Wesen und Hauptinhalt der theoretischen Nationalökonomie*, Leipzig, 1908; and "Il ministro della produzione nello stato collectivista" in *Giornale degli Econ. II, 1908*.

sel's simpler methods, that are built on those of Walras. Dr. Tisch thinks that Professor Cassel has shown that prices for the means of production can be determined merely by use of the principle of scarcity and costing. However, she does point out that Cassel has been guilty of an inadmissible simplification in assuming the technical production-coefficients as given. This, of course, they are not, as they vary with the price of the means of production (and, she might have added, with technical developments). She maintains, though, that by producing each of the production-coefficients in a concern as a function of the price of the means of production and by doing this for every existing concern, one will get "as many equations as unknowns."

Later we shall discuss these mathematical solutions on which Dr. Tisch also touches. It will suffice to say here that Professor Halm in his criticism of Dr. Tisch's solution (*The Possibility of Adequate Calculation*)[7] agrees that Professor Cassel, by saying that price-equations were all that was necessary, has given grounds for misunderstanding. But Professor Halm concedes that Cassel did not mean to explain actual price-processes, but merely to set up an ideal scheme for prices to which actual price-processes would have to be adjusted. And, instead of a factual explanation Cassel has given us rules and principles.[8] He does not help us, says Professor Halm "to understand the type of connection between cause and effect that is characteristic of the

---

[7] In *Collectivist Economic Planning.*

[8] Professor Alfred Amonn says in his review of Cassel's book in *Archiv für Sozialwissenschaft und Sozialpolitik,* 1923, that Cassel does not give a principle for arriving at such price-equations and that his presentation of the process of price-formation is no explanation of that process, but only the prelude to an explanation.

social economy," which Cassel himself has demanded.[9] The author of this treatise can confirm that Halm is right and that Professor Cassel never regarded his equations as a basis for an arithmetical or a mathematical computation of prices, but merely as an expression of principles that are generally applicable to an exchange economy.

H. D. Dickinson's treatise is rich in suggestions for solving the problem and will have to be discussed in different places. It is mentioned here, because Dickinson, too, has referred to Cassel's price-equivalents, for which Dr. Lerner has taken him to task.[10]

Dr. Herbert Zassenhaus has put forward another suggestion for a mathematical solution.[11] He first discusses the question on the assumption that the members of the community do not have free choice of consumer goods, and then on the assumption that they do. The former will be discussed in Chapter 14 together with the other solutions in this main group; the latter is built on Barone's system of equations. Zassenhaus says that Barone "reduces the task of the Minister of Production, for our case, to an exceptionally simple formula."[12] After a short survey of Barone's equations Zassenhaus arrives at the conclusion that the magnitudes required to solve the equations are (1) the quantity of means of production, (2) the function of demand, and (3) the function of the production-coefficient.

---

[9] "Der Ausgangspunkt der Theoretischen Nationalökonomie" in *Zeitschrift für de gesamte Staatswissenschaft,* Year 58, 1902, p. 592.

[10] "Economic Theory and Socialist Economy" in *Review of Economic Studies,* 1934–35, p. 52.

[11] "Über die ökonomische Theorie der Planwirtschaft" in *Zeitschrift für Nationalökonomie,* Vienna, 1934.

[12] *Op. cit.*

Of (1) he says that is *eo ipso* given. However, it is not so evident as that. In the first place it is very difficult to determine what really are resources, what can be made to serve production and what not. In this connection one has to discuss the conditions for stimulating those who take the initiative in the community in question, so as to make the maximum use of potential possibilities. This, however, introduces problems which, for various reasons, we shall not go into here (see p. 294). In the second place the importance of production-factors does not only depend on their number, but also on existing possibilities for combining them. This raises questions of the geographic position of the means of production, the labourers' place of dwelling, cost of possible transport, and once again one is brought up against the old difficulty, that *a priori* there are no prices for means of production (and transport) in the socialist society. In the third place, the magnitude of a production-factor like that of human labour will within certain limits vary with the size of its reward and will also depend on regulations governing working hours, child-labour, etc. This data can at any time be said to be given, but not the extent to which people are prepared to work for given wages. Let it be remembered that we are for the time being discussing under the assumption that there is a free choice of occupation.

Zassenhaus' attitude to (2), the function of demand, is rather sceptical and there is reason to be even more sceptical than he is (see Chapter 6).

He says of (3) the function of the production-coefficients, that in any concern and with a given amount of production they depend on the prices of the means of production. In this connection he, like Professor Halm, has a word of reproach for Professor Cassel for replacing this dependence in his system of equations by the adoption of constant co-efficients "which is not quite correct." However, this re-proach appears in rather a curious light, when one considers that Zassenhaus himself avoids this difficulty by assuming a static community. He goes on immediately to say:

> And as we have assumed certain technical conditions, along with static conditions, we may conclude that the Ministry of Production knows them as well.[13]

Elsewhere he puts this assumption of staticness more concisely:

> Finally, everything so far pictured belongs to the static the-ory of planned economy (and we are confining ourselves to that); that means that we have assumed that the data of the system are known and do not alter during the period of ob-servation, not even as a result of any movement of the system against equilibrium. This later assumption could also be ex-pressed as the assumption that the variable magnitudes of the system have an infinitely large speed of reaction.[14]

The problem, however, is precisely *how* these data can be procured. Zassenhaus' assumption of them as given re-duces the value of his views, and the fact that he argues on completely unrealistic assumptions, destroys their practical value. However, he himself realizes that they only have a "mittelbare Anwendungsfaehigkeit."

The group of solutions based on *the trial and error method* is closely allied to the mathematical solutions. To save them from being entirely superficial, they assume some

---

[13] *Op. cit.*, p. 529.
[14] *Ibid.*, p. 515.

sort of computation based on various data. The greatest exponent of this trial and error method is Professor Fred M. Taylor, who thinks that the central authority, by taking account of the consumers' demand as expressed in surplus or shortage of consumer-goods (see Chapter 6, p. 126), will

> ascertain with a sufficient degree of accuracy these effective importances or values of all the different kinds of primary factors, and that they will have embodied the results in arithmetic tables, which I shall usually designate factor-valuation tables.[15]

It is this reference to "arithmetic tables" and "factor-valuation tables" that makes it possible to put Professor Taylor's solution with the mathematical solutions. It has been rosily described by Dr. Oskar Lange as the only step forward made in the discussion since Barone's treatment of the problem, and he regrets that not only has Professor Hayek omitted to print Professor Taylor's paper in *Collectivist Economic Planning,* but also that he has called it a theoretic solution alongside those of Barone, Dickinson, etc., "whereas Taylor indicates a solution by trial and error."[16]

Such eulogy is very surprising, as is the reproach against Professor Hayek. In the first place Professor Taylor's "method" had already been suggested by Barone, and Dr. Leichter has also mentioned it. In the second place, it is a very obvious method and the one which anyone with a little knowledge of the price economy would think of first. In fact, it is so far from being sensational that it was not

---

[15] *American Economic Review,* 1929, p. 4.
[16] "On the Economic Theory of Socialism" in *Review of Economic Studies,* October, 1936, p. 56.

even mentioned during the discussion on Central Planning of Production in Soviet Russia held by the American Economic Association the day after Professor Taylor had discussed it in his paper opening the congress.[17] And, in the third place, the problem can by no means be said to have been solved by the suggestions put forward by Professor Taylor. Dr. Lange's own and much more thorough treatment of the question shows that not even he regards it as the last word on the subject.

Professor Taylor ended his paper by saying that he found himself inclined:

> to affirm rather dogmatically that, if the economic authorities of a socialist state would recognize equality between cost of production on the one hand and the demand price of the buyer on the other as being the adequate and the only proof that the commodity in question ought to be produced, they could, under all ordinary conditions, perform their duties, as the persons who were immediately responsible for the guidance of production, with well-founded confidence that they would never make any other than the right use for the economic resources placed at their disposal.[18]

One cannot accept Professor Taylor's assertion that he has solved the problem. The main objection is that he assumes that both cost of production and demand price of the buyer are given, whereas the real problem is to determine how a socialist community is to obtain these data. The reader is referred here to our objections given in Chapter VI, and we shall only add that Professor Taylor's solution clearly, though not expressly, presupposes that the community is static.

---

[17] *American Economic Review,* 1929, Supp. pp. 90–130.
[18] *Op. cit.,* p. 8.

Dr. Lange's attempt to solve the problem deserves special attention, if for no other reason than that Dr. Lerner has called it "the most up-to-date of what has been written so far on the subject . . . these words (used) in a rather specialized sense."[19] Dr. Lange's most important contribution to the discussion is in his two papers "On the Economic Theory of Socialism" in *Review of Economic Studies* of October, 1936, and February, 1937, in both of which he discusses the question of economic calculation. The papers are very different in character. The second is prefaced by a section "The Economist's Case for Socialism" and comprises arguments in defence of the socialist society that would seem unusually dogmatic for an economist to put forward as such, and which do not directly concern our discussion. In the first paper, however, Dr. Lange discusses the problem of calculation, assuming both that free choice of goods and occupation exists, and that it does not. We shall continue to assume that it does. The other alternative will be discussed in Chapter 14.

Dr. Lange is one of the few to make a straightforward attack on Mises' view. He pays him, though ironically, the honour due to him for having got the socialists to discuss the problem of calculation systematically (see p. 4). But he says that Professor Mises' view is based on a "confusion concerning the nature of prices," and recalls that Professor Wicksteed pointed out that the term "price" has two meanings. It can either have its popular meaning of the exchange-relationship between two goods on a market, or it can have the more general meaning of the "terms on which alterna-

---

[19] See "A Note on Socialist Economics" in *Review of Economic Studies,* October, 1936, p. 76.

tives are offered."[20] He goes on to say that it is only prices in this generalized meaning of the word that are necessary to solve the problem of the distribution of resources.

There is, however, no justification for accusing Mises of "confusion concerning the nature of prices," since he has expressly stated that it is prices in the sense of exchange-relationship and value-relationship that are needed.[21]

It is also questionable whether Dr. Lange has not misunderstood Wicksteed when he uses his expression "terms on which alternatives are offered" in the way he does. The point Dr. Lange wants to make, and it is an important one for his point of view, is that the prices do not need to be market-prices. It is enough for him that they are parameters. Now, Dr. Lange says that by "terms on which alternatives are offered" he understands "the functions of production" and "the technical possibilities determining the transformation of goods."[22]

Professor Wicksteed, however, uses the term in quite another sense. As he himself says in the first two lines of his introduction, his whole work is "intended primarily as a popular but systematic exposition of the 'marginal' theory of economics." The "terms on which alternatives are offered" that he has in view, are the subjective balancings and value-judgments made by the individual person. Far from indicating non-market prices, Wicksteed tries to show that the principles that held good in a market are those

---

[20] Dr. Lange refers to *The Common Sense of Political Economy*, 2nd Edn., London, 1933, p. 28.

[21] See *Socialism*, p. 120.

[22] *Op. cit.*, p. 55.

more or less consciously used by the individual when making his choice.

> Whatever the nature of the alternatives before us, the question of the terms on which they are offered is always relevant. If we secure this, how much of that must we pay for it, or what shall we sacrifice to it? And is it worth it? What alternatives shall we forgo? And what would be their value to us?
>
> In the market this problem presents itself in terms of money prices.[23]

And then he gives an example of the individual's thoughts when weighing up advantages and sacrifices. What Wicksteed wishes to emphasize is the individual's often irrational and unconscious, but ever subjective, weighing-up of "terms," of stronger or lesser need, of desire and dislike.

In the author's opinion Wicksteed's treatment of the "terms on which alternatives are offered" does not in any way permit the inferences made by Dr. Lange. However, they give rise to another question of importance for his alternative solution, but which Dr. Lange has evidently overlooked. Is it possible for a third person, e.g., the central authority, to draw up a scale of preference giving a satisfactory picture of the heterogeneous and constantly shifting needs of the members of a community? As we shall see Dr. Lange seems also to have overlooked the fact that the chapter in Professor Wicksteed's book to which he refers us, in another respect too constitutes an argument against his own point of view.

Dr. Lange says that the economic problem is a problem of choice between different alternatives and maintains that for that reason three data are necessary to solve it: (1) a

---

[23] *The Common Sense of Political Economy*, London, 1910, p. 21.

scale of preferences to guide people in making their choice, (2) knowledge of "the terms on which alternatives are offered," and (3) knowledge of the extent of existing resources. With these the problem of choice is solved. Dr. Lange maintains that (1) and (3) are given, at least to the same extent as they are in capitalist society, and that the only thing on which there may be some doubt is whether the data for (2) are available. He mentions that Mises denies that they are, but says that a careful study of the theory of price and production shows convincingly that once the data for (1) and (3) are given, so, too, the terms on which alternatives are offered are, in the last resort, settled by the technical possibilities of transforming one good into another, that is to say, by the functions of production. The leaders of the socialist society will have exactly the same information, or lack of information, concerning the functions of production, as has the capitalist producer, he says. He then goes on to repeat that Professor Mises has confused the two forms of prices and concludes by saying that Mises' denial of the possibility of economic calculation in the socialist society must be dismissed.

Neither of these assertions can be considered tenable. In the first place, it is highly doubtful whether the economic leaders of a socialist society would agree that they had solved the problem (rational distribution of thousands of individual means of production), even if they were handed these three data. They will rather be inclined to agree with the assertion that there are just as many equations as unknown quantities. Dr. Lange ought, in any case, to have said that his alleged solution was not of practical value.

In the second place the data for (1) and (3) are not given to the same extent in the socialist society, as they are in the capitalist one. To get his "scale of preferences to guide people in making their choice" Dr. Lange falls back on Professor Taylor's solution. He says:

> *Any price difference from the equilibrium price would show at the end of the accounting period as a surplus or a shortage of the commodity in question.*[24]

Since Dr. Lange has brought up this side of the question, it must be asked to what extent a surplus or shortage of consumer goods can be considered satisfactory data for evaluating consumers' preferences in a socialist society. As we attempted to show in Chapter 6, this cannot be said to be the case except under certain, very unlikely, assumptions.

As to (2) ("the terms on which alternatives are offered") Dr. Lange obviously means by that the functions of production, and to this one can only say that the functions of production do not depend only on the technical possibilities. If only technical coefficients are to be taken into consideration, one will run the risk of molybdenum being used for the manufacture of toy swords and microscope lenses for schoolboys' magnifying glasses. The use of technical coefficients must depend, too, on the values (prices) of the means of production and these are not determined only by quantities. As far as information on the extent of resources (3) is concerned, we have already pointed out that accurate data are not easy to obtain. In addition comes the fact that the possibilities of production also depend on existing possibilities for *combination.*

Dr. N. Kaldor's review of Dr. Carl Landauer's *Planwirtschaft und Verkehrwirtschaft* in the *Economic Journal* of

---

[24] *Op. cit.,* p. 164. Dr. Lange's italics.

June, 1932, contains some valuable comments on the method of trial and error, that are worth quoting:

> . . . in order to find out anything at all in this way, the different factors must be moved simultaneously, and not alternatively . . . So long as 'factor movements' are carried out alternatively (i.e. under no simultaneously valid conditions) the results disclose little about the true situation; while if all factors are moved simultaneously, any attempt to deduce factor-prices from the existing price-relationships of consumption goods becomes impossible; even if the above objections did not hold, such a process of trial and error would prove to be absurdly uneconomical, as all factors would have to be tried in all employments; and carrying factors from one employment into another involves a special cost—even in a Socialist State.[25]

It must be added, that Dr. Lange, like Professor Taylor, obviously assumes that the community is static. In a dynamic community technical development, among other things, would make Dr. Lange's coefficients change continually. Dr. Lerner, too, for all his appreciation, has to call Dr. Lange's solution "reactionary and static."[26]

Another solution based on the trial and error method is that of W. Crosby Roper Jr. He, too, says that lack of a consumer good is a clear indication that the central authority must revise its prices for its means of production, until "a sort of equilibrium" is found. At the same time he expresses strong doubt as to the practicability of the method. He realizes that a mistake will entail changes in the whole system (see the quotation on p. 127), and also that equilibrium can only be achieved in this way in a static community, which cannot exist.

---

[25] P. 280.
[26] *Op. cit.,* p. 75.

In his short essay Crosby Roper, while expressing his strong sympathy for socialism, is obviously of the opinion that the best that can be achieved is a system approaching that used in the capitalist society. He writes:

> Our socialist state would be justified in claiming success, if it could point to a productive structure based on a pricing mechanism as near exactness as that of present economy. . . . Economically it is perfectly conceivable.

But he adds later that:

> The great obstacle is in the limitation of human abilities. The complexities of a national pricing structure would be far beyond those of any present system of accounting. Added to the generally recognized difficulties of managing a centralized state's productive apparatus, these problems would almost certainly prove insurmountable obstacles to successful administration. It seems safe to say that the pricing apparatus necessary for an efficient centralized collectivism, is, at best, only a remote possibility.

He ends by saying:

> It (his argument) indicates that the best chance for success of a socialist society lies in a decentralized organization which retains, so far as possible, the strong features of capitalism.[27]

Professor Hayek has said of these mathematical solutions that the apparatus by which theoretical economics explains the formation of prices and the direction of production in a competitive system may determine the value and quantity of the various goods that are to be produced, *provided* there is complete knowledge of all relevant data. It is not an impossibility in the sense of being logically

---

[27] *Op. cit.,* pp. 60–62.

contradictory, says Hayek, but that is only one side of the question. To argue that because it is logically conceivable to determine prices by such a procedure, it in any way invalidates the contention that it is not possible, only shows ignorance of the real nature of the problem. It is only necessary to try to visualize what the application of that would imply in order to reject it as "humanly impracticable and impossible."[28]

If the central authority is to reach the same degree of economy as in a competitive society, it will in its calculations have to treat the means of production as being of about as many different types of goods as there are individual units. Two technically similar goods in different places, differently packed and of different age, says Hayek, cannot possibly be considered similar as regards utility and serviceability, if even a minimum of effective use is to be secured. Since the manager of a factory in a centrally directed community will have no powers to substitute one good for another as he wishes, all the innumerable different units will have to appear separately in the calculations of the central authority. This would be a greater statistical task than anyone has ever dared to attempt.

But as Professor Hayek says, this is not all. The information the central authority will need must also include a comprehensive description of all relevant technical characteristics of each single good, including the cost of transport to each and every other place where they might conceivably be employed to greater advantage, costs of possible repairs, alterations, etc., etc.

Professor Hayek points out that this choice of suitable

---

[28] *Op. cit.,* pp. 207–208.

uses is only possible if all this information is taken into consideration in the calculation, which in practice would mean that it was concentrated with one or two people who could formulate the necessary equations, and this is patently absurd even if one assumes that the information "exists" at a given moment. In reality this knowledge consists of the ability to take quick decisions in respect of a given set of circumstances. With regard to the data concerning consumer goods Professor Hayek points out that previous experience is of no value, since tastes are constantly changing, so that the list would have to be constantly revised, while hundreds of thousands of comparisons will be needed to fulfil the task, and that is beyond man's capacity.

Professor Lionel Robbins has the same objection, only he says that the central authority will have to solve millions of equations.[29] He has also discussed the question in his *Economic Planning and International Order,* where he says:

> In a world economy, with hundreds of thousands of types of commodities and hundreds of thousands of ways of producing them, the attainment of one solution, let alone the continuous change of solution which changing conditions will involve, would be completely out of the question.[30]

To this Dr. Lange has objected that consumers also solve equations without taking an examination in higher mathematics; that Professor Hayek and Professor Robbins themselves "solve" hundreds of equations every day when buying a paper or deciding to eat in a restaurant. Dr. Lange's objection, however, does not hold. Quite apart from the fact that the equations the central authority would have to

[29] *The Great Depression,* London, 1933, p. 151.
[30] P. 201.

solve are of quite a different nature to those of the private individual, the latter tend to solve themselves automatically, which Dr. Lange must admit the former do not. However, the best argument against this objection is to be found in the chapter of Professor Wicksteed's book to which Dr. Lange has himself appealed, where Wicksteed says:

> We are not obliged to be constantly considering alternatives, because in a fairly well regulated mind the suggestion of any particular item of expenditure does not as a rule arise until it is approximately in its proper turn and place for gratification.[31]

It may be as well, in conclusion, to draw attention to what is not devoid of significance in our appraisal of these mathematical solutions; that those who first suggested them, Vilfredo Pareto and Enrico Barone, themselves stated that their systems of equations were not capable of being put into practice. Pareto wrote:

> Remarquons, d'ailleurs, que cette determination (de l'équilibre économique) n'a nullement pour but d'àrriver à un calcul numérique des prix. Faisons l'hypothèse la plus favorable à un tel calcul; supposons que nous ayons triomphé de toutes les difficultés pour arriver à connaître les données du problème, et que nouns connaissions les ophélimités de toutes les marchandises pour chaque individu, toutes les circonstances de la production des marchandises, etc. C'est là déjà une hypothèse absurde, et pourtant elle ne nous donne pas encore la possibilité pratique de résoudre ce probleme. Nous avons vu que dans le cas de 100 individus et de 700 marchandises il y aurait 70699 conditions (en réalité un grand nombre de circonstances, que nous avons jusqu'ici négligées, augmenteraient encore ce nombre); nous aurons donc à résoudre un système de 70699 équations. Cela dépasse pratiquement la puissance de l'analyse algébrique, et cela la dépasserait encore davantage si l'on prenait en considération le nombre fabuleux d'équations

---

[31] *Op. cit.,* p. 35.

que donnerait une population de quarante millions d'individus, et quelques milliers de marchandises. Dans ce cas les rôles seraient changés: et ce ne seraient plus les mathématiques qui viendraient en aide à l'économie politique, mais l'économie politique qui viendrait en aide aux mathématiques. En d'autres termes, si on pouvait vraiment connaître toutes ces équations, le seul moyer accessible aux forces humaines pour les résoudre, ce serait d'observer la solution pratique que donne le marché.[32]

Enrico Barone wrote:

Many of the writers who have criticized collectivism have hesitated to use as evidence the practical difficulties in establishing on paper the various equivalents; but it seems they have not perceived what really are the difficulties—or more frankly, the impossibility—of solving such equations *a priori*.[33]

The following is the first of his conclusions:

From what we have seen and demonstrated hitherto, it is obvious how fantastic those doctrines are which imagine that production in a collectivist régime would be ordered in a manner substantially different from that of 'anarchist' production.[34]

It is amazing that the many who have proposed a mathematical solution of the problem, basing it on Pareto's and Barone's systems of equivalents, have not been aware of these reservations. When, in addition, it is realized that the data which are a prerequisite of such mathematical solutions are partly difficult and partly impossible to obtain in a socialist society, and that equivalents of this kind, more or less *explicite,* assume a static community, one is entitled to conclude that the mathematical suggestions do not solve the problem.

---

[32] *Manuel d'économie politique,* Paris, 1909, pp. 233 and 234.
[33] *Op. cit.,* p. 287.
[34] *Op. cit.,* p. 289.

12

Other Solutions, Marginal Costs as Criteria

The *Economic Journal* of December, 1936, carried an article by E. F. M. Durbin, "Economic Calculus in a Planned Economy," in which the author attempted to show that there was no theoretical or logical difficulty in having an exact pricing system in a planned economy. In his opinion there was no reason to abandon the search for economic or utilitarian calculus in an industrial system controlled by a Central Authority. He agreed with Professors Robbins and Hayek that the mathematical solutions and any system involving simultaneous equations were impracticable, but asserted that he could point to an alternative system, thus refuting the arguments advanced by Mises, Halm and Hayek in *Collectivist Economic Planning*. Dr. Durbin based his argument on "the well-established fact of economic scarcity." The consumers must be consulted about what they want "unless democratic doctrine is rejected root and branch." If there is no wastage of resources, the costs of one commodity must be assessed in quantities of sacrificed alternative goods. "There must, therefore, also be a free market for the factors of production."

Now, says Dr. Durbin, it is the best known truism of

the theory of value, that perfect competition, including perfect foresight, will secure the right adjustment of production to the preferences of consumers.[1] This basic doctrine has been advanced in three separate ex-positional forms of very different value for solving the problem of a planned economy. There are Marshallian supply and demand curves, the Austrian School's solution by way of marginal products, and the equational systems. Dr. Durbin considers that it is "almost certain" that the second (the marginal product method) can be equally well used in a planned society, as in one of *laissez-faire*. Were the central authority to instruct the various producing units (1) to calculate the marginal productivity of all mobile resources and (2) to move all mobile resources to the positions of highest calculated product, there would—according to Dr. Durbin—seem to be no reason to suppose that the distribution of resources would be any different in such a community than it would be in one with complete competition, "since all logical, theoretical and accountancy problems are the same in both systems."

Dr. Durbin grants that it might be very difficult to calculate the marginal products, but the technical difficulties will be the same in both societies. There are problems that can only be solved after a comprehensive sociological and psychological analysis, but in the realm of economic theory the marginal productivity solution would seem adequate. The ability to discover marginal products does not depend upon

[1] Dr. Durbin adds in a footnote that he has expressed his doubts about the validity of this doctrine and refers the reader to his article, "The Social Significance of the Theory of Value," in the *Economic Journal*, 1935.

the existence of a particular set of social institutions—and certainly not on those of *"laissez-faire,"* he thinks.

On the other hand, Dr. Durbin is not satisfied with a solution exclusively based on marginal products. He admits that the estimates of marginal value products are extremely liable to error. Demand curves will have to be calculated. In either calculation the margin of error is likely to be great, and in the resulting value product doubly so. There can be no complete solution of the problem, unless the process can be submitted to another check and assessment. This raises the question of applicability of the English *cost* analysis to the problems of the planned economy.

Then Dr. Durbin discusses the position of a socialized trust and assumes that there will be competition between trusts, in which connection he mentions a rate of interest, established in the free market, for new capital.

He also discusses the possibility of inaccuracies occurring and what a trust could do, if demand sinks. The treatise also criticizes Professor Hayek's views on the question of depreciation in *Collective Economic Planning* and here the author of this book is largely in agreement with Dr. Durbin.

Dr. Durbin concludes by saying that in his opinion he has refuted the main charge offered by economists against a planned economy, that it has no method for the rational calculation of relative productions. He thinks the real arguments for and against a planned economy lie elsewhere. He does not specify where, but thinks that not economic theory, but only social science, can hope to find an answer to them.

Many of Dr. Durbin's comments are interesting and some of them help to throw light on the problem, but it is difficult to agree with his assertion that he has solved the problem. He has managed to maintain the discussion on a high theoretical level, but in his anxiety not to "dogmatize on practical questions" he has overlooked the crux of the whole problem, namely, how the data on which the socialist trusts are to base their calculations are to be obtained.

It is all very well to say that competition and market prices are preferable to mathematical computation of thousands of questions, but that is no solution. The great questions are: to what extent can market prices be obtained in a socialist community, and how far are competing trusts compatible with the central authority which Dr. Durbin assumes to exist? On these questions he does not touch. He speaks of "interest rates, established in the free market, for new capital," but never says who is to offer this new capital. If he means that it is to come from the savings of the members of the community, this would involve a number of questions that ought to have been discussed (see Chapter 8). If, however, he means that the new capital is to be supplied by the central authority and that the various trusts shall compete for it, this, too, raises interesting problems that must be solved before one can accept his assumption of a free interest market.

Nor does Dr. Durbin say exactly whether it is vertical or horizontal trusts he has in mind. Even under the assumption that there will be markets with several buyers and sellers of all intermediary products, there will be only one supplier of natural resources (obtained from the soil) and the fixing of prices in such a market would be as imperfect, as though the capital was merely supplied by the central authority.

When assuming the simultaneous existence of a planning authority and competing trusts, as Dr. Durbin does, one has at least the right to expect an indication of the extent of the trusts' autonomy and of whether they will be able to expand or diminish their activities, even though this ran counter to the plan, or not. Had Dr. Durbin embarked on a discussion of these points, he would presumably have seen that his solution gets us no further, not even on paper. The free right of disposition and competition in order to achieve maximum marginal productivity, production according to a central plan, and production according to the consumers' preferences, are three things that cannot be combined. Dr. Karl Polanyi, whose attempted solution, to which we shall return, also assumes the existence of competition, fully realizes the implications of such a proposal and says straight out that calculation is out of the question in a community directed by a central authority.

Dr. Durbin's idea, that special institutions are not required to determine marginal products, at any rate not those found in a *laissez-faire* society, is interesting, and it is to be regretted that he neither pursues it, nor gives his reasons. Perhaps he thinks that it is not within the scope of a treatise on theoretical economics to give reasons, but in that case the opinion should never have been expressed. Dr. Durbin's tendency to advance views on matters that he considers to lie outside the scope of the economist, appears again in his conclusion where he has beautiful things to say of the "better and juster type of society" called a Planned Economy, but declines to justify his views.

In actual fact, much of Dr. Durbin's treatise does not touch on our problem: the possibility of economic calculation in a socialist society, but on an extraneous and in itself interesting problem, namely, the production policy that autonomous monopolistic trusts in such a society ought to conduct.

One solution that commands respect is that of Dr. A. P. Lerner, who has made many important contributions to the discussion. His criticism of the solutions of others has at times been so severe that one might almost think that he himself doubted the possibility of economic calculation in the socialist community; but this is not the case. His views were, however, somewhat difficult to grasp and it was not till Dr. Maurice Dobb accused him of being an "elusive" and "invisible opponent" that he made them clearer. In his *Economic Theory and Socialist Economy: A Reply* he treats first the difficulties encountered in other solutions:

> Where there are thousands of products and thousands of factors, being combined in thousands of different ways in millions of different, productive units, and where a reshuffling of factors may have to be of a most complicated kind, it seems to me that it would not be so easy to find the technical expert who knows all that is going on everywhere.

and he continues:

> If every producer so regulates his production as to make the marginal productivities of factors proportional to their prices on a market, and if the prices are moved so as to equate the producers' demands to the supply, the problem can be solved without waiting for the super-technician.[2]
>
> And by a price system I do mean a price system. Not a mere *a posteriori* juggling with figures by auditors, but prices which will have to be taken into consideration by managers of factories in organizing production.

One must agree with what Dr. Lerner says here, but it is

---

[2] On the preceding page he writes:

difficult to see how this represents a solution of the problem. True enough, with both markets and prices there is no need for the super-technician, but it is just the assumed absence of markets and prices that has called forth the proposals for mathematical solutions, which in their turn call for the technical expert who knows everything that is going on everywhere. With both markets and prices the problem ceases to be a problem. The question is: How are these to be obtained? Of that Dr. Lerner has nothing to say.

Considering that Dr. Lerner with wit and acuteness has demanded clarity in the discussion, and considering the light he himself has shed on the problem, one hesitates to think that he could have overlooked the importance of how markets and prices are to be achieved in the socialist society. Unfortunately, one's doubts are not removed, but strengthened by a later article of his,[3] criticizing Dr. Durbin's article. He himself describes it as a protest against

> the developing tradition, in approaching the problems of socialist economics, of starting from the consideration of competitive equilibrium, instead of going direct to the more fundamental principle of marginal opportunity cost. This approach is not only subject to methodological criticism as indirect and cumbersome, but is a fertile source of actual error deriving from unrealized implications of the static nature of competitive equilibrium.

There is no doubt that the method is cumbersome, that it makes mistakes possible, and that it is natural to assume static conditions when discussing competitive equilibrium, but it is difficult to see how one can avoid consideration of

---

[3] "Statics and Dynamics in Socialist Economics," in *Economic Journal,* June, 1937.

underlying conditions and difficulties, if the task is to elucidate the problem before us.

Dr. Lerner's treatise is first and foremost a criticism of Dr. Durbin's solution.[4] In his opinion it is more practical than Dickinson's and

> also refutes anew the well-known thesis of Professors Mises, Hayek and Halm that a socialist economic calculus is impossible.

This "also" is rather surprising in view of Dr. Lerner's almost deadly criticism of Dickinson's solution. There are many valuable points of view in Dr. Lerner's treatise, but it does not mention what, in our opinion, is the greatest weakness in Dr. Durbin's proposal, namely, the lack of any indication of how the necessary data for calculation are to be obtained. This is where Dr. Lerner's own solution, too, falls down.

As far as Dr. Lerner is concerned, the matter is simple. He writes:

> If we so order the economic activity of the society that no commodity is produced unless its importance is greater than that of the alternative that is sacrificed, we shall have completely achieved the ideal that the economic calculus of a socialist state sets before itself.

This immediately and obviously raises the question of how the "importance" of products is to be determined. Later Dr. Lerner writes:

---

[4] Dr. Durbin has himself in "A Note on Dr. Lerner's 'Dynamical' Propositions," *Economic Journal,* September, 1947, accepted some of Dr. Lerner's objections and refuted others. He also repeats that he and Dr. Lerner agree on the most important thing of all, "the applicability of the logic of the theory of value to the circumstances of the Planned Economy."

We must therefore aim *directly* at our real object, *the most economic utilization of resources*. What does this imply? . . .
. . . If we assume that the members of the society, in spending their income, do not take into account the effect of their individual purchases on the prices of consumption goods, we can take the ratio between the prices at which goods sell freely on the market as measuring the ratio between the marginal significance of the commodities. This is because every individual, in using his income to the best advantage, will purchase more significant shillingworths . . . until all the shillingworths have . . . the same marginal social significance.

This means that the central authority is to take its indications of the importance of products from a free consumers' market. If that is the case, then one ought to go into the question of whether alterations in prices are to be made by the central authority or by autonomous retail shops, and to clarify the conditions under which "ratios of prices" can be said to give reliable indications.

Dr. Lerner says in a footnote:

This assumes that individuals choose best for themselves. Whenever this is not considered to be the case, others—normally in the form of the State—can choose for them either wholly or partly (i.e. by influencing particular prices by taxes or bounties). These others are then the consumers and the whole scheme formally remains the same.

There are two reasons why this is a noteworthy statement. First, because Dr. Lerner had earlier said that to let the central authority determine the scales of needs would be irreconcilable with democracy and socialism (see footnote on p. 110). In the second place, because—and this is the main point—this is of decisive importance for assessing the possibility of calculation. Dr. Lerner has rightly said that the question of the extent of the free choice of goods and occupation the community shall have is not one that can be settled by an economist as such. This, however, does not mean that it is not of great economic consequence and of essential importance in solving the problem of calculation, which of these alternatives is chosen. This will be discussed in greater detail in Chapter 14, but it can be said here that the valuation of capital goods (that is, the obtaining of the necessary cost data) is another—and easier—task, when the valuation is to be made by the same individual (or individuals) who determine what the members of the community are to have, than when the valuation is made by a different method. The problem is quite different, if production is, for example, to be adapted to (and the means of production valued according to) the constantly shifting needs of the members of the community. It is thus wrong in principle to discuss the question on the basis of both assumptions simultaneously.

That Dr. Lerner assumes the community to be dynamic is a step forward. He calls his treatise *Statics and Dynamics in Socialist Economics* and points out that his hypothesis includes variable marginal costs, at the same time taking Dr. Durbin to task because the relationship between short-period and long-period problems "is left beautifully vague in the simplified directives given by Dr. Durbin to the managers."

He considers that Dr. Durbin's expression "in the fullness of time," which is the only clue he gives of when and how quickly a new factory is to be built,

> must surely be the nearest English expression for the untranslatable word by which the citizens of such countries as Russia and Spain show their refusal to recognize time as an economic factor.

As the community is assumed to be dynamic, it would have been natural to discuss the effect on demand of alterations in, for example, the size, age-composition and tastes of the population. This is not the only point on which Dr. Lerner, to use his own expression, is "beautifully vague." He is vague, too, in regard to data on costs. Besides the general directions, which have already been quoted, he employs two rules. The second, which he mentions first,

> suggests that if all the officers of the economic administration equalize their marginal revenues to their marginal cost—and this is what they would do if each is simply enjoined to maximise the profits of the enterprise under his control—this will suffice to set in motion all the forces necessary to achieve the equilibrium. We may call this rule, suggested by the second method, Rule Two. . . . If the application of Rule Two results in a deviation from this norm, the officers may be instructed to subordinate Rule Two to another rule, which we may call Rule One, derived from the first method and calling for the equalization of price to average cost.

His final word is:

> Price must be made equal to marginal cost. This is the contribution that pure economic theory has to make to the building up of a socialist economy.

Of the definition of marginal costs and marginal productivity Dr. Lerner writes, that instructions should be issued that:

> the use of every factor is to be extended up to the point where the marginal physical product multiplied by its price is equal to the price of the factor. Or, in other words, up to the point where the price of the factor needed to produce another unit of product multiplied by the product is equal to the physical quantity of any price of the factor. This value, which has to

be equated to the price of the product, we shall call the marginal cost.

And in a footnote to this extract he writes:

The concentration on the price of a factor is achieved under conditions of perfect competition because then the price happens to be equal to the extra cost of buying one unit more. This has very aptly been called the parametric function of prices under perfect competition. See O. Lange, 'On the Economic Studies of Socialism, Part One,' *Review of Economic Studies,* October, 1936, p. 59. With our rule we need not rely on the conditions of perfect competition being present, and we are not upset if, because of the growth of the unit of production or for any other reason, the parametric function of prices break down.

The views expressed in this footnote will be discussed later, but it must be pointed out that Dr. Lerner, although using the term "marginal physical product," is really operating with prices and values. In one place he says that marginal costs result from multiplying with the price and elsewhere he says that in evaluating the greater or lesser marginal (physical) productivity of the various factors, the price of the factors must be taken into account. Apart from the obvious objection that Dr. Lerner omits to say how he will arrive at these prices, his argument can also be criticized for circular reasoning. As Professor Fritz Machlup wrote in "On the Meaning of the Marginal Product."[5]

By measuring units of factors in terms of their market value, marginal productivity analysis is, to my mind, reduced *ad absurdum*. One must bear in mind that marginal productivity analysis as a part of the theory of distribution is to serve as

---

[5] See *Exploration in Economics. Notes and Essays Contributed in Honour of F. W. Taussig,* New York, 1936.

explanation of the market values of factors or services. To define these services in terms of their market values is to give up the task of explaining them.

It is also of importance to point out that all forms of marginal consideration assume the possibility of choice and of a selection of goods, and that the more imperfect the markets are, the more valueless become the decisions taken. This is a question that Dr. Lerner might well have discussed, but has not.[6]

Even though we accept, as Dr. Lerner does, the importance of supply and demand and the importance of relating prices to costs, it is obvious that his directions do not solve the problem of economic calculation in the socialist community. In his positive solution he moves within a narrow field, where he—without even stating it—assumes all the relevant data to be given, both those needed for determining costs and those required for determining demand. In other words, he assumes that the most difficult part of the problem has already been solved.

---

[6] It is no elucidation that Dr. Lerner has elsewhere written: ". . . the competitive price system has to be *adapted* to a socialist society. If it is applied *in toto* we have not a socialist but a competitive society." See "Economic Theory and Socialist Economy," in *Review of Economic Studies,* 1934–35, p. 55.

13

Other Suggested Solutions—Competition in the Socialist Community

Professor Hayek reports in his book that many of the younger economists, after serious study of the problem of calculation, have lost all faith in the possibility of its being solved in a community governed by a central authority. In its place they suggest restoring competition in as far as that is compatible with the abolition of private ownership of the means of production. Nothing has been published on this subject, but from conversations Professor Hayek has had with younger (English) economists this would seem to be the direction in which they are thinking. A similar proposal has already been made in Germany, and H. D. Dickinson has himself taken a step along the same path.

Before discussing this proposal, we must point out, as does Professor Hayek, how significant it is that socialist economists should recommend competition. That means that they will abandon the idea of a planned economy directed by a central authority, which so far has generally been called the only rational form of society. They began by looking for a form of society that will eliminate "hazard" and "anarchic production" (which they hold to be the result of free competition) and end by proposing that free competition should be copied. "The wheel has gone full round."

With the generally accepted definition of socialism, which is used here, any solution which did away with the central authority would lie outside the scope of this discussion, for such a community would not be socialist. However, it is of such wide interest to examine how such a modified form of socialism might work, that we must devote some space to it.

The proposals for making use of competition are vague and for that reason difficult to discuss. Professor Hayek states that H. D. Dickinson has made a small step in the direction of competition, but in reality, it is a big step. It is true that among his original postulates Dickinson demands that "all production is undertaken by the community,"[1] but he later assumes "a free market at each end of the chain of production, for finished goods and for productive services."[2]

Dr. Durbin and Dr. Lerner have obviously assumed that there will be some sort of competition too, but they have been so vague about their assumption, that it is not clear what kind of competition they had in mind. All the same, it is obvious from Dr. Durbin's answer[3] to Dr. Lerner's criticism that he envisages the possibility of the simultaneous existence of a socialist planned economy and of independent competing production units. In reality these two forms are incompatible, a fact overlooked by most of those making proposals of this kind. In this answer Dr. Durbin writes that he had not succeeded in making it clear in his original

---

[1] *Op. cit.,* p. 238.

[2] *Op. cit.,* p. 242.

[3] *Economic Journal,* September, 1937.

article, that one of his important principles was "the practical necessity for retaining as much financial independence for the management units of, and as many management units in, a socialized industry as possible." He enlarges on this in a footnote, saying that it is "the independence, rather than the simplicity, that is valuable."[4]

Let us recall in passing that W. Crosby Roper, Jr., who has also insisted on the need for competition, said that the degree of efficiency that can be expected to be achieved in the socialist society will depend on the degree to which it has been able to attain the same competition as in a capitalistic society.

G. D. H. Cole, one of the protagonists of Guild Socialism, is well aware of the difficulties in carrying it through. In his *Principle of Economic Planning* he wrote:

> On this issue I remain an unrepentant Guild Socialist, though I am conscious that the way to industrial self-government in any full sense may be longer and more difficult than I used to think.

Not even he is very clear about the important question of the autonomy of the guilds. It is his opinion that "in the long run the aspiration of a planned economy must be to make each industry to the fullest possible extent a democratic self-governing Guild," but almost in the same breath he says: "I do not, of course, mean that each industry or service can be left free to do things which militate against the national plan as a whole."

It must be stressed that Cole's proposal comes from an idealistic desire to improve social conditions and is not put forward as a solution of the problem of economic calcula-

---

[4] *Op. cit.,* p. 580.

tion in a socialist society. He writes in the preface that originally it was his intention to discuss this and cognate problems, but that he gave it up as the question proved too difficult and theoretical.

Between 1822 and 1923 various proposals were made in Germany for a socialist community admitting of competition. One of the first was that of Dr. Eduard Heimann, who expressed the opinion[5] that he was the first to bring up the question of price-fixation in the socialist community.[6]

Dr. Heimann's point of view is in many respects individualistic. He is a moral philosopher, a Christian Scientist, and suffers, like many others who have taken part in the discussion, from discrepancies between what his ideals and sympathies lead him to desire and what his learning and reason tell him is possible and sensible. Dr. Heimann wants to have "*Gleichschaltung*" in place of "*Gegenschaltung*" and speaks of the "*ergriefende Sehnsucht*" for better distribution (of wealth). Thus, his instincts and sympathies are against the liberalistic struggle of competition. However, he curtly refuses any idea of a moneyless economy. Also he turns against those who use unjustifiable catch-words, like "anarchy," for the capitalist form of production, calling it an "*Irrlehre*" to speak of it as being planless and confused, and in many places he becomes almost panegyrical in speaking of the significance of market prices (e.g., p. 71, Chapter 4). He speaks of "*Oppenheimers schöner Lehre vom friedlichen Wettbewerb*" and it is this peaceful competition which is his ideal.

---

[5] *Mehrwert und Gemeinwirtschaft*, Berlin, 1922.
[6] "Die Sozialisierung" in *Archiv für Sozialwissenschaft und Sozialpolitik*, 1918–19, Vol. 45, p. 569.

For all its interesting ideas and valuable pointers Dr. Heimann's own solution is neither clear, nor satisfactory. Not even he explains exactly what the connection is to be between the central authority and the monopolies. Dr. Heimann has from time to time been classed as a Guild Socialist, yet he characterizes G. H. D. Cole's proposal as "exceedingly superficial and inconsistent." In fact it is doubtful whether Dr. Heimann can be classed as a socialist at all, seeing that he also maintains that there is need for private ownership of the means of production.[7]

Dr. Heimann's greatest dilemma is that, while understanding the importance of prices and markets (and also considering private property as necessary) he still wants to have socialism. He considers that the necessary and peaceful competition can be induced between the managers of the socialist concerns. Dr. Heimann's various pleas speak rather of his divided focus and inner doubts as to whether competition and socialism can really be reconciled. These doubts are understandable when it is remembered that Dr. Heimann was one of the first to draw attention to the existence of the problem of calculation, and that, as late as 1930, he said that the difficulties in Marx' and Lenin's problems *"in groteskem Masse unterschätzt würden."*[8]

A serious objection to Dr. Heimann's solution of the problem by introducing competing monopolies is, as has been stated by Professor Halm, that Dr. Heimann's main argument against the capitalist society is just its "monopolism" and the insufficient competition arising from monopolism. He has also weakened his position by originally

---

[7] *Op. cit.,* p. 178.

[8] "Sozialisierung" in *Neue Blätter für den Sozialismus,* Vol. 1, 1930, p. 23.

maintaining that Professor Cassel was wrong in saying that the formation of interest rates would remain unchanged in the socialist community on the ground that this presupposed "various contracting parties in the market" (see Chapter 8, p. 184).

In judging Dr. Heimann's theory it should also be remembered that he draws a distinction between *"Erzeugungs- und Bedarfsplan-Wirtschaft,"* which can only be considered untenable and sterile. Reference should also be made to his proposal for "imputation" (see Chapter 9, p. 194). That Dr. Heimann's proposal is of little practical significance is apparent from the fact that he assumes that the community is "mainly" static and, further, that it contains people who build on *"ursprungliche Gemeinschaft nicht auf materielles Interesse."*[9] Elsewhere he has said that he does not regard his *"primitives Denkscheme für ein praktisches Rezept"*. His view-points and opinions have been discussed and criticized by Professor Halm and—partly on other grounds—by Professor Mises[10] and Dr. Cläre Tisch.[11]

Despite all its defects, defects which are natural enough in view of the difficulty of reconciling the views he advocates, it must be said that Dr. Heimann's plea is very winning in its honest and explicit admission of the advantages of the capitalist system of competition, to which his sentiments are so strongly opposed.

The problem of calculation in the socialist society has been discussed by Dr. Karl Polanyi in his treatise *Sozialistische Rechnungslegung*. He calls it the "key problem of

---

[9] *Mehrwert und Gemeinwirtschaft*, p. 204.
[10] *Neue Beiträge zum Problem der sozialistischen Wirtschaftsrechnung* in *Archiv für Sozialwissenschaft und Sozialpolitik*, Vol. 51, 1923.
[11] *Op. cit.*

the socialist economy." What he discusses is really a particular problem, for what he wants to find is a method of calculating what humanity's ideals cost it. This is no place to discuss whether or not he has succeeded in solving that task, but what is of interest for us, is that Dr. Polanyi wants to have markets and not a central authority:

> We admit out-of-hand that we regard the solution of the problem of calculation in a centrally directed economy as impossible.[12]

Dr. Polanyi's assumptions and proposals are, like those of many other Guild Socialists, somewhat nebulous. For example, one is not told whether the guilds are merely the managers or whether they *own* the means of production of which they dispose. In the latter eventuality one would no longer be dealing with a socialist, but with a syndicalist community. Dr. Polanyi himself admits that he is discussing a "type of socialist transitional economy." Nor is it clear how he imagines prices will be arrived at in this "functionally organized" community. He says that there will be "every form of price-formation," yet admits on the same page that this is an inadmissible assumption. An elaborate criticism of his proposal has been made by Dr. Felix Weil, who says *inter alia:*

> Hence it will also appear that Polanyi's method of calculation, even if his assumption (functionally organized economy) is accepted, is impossible, even senseless.[13]

---

[12] *Op. cit.*, p. 378.

[13] See "Gildensozialistische Rechnungslegung" in *Archiv für Sozialwissenschaft und Sozialpolitik,* 1924; also Polanyi's reply "Die funktionelle Theorie des Gesellschaft und das Problem der Sozialistischen Rechnungslegung" in the same publication.

In a treatise *Wirtschaftsrechnung und Gemeinwirtschaft. Zur Mises'-schen These von der Unmöglichkeit sozialistischer Wirtschaftsrechnung* Dr. Jakob Marschak maintains that he has shown that Mises' thesis is not proved. It is difficult to accept this assertion, although Dr. Marschak makes out quite a good case for individual aspects of the question, among them the difficulties arising out of the dynamic character of economic activity. Dr. Marschak is fully aware of the defects of monopolistic fixation of prices, but his main argument is that monopolistic fixation of prices also takes place in the (private) capitalist society, and that the advantages of monopolies are greater in the socialist community.

To say that the fixation of prices is at least as imperfect in the capitalist society is no real theoretic objection, and, in fact, by his criticism Dr. Marschak indirectly concedes the rightness of Professor Mises' views (for a more detailed criticism of that point, see Dr. Tisch's paper). Added to this, Dr. Marschak's emphasis of the trade-regulating qualities of socialist monopolies is very shakily founded (see Appendix B).

Dr. Marschak is on firmer ground when he suggests an amplification of the concept of price. If one defines price in such a way that almost any numerical designation becomes "a price," that, of course, *seemingly* increases the theoretical possibilities for calculation. (The question will be further discussed in Chapter 14, but see also Chapter 11).

The form of socialism that Marschak himself suggests is a kind of Guild Socialism with so large a degree of independence that syndicalism is the right description of it, and this Marschak himself uses. Now, in actual fact, syndicalism means that the right of private ownership of means of production exists and, hence, is not socialism. Thus a syndicalist order cannot solve the difficulties of economic calculation in the socialist community.

That Dr. Marschak's treatise neither refutes Mises' views, nor solves the problem, does not hinder it from containing much that is interesting and valuable. He also shows a higher degree of psychological realism than many of the others who have taken part in the discussion, when he says:

> This much can be said here: Syndicalism is a system that demands the least departure from the contemporary type of economically egoistic man. Within the syndicates there is a far-reaching homogeneity of economic interests and in the scales of enjoyment and labour-sacrifice.

A further good thing about Dr. Marschak is that he is one of the few in this group putting forward suggestions who would seem to understand the importance that attaches to the form which the socialist monopolies and trusts are given.

One general objection to these proposals for solving the problem of calculation by introducing competition into socialist communities, is that they are far too vague about the *kind* of competition that is intended. The shape competition is to take is of decisive importance in determining the solution and, hence, in evaluating it. For example, were they to go so far as to propose the introduction of competition between individuals (or groups of individuals) owning means of production, this would mean that they had given up the attempt to solve the problem within the socialist framework. On the other hand, if it is proposed to have planned direction and competition at the same time, this would show that the problem had not been sufficiently thought out. If production is to be in accordance with the plan of the central authority, it cannot be related to price variations and the changing needs of the public. It must either be the one or the other. There is no reconciling the two principles. One of the most important tasks of the manager of a concern is to expand and diminish production. Inability to make the adjustments required would mean that conditions of competition and thus market prices, were completely illusory.

It is also very important to know whether competition between individual concerns or merely between various trusts is intended, and, in the latter case, whether these are to be horizontal or vertical trusts.

In this discussion of the possibility of calculation in the socialist society there seems to be considerable confusion in the estimation of the importance of trusts and monopolies for the formation of prices. There is a tendency to drop the usual objections to trusts and monopolies, since in the socialist society they are to be owned by the state or the community. One result of this is that it is apparently considered of no importance what prices the monopolies (state trusts) demand of their customers. For example, H. D. Dickinson suggests that the prices should be such as "the traffic will bear."[14]

If a monopoly is owned by the community and its profits go to the community instead of to possible private owners, this will make possible a change of the distribution of the community's income and, of course, a monopolist restriction of production, which can be criticized in the socialist

---

[14] *Op. cit.*

society with as much, or as little, justice, as in a capitalist economy. It does not mean that monopolies in a socialist society exert a less unhappy influence on price-formation than they do in a capitalist economy. On the contrary, the fact that socialist societies must, by definition, forbid all production and trade for private accounts, means that monopolies in a socialist community will have more power than in a capitalist economy. What interests us here, is not the distribution of possible profits from monopolies, but the possibility of arriving at prices that could serve as data for calculation. In this respect socialist monopoly-markets will be even more imperfect, than the capitalist markets. For this reason the proposal that there should be competition between trusts or monopolies is no satisfactory solution of the problem of calculation.

Let us assume that the socialist community with which we are concerned goes in for horizontal trusts and monopolies. This means that there will be a monopoly for each intermediate product within each branch of industry. For that part of the factors of production which are used by all the monopolies there will be competition on the buying side, but not on the selling side, for here there will by hypothesis be a monopoly. One production-factor which all will use to a greater or lesser extent, is power. The others for which there will be competition (to buy) will, with the exception of labour, be of smaller significance for the price of the final product. The important thing will be materials, tools, and machinery of a general kind (including office equipment) which can be used in any branch of industry. As regards the market for the supply of power, there will be competition from purchasers, but the market will be particularly imperfect in character. The monopoly for the supply of power will, like the other monopolies for land and natural power, have no sales- or cost-data for the provision of its main product, whether this be land, metals, timber, etc. They can take as this basis, prices known to have been used in the past, or the prices ruling at the time of nationalization (if compensation was paid), yet the changes that are continually taking place in a dynamic society carry with them the necessity for continual revaluation of the factors of production, if hazard and gambling are to be avoided.

In a socialist society with horizontal monopolies it will, by definition, be impossible to have competition on the selling side for land and natural power. These monopolies, in contrast to the others, cannot be links between buyers and sellers, but will only have to do with buyers. One may add that, if a mistake is made in price-fixation (or, rather, in the more or less arbitrary valuation) of these production-factors, a mistake in the sense that the price or valuation does not express the relative scarcity of the factor concerned in relation to the preferred alternative uses, this mistake will be felt throughout every link in the chain of production.

An ostensible advantage of horizontal monopolies is that you get markets for goods at every stage of production. However, the price-formation obtained from such markets will be the poorest possible for the main product of each monopoly. This will lead to so-called cases of bilateral monopolies: one monopoly-seller against one monopoly-buyer (monopsonist). That in such cases prices will be fixed within very wide limits is self-evident and well known from the monopoly theory.

Assuming that the monopolies are vertical ones, there will also be competition for those production-forces (including labour) that can be used by all monopolies. One fundamental deficiency, from the point of view of price-formation, is that there will be no markets for the intermediary products typical of the branch of industry concerned. In this event there will be arbitrariness, not only in fixing the prices of the original factors of production, which are allotted to the various trusts, but also for all intermediary products—right down to the final products, which are typical of the trust concerned. In other words, the formation of prices will be even more imperfect than with horizontal trusts. One has, therefore, to conclude that competition between monopolies will neither give such markets nor such prices and data for calculation, that the problem of calculation can be said to be solved by the proposed introduction of this kind of competition.

The fact that competition between monopolies means that both the competition and the formation of prices will be imperfect, has naturally brought up the question of whether more trustworthy data for calculation can be obtained by having free competition between individual units of production and trading, whatever the branch of industry. Were this so, we should get a form of community that not everybody would accept as socialist, and which would conflict with our definition, in as far as it would entail weakening the authority of the central authority and delegation of its power and economic initiative. Such an order would in reality come very close to that which one finds to-day in the capitalist societies. The only difference would be that in the socialist community the means of production would be owned by the community and not by individuals or groups of individuals.[15]

The introduction of free competition between individual concerns in a socialist society would meet with so many difficulties, that it is doubtful whether such a thing could be carried out effectively. Even though the socialist society had it in its power to eliminate monopolies (including labour-monopoly), there would still be one which, by definition, could not be abolished, that is: the monopoly right to the ground and all that it contains. In that market there cannot be more than one real seller and therefore fixation of prices would be very imperfect. By virtue of the importance of these production factors for prices of all social goods, arbitrariness is at once introduced into the fixation of all prices right from the beginning.

There are also other factors militating against the possibility of creating free competition and free markets in socialist societies, even if the central authority honestly wished to do that. If the community's right of ownership

---

[15] To most people this difference will seem both great and fundamental. Among those whose opinions ought to count, that is, the owners of means of production in capitalist societies, there seems to be a growing tendency to think that the difference is not so great. It is pointed out that the actual right to own and dispose of means of production is being continuously whittled down: the ability to enjoy and dispose of the surplus is being more and more limited, as the public authorities take a continually mounting proportion of the surplus in taxes. It is also objected that restrictions and state interference so greatly restrict the sphere of activities and make business men so dependent on government departments, that they are really becoming a kind of state official. If this view is right, it means that those who want to solve the problem of calculation by having competition between individual links in the chains of production and disposal, are really proposing an order which is approximately what we already have to-day in the capitalist societies. Whether the results are desirable is another story.

is to mean anything at all, it must be accompanied by a certain degree of control over the surplus (which is to be transferred to the community) and by means for making changes in personnel. The central authority can give the managers of concerns complete freedom and full right to do as they think best, but it must of necessity reserve to itself control of the concern and the appointment of its managers. Such control is all the more natural, since in the capitalist society such changes are automatic, as managers who run their concerns at a loss are sooner or later eliminated, whether they work for their own or another's account.

Unless the positions of managers of concerns are to be made hereditary or for life, the central authority (which in such a socialist competitive society ought to be rechristened the control department) must have a scale for measuring the ability and suitability of managers. The qualities which are needed for managing a concern, such as the ability to assume responsibility and to get things done, are not such as can be determined by either examinations or psychotechnical tests. Thus another yardstick must be found. Maximalization of profits[16] is a natural yardstick for the efficiency of managers of concerns in a socialist society that aims at competition between individual links in the chain of production and distribution. In practice it will result in managers also aiming at minimizing costs, and this, in its turn, means that what is aimed at is maximalization of the profit-rate. As long as interest is taken into account—a necessary assumption for an economic calculation (see

---

[16] For others, but in this case, impracticable yardsticks, see Professor Ragnar Frisch: *Innledning til produksjonsteorien* (stencilled), Oslo, 1937, p. 136.

Chapter 8)—interest must appear as an element of cost, and is thus an invitation to reduce the use of capital or, in other words, to maximalize the total net profit in relation to the capital used. To avoid being misunderstood, it must be explained here that we are only talking of profit-max-imalization (based *inter alia* on maximalization of prices) in those branches of industry where there is free competition between individual links in the chain of manufacture and distribution. As long as this assumption holds good, one need not scruple to allow managers to increase prices as far as they can, since competition will prevent the consumers being exploited.

However, there is one branch of production where, in socialist societies, there can by definition be no competition between individual concerns, and that is where land is the production factor. Here price-fixation must be monopolistic. The significance of this and its dependent factors for fixation of the prices of all social goods means that in such a community this would afford an opportunity for possible exploitation that could not be eliminated.

If maximalization of profits is to be a real measure of managers' efficiency, it is self-evident that one manager cannot be handicapped in relation to others in the same branch. As competing units, they must all have the same opportunity to modernize and expand. This means that they must all have the same access to capital (by which is understood production factors or purchasing power capable of acquiring production factors). On the other hand the control department can hardly be expected to supply the managers with capital in the dark, without taking their efficiency into account (and this is measured by their ability to maximalize profits). A state bank or some other authority must take over the function of the banks in capitalist societies, and decide whether a manager deserves to be given capital or not.

This raises the question of whether the state bank (or the control department) is to take into account, as well as the manager's efficiency, the other factors that in the capitalist society influence the granting of loans, such as the concern's prospects for the future. The danger of employing this criterion in the socialist community is that it easily leads to that complete and central direction which is by assumption to be avoided. (This danger is not present in the same degree in capitalist societies, since there are competing loan-institutions and since the existing right to own capital equipment makes it possible to obtain capital in other ways.)

The state bank or control department will not only have to decide on the supply of capital to new concerns, but also the extent to which those concerns, or rather those managers who show the greatest aptitude in maximalizing profits, shall be allowed to increase their capital. As is known, there is in the capitalist society a constant transference of capital from the less efficient to the efficient managers and concerns, because the former show deficits and the latter surpluses. This amounts to an automatic supply of capital (modified by more or less progressive taxation) to the best risks and to those who have proved the greatest ability to maximalize profits. If the socialist society is to achieve the same "natural selection," the state bank must not draw all profits from the concerns, but must let them remain there, for the more capital—both absolute and relative—the greater the surplus.

If maximalization of profits is to be a reliable measure

of managers' efficiency, there are other inequalities, such as geographical position, which will have to be reckoned with. Managers must be able freely to move their factories or their shop to another town or another part of the country, if they consider they can function with greater profit there. The liquidation of a concern will, like its shifting, contain the same element of "waste," of which the capitalist system is accused. This apparent waste is, however, a consequence of free competition. In reality it is no waste at all, but an adaption necessitated by altered circumstances such as find expression in changed demands of the community or the discovery that it is possible to operate with lower costs elsewhere.

Free competition means that branches of activity are not exclusive, but open to new competitors, but on the other hand, as the right of private ownership of means of production is by definition abolished in socialist societies, the starting of a new concern, which will demand the right to dispose of means of production, will depend on the state's granting its concurrence. There is an element of contradiction here, which is difficult to reconcile unless all who are regarded as qualified to manage a concern are supplied with money or purchasing-power, that is to say, access to means of production of which they can have the use. A manager must not only be able to operate where the possibility of maximalizing profits is greatest, but also in that *branch* of industry where that possibility is considered greatest. Otherwise, the central authority or control department, will reserve to itself such powers of deciding who and how many shall begin new activities, as will be tantamount to abandoning the free competition we assumed to exist.

There are other reasons why it is probable that competition will be illusory and even consciously eliminated. In order to maximize profits, or, at any rate, to avoid losses, managers will be strongly tempted to form cartels or agree on prices with their colleagues in the same branch of industry, in other words, to exploit, in the last resort, the consumer. It will, in practice, be easier to form cartels and make price agreements in the socialist competitive society, than it is in the capitalist competitive society, since, as a general rule, the difficulty in the way of making private cartel agreements in the latter is that those concerns that are in a superior competitive position have no reason to form cartels. This will not be the case in the socialist competitive society, since the surplus does not go to those who conduct the concern, but to the community.

It has already been mentioned that the socialist society must set aside a certain proportion of the community's production as a risk-quota (see p. 132). At that point, it was only pioneer activities that were being discussed. The far larger possibilities for expansion that exist within the individual concerns will not be covered by such a risk-quota. In the capitalist society concerns are developed because there are prospects of greater profits. In the socialist society, however, there is no possibility of profit in the capitalist sense and herein lies a danger of passivity, in so far as expansion always implies an element of uncertainty, being aimed at the future. Managers will have much to lose, when they develop and take chances, and little to gain.

It has already been pointed out (see Chapter 7) that this danger will persist even if the managers' attitude is one of complete altruism, since expansion or any form of sharpened competition will involve all competitors and make them less favourably regarded by the control department and even lead to their losing their posts, which is something an altruistic manager may be expected to wish to avoid.[17] For the same reason one can conceive a manager not wanting to strive to minimalize his costs, as this could give his own concern an advantage or produce a better balance-sheet than that of his competitors. Should such opposition to competition ever become general, it would mean—in a socialist society where there is competition between autonomous unit concerns—a serious reduction of the community's level of production and smaller possibility of achieving the maximum production for needs.

The conclusion must be that the sort of competition that can be created in the socialist society will be an imperfect quasi-competition and that the data it will provide will be unreliable as a basis for economic calculation. If one assumes that there is competition between monopolies, the range of prices will be so wide, that they will have little or no value as data for calculation. Even if a form of free competition between manufacturing and distributing units is chosen, the prices for all goods at all stages of production will be arbitrary, for the simple reason that there will be no competition on the supply side for land, sites, fuel, power, timber and metals, since such means of production are by definition in the hands of the one owner.

Any attempt to introduce competition into the socialist society will also be countered by a tendency to abolish and restrict competition (which means unreliable prices, unreliable data for calculation and reduced efficiency). One must regard these tendencies as being stronger in the so-

---

[17] Barbara Wootton takes the same view in her *Lament for Economics*, p. 224.

cialist society, than in the capitalist society with its right to private ownership of the means of production; this irrespective of whether the managers of the socialist concerns are assumed to be egoistic individualists or altruists.

Finally, it must be stressed that a solution which assumes the existence of competition, irrespective of whether it is between monopolies or atomic concerns, excludes the possibility of a planned economy and of a central authority as the directing organ. For this reason many will deny that proposals of this kind can be regarded at all as solutions of the problem of calculation in the socialist society.

14

Economic Calculation in a Socialist Society Where There Is No Free Choice of Goods or Occupation

Those to whom the King had entrusted me, observing how ill I was clad, ordered a Taylor to come next Morning, and take my Measure for a Suit of Cloths. This operator did his Office after a different Manner from those of his Trade in Europe. He first took my Altitude by a Quadrant, and then with Rule and Compasses, described the Dimensions and Out-Lines of my whole Body; all which he entered upon Paper, and in six Days brought my Cloths very ill made, and quite out of Shape, by happening to mistake a Figure in the Calculation. But my Comfort was, that I observed such Accidents very frequent, and little regarded.
—A Voyage to Laputa.

The suggested solutions of the problem of calculation which we are to discuss here, are a class in themselves. Whilst the other suggestions have all more or less explicitly assumed that the aim of economic activity is to satisfy the needs of the members of the community, and that they are to have free choice of goods and occupation, those who put forward these suggestions have stated that socialism is only possible if the members of the community are deprived of their freedom in these respects. They agree with the more perspicacious of those who have suggested solving the problem by competition, that competition and a planned economy are irreconcilable; but, while the others deduced from that, that it was the planned economy which would have to be abandoned, those in this group take the view that one must cease to let the wishes of the members of the community be the decisive factor.

The sharpest criticism of those solutions which assume free choice of goods and employment has been made by Dr. Maurice Dobb[1] but, as we shall see, he has not realized all the implications of his attitude.

Dr. Dobb begins by attacking the generally accepted conception of the universal applicability of the economic theory.[2] He mentions Mises' and Brutzkus' view that socialism cannot be carried out, because the socialist society will lack a free market and a free price system, and that H. D. Dickinson has disputed this, maintaining that it is a question of combining socialism with a price system. In a footnote Dr. Dobb explains that he used to hold the same view, but that he now considers it to be false. He goes on to point out that both Mises and Brutzkus on the one hand, and Dickinson on the other, assume that the economic theory will be as applicable in the socialist, as in the capitalist, society, and this he disputes. (In this connection, see Chapter 3, p. 12.)

Dr. Dobb says that in these days it has become general to abandon the old hedonistic basis for the modern theory of value, and to treat social economy as a non-normative equilibrium theory. He mentions Professor Robbins as having carried this view-point to its logical conclusion and defined the entirely formalistic character of the economic the-

---

[1] *Economic Journal*, December, 1933.

[2] Dr. Dobb refers in a footnote to H. D. Henderson (*Supply and Demand*, pp. 11 and 14), Wieser (*Natural Value*, p. 164), Pareto (*Cours*, Vol. 11, p. 364) and Cassel (*Theory of Social Economy*, Vol. 1, p. 76).

ory, but without, in Dr. Dobb's opinion, entirely realizing what this involves. Let us quote Dr. Dobb:

> Yet, when it comes to such judgments, the equilibrium theorist, of course, tacitly appeals to a norm. Despite his trumpetings against the welfare-economists, he in fact secretly imports an assumption which at once places him precisely on the same ground as the Hedonist whom he has pretended to disown. And in this assumption the whole apparatus of Utility and Welfare, which it was his pride to dispense with, is implied. But the manœuvre has not been for nothing: it has enabled the scientific dignity of an ethical neutrality to be combined with an undiminished capacity to deliver judgments on practical affairs. The crucial assumption is as simple as it is questionable: it amounts to the sacredness of consumers' preferences (as a general rule, and subject to unimportant exceptions here and there).[3]

Dr. Dobb then says that this "sacredness" is attacked by advertisers and the magnates of the Press, and that in the economic market there is not equal voting rights, but plural voting.

In his view, the "central dilemma" is the following:

> Precisely because consumers are also producers, both 'costs' and 'needs' are precluded from receiving simultaneous expression in the same system of market valuations. Precisely to the extent that market valuations are rendered adequate in one direction they lose their significance in the other. Mr. Dickinson cannot have it both ways.

Dr. Dobb sees no reason to expect the consumer to be any cleverer under socialism. In a competing market they will be just as much subject to influence, whether the society

---

[3] *Op. cit.*, pp. 590–591. (A footnote with reference to the assumption of Marshall is here omitted.)

is socialist or capitalist. His main objection to the price system—in both communities—is that there is no basis for a relationship between the two categories of costs: hire of a tool for one day and hire of a man for one day. What is this basis to be?

> On the answer to this question the whole costing problem turns, and the whole 'balance' between different types of industry depends. But the question receives no answer from any spontaneous verdict of a free market; since the two categories of cost are incurred by dissimilar agencies (or persons). Neither is it answered in a socialist, any more than in a capitalist, economy.

Dr. Dobb calls it an illusion to believe that a free market can provide the relation mentioned above, and he then goes over to a relatively long discussion of the question of interest.

Dr. Dobb's views have been attacked, first and foremost by Dr. A. P. Lerner in his paper "Economic Theory and Socialist Economy" in the *Review of Economic Studies,* 1934–35. Dr. Lerner maintains that Dr. Dobb seems to think that a free price-system is necessary to give people what they want, but that he does not want to give it them. "It is only by disputing this end, that Mr. Dobb rejects the means," writes Dr. Lerner, who then says that as an economist he cannot "adjudicate" the correctness or legitimacy or goodness of such an end, but that as a human being and a sympathiser with socialist ends he has a different view (for this quotation see p. 110, footnote). "But if it is impossible to argue about attitudes, it is still possible to show that, even if Mr. Dobb's attitude is accepted, his conclusion does not follow."

Dr. Lerner thinks that the problem remains the same

whether it is the consumer himself or somebody else who decides what is good for him. In this event, this other person or group becomes the consumer.

> Without the pricing system that Mr. Dickinson, and once Mr. Dobb, were seeking to develop, it is impossible for an economic system of any complexity to function with any reasonable degree of efficiency. All Mr. Dobb's arguments and illustrations to the contrary are erroneous or irrelevant. While starting out with the argument that pricing is not necessary, Mr. Dobb soon finds himself in the company of 'Mises' in dogmatic assertions of its impossibility.

He goes on to say that Dr. Dobb's demand for exact equality of voting goes ill with his bureaucratic contempt for the intelligence of the voter. He also points out that Dr. Dobb has not drawn the natural conclusion from his allegation that voting is destroyed by advertisers and Press magnates, namely, that the Press magnates and harmful advertisements should be abolished in a socialist state, but reaches the surprising one that the popular verdict is to be ignored.

After some interesting remarks about Dr. Dobb's political views, which, though irrelevant, do give the psychological background for the change in his ideas, Dr. Lerner goes on to discourse eloquently in favour of the price system, without which, according to him, we should just be playing Blind Man's Buff. He says that the loss from not having an adjustment of factors (with the help of the marginal productivity of different factors) will be seen in a difference in the concrete commodities produced.

Dr. Lerner adds that this will be distinct from the loss caused, because the consumers are unable to get the goods they desire, a loss that cannot be objectively demonstrated. In his opinion, a price system tends to eliminate both kinds of loss. Dr. Lerner himself is inclined to consider the loss due to the replacement of consumers by bureaucrats the more important, but he is mainly concerned in his article with the first form of loss, since even the most avowed bureaucrat must recognize departures from the objective maximum.

Dr. Lerner upholds the democratic character of the price system:

> Just as the bureaucracy tries to free itself from the direct democratic control of the masses whom it comes to despise, so it is anxious to be above and beyond the external control of a still more democratic pricing machine to which it would in certain respects be subservient.

He then quotes Dr. Dobb's recipe:

> In a socialist society the rate of interest, the level of wages, and the distribution of resources between constructional and finishing trades are all elements in a single decision taken by the State as to the distribution of resources between present and future.[4]

and counters this with certain sayings of Leon Trotsky, "a great revolutionary leader who has had practical experience of the problems."

> If there existed the universal mind, that projected itself into the scientific fancy of Laplace; a mind that would register simultaneously all the processes of nature and of society, that could measure the dynamics of their motion, that could forecast the results of their inter-reactions, such a mind, of course, could *a priori* draw up a faultless and an exhaustive economic plan, beginning with a number of hectares of wheat and down

---

[4] *Op. cit.,* p. 58.

to the last button for a vest. In truth, the bureaucracy often conceives that just such a mind is at its disposal; that is why it so easily frees itself from the control of the market and of Soviet democracy.

The innumerable living participants of economy, State as well as private, collective as well as individual, must give notice of their needs and of their relative strength not only through the statistical determinations of plan commissions but by the direct pressure of supply and demand. The plan is checked and, to a considerable measure, realized through the market. The regulation of the market itself must depend upon the tendencies that are brought out through its medium. The blueprints produced by the offices must demonstrate their economic expediency through commercial calculation.

Economic accounting is unthinkable without market relations.[5]

Dr. Lerner, after having said that several of Dr. Dobb's points are not in harmony with the main contentions, goes on to show that Dr. Dobb does not actually despise consumers' preferences so much. His statement that the same pricing principles cannot be used for capital and labour "since the two categories of cost are incurred by dissimilar agencies (or persons)" Dr. Lerner calls obscure, and also contests several of Dr. Dobb's views on interest, saying that he has got hold of an inadequate formulation in Dickinson's scheme.

In his reply[6] Dr. Dobb comments on the strangeness of Dr. Lerner's view that it makes no difference to the theory whether the consumer himself makes his choice, or someone else does it for him. He says that it will, of course, make no difference in a "formal analysis," but that, in his view,

---

[5] Leon Trotsky, *Soviet Economy in Danger,* New York, 1933.

[6] "Economic Theory and Socialist Economy", in *Review of Economic Studies,* 1934–35, p. 144.

it puts things on the "plane of abstraction" where all discussion becomes meaningless. Dobb says that he understands Dr. Lerner's contention as being that unless an economic system achieves, or approaches, a maximum, it will be inefficient, and to achieve a maximum the concept of marginal productivity must be employed. Since the concept of marginal productivity is merely part of the definition of a maximum, this cannot be refuted, but what use is it to talk of maxima, without knowing what it is one is maximizing? Dr. Dobb maintains further that, when one speaks of a maximum in economics, the maximum must necessarily be expressed as a quantum of *values*. According to Dr. Dobb economic value is not a simple objective quantity, like energy or weight or height, or any of the things with which the technician deals.[7]

On closer examination it appears that Dr. Dobb does not wish to neglect consumers' preferences altogether; but when it comes to the valuation of intermediary products and factors of production, he sees no adequate grounds for having a competitive price system. Dr. Dobb's main point is that a discussion of the extent to which a special form of produc-

---

[7] Economists are often inclined to overestimate the stability of the quantitative measures used by technicians. A pint of milk is a very variable magnitude, if account is taken of fat-content, vitamins and other ingredients, to say nothing of bacteria. A certain quantity, measured by volume, will vary in weight according to the dampness of the atmosphere. A yard of wet cloth will usually be different in length once it is dry. Even technicians, therefore, operate with variable yardsticks, but it is important to remember that the economist is up against the additional difficulty that value is also influenced by subjective factors, by the individual's "private" yardstick of quality not to mention the fact that the yardstick for expressing value, the monetary unit, is exposed to variations, *inter alia*, because its possible gold-content may be altered or done away with.

tion is "economic," implies a judgment of the production result in terms of value, and that this of necessity must stand in relation to the scale of valuation which is used.

In "A Rejoinder" (see *Review of Economic Studies,* p. 152) Dr. Lerner explains that he disagrees with Dr. Dobb on two issues. The first is purely one of values, his point being that individuals ought to have the maximum of freedom in the conduct of their lives. He believes that this can only be approached if there exists a free market in consumers' goods. He also says that the "average man" does not exist, and illustrates this by pointing out that Procrustes' bed would not be much more comfortable even if it were fitted with scrupulous exactitude to the length of the average man. Dr. Lerner stresses, however, that this issue being a value-judgment does not lend itself to useful discussion. If Dr. Dobb does not consider the fulfillment of the individual's choice as important, there remains nothing but to record a difference in outlook.

On the other hand Dr. Lerner maintains that, once the State has decided what is to be done to fulfil or not to fulfil the individuals' choice, and has established its priorities, those ends will not be achieved with any reasonable degree of efficiency without the use of a price-system, and by price-system he does not mean *a posteriori* juggling with figures by auditors, but prices which the managers of factories will have to take into account. (See the quotation on p. 229.)

Dr. Dobb has discussed the problem further in his *Political Economy and Capitalism,* a book that is a curious mixture of interesting theoretical reflections and demagogical statements, unproved and unprovable. His attitude to the problem of calculation is both defined and impaired in the chapter on "Economic Law in the Socialist Economy," where he writes: "Either planning means overriding the autonomy of separate decisions, or it apparently means nothing at all."

He reiterates that any scale of priority whatsoever will do to make quantitative calculation possible. With a given quantity of resources and the relative value of consumer goods given, he considers that the only other thing required to be known is the "real productivity of these resources, used for various ends"; and this, he says, is a "concrete" detail of technical character.

Here, as often elsewhere, Dr. Dobb seems to overlook the fact that the technical decision—in a community employing more than one factor of production—must vary with the value of the factors of production. This factor of value, which Dr. Dobb rightly shows as being implicit in the word "economic," and which he would so gladly do away with, will crop up also in technical decisions in communities with scarce means. (The question will be further discussed later.)

However, as Dr. Dobb begins considering how his system will function, he seems to become doubtful of its suitability. His planned economy ceases to be "unified," and he says that in practice it will naturally be cumbersome and unnecessary to distribute every little factor of production in accordance with a fixed plan. He counts, too, on the possibility of decisions "outside the plan," that a factory on its own initiative can buy directly from another factory, or directly from a co-operative farm. In such cases Dr. Dobb seems to assume free formation of prices, and he writes of "a kind of competitive market" for such goods.

He also reaches the conclusion that the questionnaires he advocated earlier will probably not give very good results, and begins to talk of a "consumers' market" which can give facilities for the consumers' free choice, though without going into the question of how far the consumers' choice is to influence the formation of prices and determine future production. The members of the community are to be able to choose their occupation according to differences in wages, so it is obvious that he has come to doubt, or, possibly, found it inopportune to maintain, his demand for an authoritarian planned economy.

The contribution to the discussion made by Drs. Dobb and Lerner has been quoted so extensively, both because it raises interesting theoretical questions and because it throws light on the problem we are discussing. Before further examining their two points of view, we shall mention what has been said by two other economists who have assumed the abolition of free choice of goods and employment, namely, Herbert Zassenhaus and Oskar Lange.

We have already mentioned[8] Dr. Zassenhaus' subsidiary solution of the problem of calculation, which is mathematical and put forward on the assumption that there exists free choice of goods and employment. This, however, he regards as a "special case," and his principal solution implies the abolition of free choice of goods and employment.

According to this, one is led to believe that Dr. Zassenhaus considers that the central authority will control production. Much of what he says points to this; he writes, amongst other things, of "valuation of consumers' goods by the Ministry of Production," but all the same it is not clear what he is really proposing. He apparently wants to have free competition, too, for he says:

---

[8] "Über die ökonomische Theorie des Planwirtschaft" in *Zeitschrift für Nationalökonomie*, 1934.

We assume for the time being, still keeping to the *modus procedendi* of the Theory of Individual Business, that free competition exists.[9]

That regard for the consumers' preferences is not to be set aside appears from other of his statements, such as:

This scale of valuation for the final products will, under pressure from individual influences, alter continuously until it achieves an appearance of equilibrium.[10]

For all its lack of clarity Dr. Zassenhaus' treatise now and again throws valuable light on the problem. With many of his views one must agree, for instance, with that on the unit of calculation, and, partially, with those on interest. Where he makes positive suggestions, however, he tries to combine solutions that are irreconcilable, such as a planned economy and free markets, authoritarian fixation of prices and regard for consumers' preferences. Nor does he discuss how "individual influences" are to exercise "pressure." To say that the Ministry of Production should follow Gossens' laws (apart from the fact that their validity has been disputed) is devoid of sense, when there is no indication of how the individuals' constantly varying interest-curves for the different goods are to be obtained. As a final example of the lack of reality in Dr. Zassenhaus' discussion, it may be mentioned that he assumes throughout that the community is static, and that there is an "infinite rate of reaction." (See p. 183.)

The greatest interest attaching to his treatise is that he, in common with Dr. Dobb, maintains that the prices fixed

[9] *Ibid.,* p. 513.
[10] *Ibid.,* p. 515.

by the Ministry of Production can serve as a basis for calculation. He has, however, defined his point of view more closely in a later article,[11] but here, too, he writes of a free market for consumer goods and of the managers of concerns having a free hand in their decisions.[12] The real basis for calculation is, however, something different.

> Income and prices, in as far as they are actually paid, are merely technical means for the distribution; it is only those valuation-indices of the Ministry of Production that are the basis for calculation.

While Dr. Dobb sharply defines the fundamental difference between socialist and the capitalist societies, Dr. Zassenhaus says:

> The importance and place of the free markets in private capitalist societies are taken by the Social Distribution of Products; there is no fundamental difference between the two forms of economy.[13]

Here it is well to remind oneself that public retail-sale in the socialist society will not necessarily provide satisfactory data for determining demand-curves, wishes and needs, as Drs. Dobb and Zassenhaus and others who have taken part in this discussion, wrongly assume. (Cf. Chapter 6.)

If one accepts the assumption, as has generally been done in this discussion of the socialist society, that the central authority in determining wages, or in distributing a social

---

[11] "Neüre Planwirtschaftsliteratur und die Theorie der Planwirtschaft" in *Zeitschrift für Nationalökonomie*, 1936.

[12] *Op. cit.*, p. 114.

[13] P. 520 in the first mentioned treatise.

dividend, is to see that the whole of that part of the social income which is allotted for distribution really is distributed, the statistics of sales will not give the data required. This assumption means that the whole quantity will have been sold, and that the central authority in consequence will not know whether one quality or group of goods is in greater demand than another.

Should more money be distributed than there are goods, with the result that there occur periodical partial or complete shortages of goods, the value of the statistics as a barometer will likewise be minimal, as the members of the community would in that event be inclined to take what they could get, so as to have something at least for their money.

A tendency to buy all the goods obtainable at any time for the money distributed (and a corresponding lessening of the reliability of the statistics) would also be a natural consequence of lack of confidence in the value of money, e.g. as a result of the socialist society having been transformed from a former capitalist society and having gone through a period, when distrust, flight of capital and other circumstances had occasioned a fall in the value of its currency.

Dr. Lange, too, has discussed the possibility of disregarding the wishes of the consumers.[14] He asserts that his trial and error method can also be used in cases where the central authority establishes a scale of preferences to serve as a basis for evaluating consumer goods. He says that just as the consumer in a competitive market never has to work out a mathematical formula of utility or preference function

---

[14] "On the Economic Theory of Socialism" in *Review of Economic Studies,* Vol. IV, No. 1, October, 1936.

before knowing what he shall choose, so, too, the central authority will not need to do so.

> By simple judgment it would assign, for instance, to a hat the valuation of ten monetary units, when 100,000 hats are produced monthly, whereas it would assign a valuation of eight monetary units to a hat, when 150,000 hats per month are produced.[15]

Such a simplification of the problem is not permissible, and Dr. Lange here again makes the mistake to which we have already drawn attention: he overlooks the fact that the individual undertakes a partially subconscious weighing of his need against the sacrifice entailed, while the problem is quite different and far more complicated for a central authority. (See p. 221.)

While Dr. Dobb admits the need for certain competitive markets, Dr. Lange insists that all prices shall be "accounting prices." The instructions which Dr. Lange considers the central authority should give to managers of concerns appear somewhat confused, for his idea seems to be that their aim should be (1) to produce a given quantity, (2) to minimalize costs, and (3) to operate with "given" prices. How this problem is to be solved, he does not mention, but, according to him, his trial and error method will function splendidly in this case, too.

Dr. Lange indicates, however, that if the accounting prices are made too low for a factor of production, the demand will be too great, and this will lead to rationing. Such rationing will lead to a point where "equilibrium prices" have been attained. However, such rationing has certain

---

[15] *Op. cit.*, p. 68.

unfortunate consequences, which Dr. Lange himself describes in eloquent language:

> But if rationing becomes a general procedure the rules enumerated above cease to be reliable indices of the consistency between the decisions of the managers of production and the aims established by the plan. The consistency of those decisions with the plan can be, instead, measured by fixing quotas of output and comparing them with the actual achievement (as is done in the Soviet Union). But there is no way of measuring the *efficiency* in carrying out the plan without a system of accounting prices which satisfy the objective equilibrium conditions, for the rule to produce at the minimum average cost has no significance with regard to the aims of the plan unless prices represent the relative scarcity of the factors of production.[16]

In a footnote Dr. Lange asserts that prices are not needed to carry out the plan satisfactorily, if one assumes constant production "coefficients," which assumption, however, is, as he says, "extremely unrealistic."

Dr. Lange ends by saying that it was by no means his intention to recommend a system in which consumers' free choice of goods is to be replaced by preference scales calculated by the bureaucrats of the central authority. He says that Dr. Lerner has clearly shown how undemocratic such a system would be and how at variance with socialist ideals, and that hardly any civilized nation would tolerate it. The rationing of consumers' goods in the Soviet Union he attributes to the fact that the standard of living was so low, that any increase was welcome.

Dr. Lange's continual references to an existing society, that is, the Soviet Union (of which he speaks with great

---

[16] *Op. cit.,* pp. 69–70.

respect) are somewhat disturbing in so far as his trial and error method is, actually, based on the assumption of a static community. (See p. 218.)

Even though objections can be raised against the form of those proposals that assume the elimination of free choice of goods and employment, and even though those who put them forward have been unable to maintain them consistently and unreservedly, these proposals are very interesting from a theoretical point of view. They represent, in fact, a solution of the problem of calculation that can be said to be formally satisfactory, provided one is willing to define calculation and prices in such a way, that these concepts do not require any rational content.

In a society with an authoritarian central authority that can make decisions without taking the wishes of the individual into consideration, all data necessary for calculation is obtained by the authority's arbitrary fixation of prices. The prices of means of production can be the historical, previous prices, those at which they are taken over, or arbitrary prices, fixed once for all, or periodically, by the central authority. The prices of intermediate and final products can be fixed beforehand or be calculated at the various stages of production and have added to them the costs incurred (the magnitude of which is determined by the central authority). The costs can—or not—include all costs, including profit, depreciation, obsolescence, rent and interest. The wages that figure in the calculation can correspond to those actually paid out, but they don't need to. The position really is that, *since the central authority in such a society* ex hypothesi *fixes all prices, it can—irrespective of how it calculates and what use it makes of things—logically claim that its calculation is economic.*

The first objection to such an arrangement is that made by Dr. Lerner, Dr. Lange, and many others, that it conflicts with democratic and socialist ideals, and that it would not be tolerated in a civilized society, etc.[17] These arguments, however, are irrelevant from a theoretical and logical point of view. The decisive question is whether or not the central authority can calculate economically under the given hypotheses. In this connection it should be noted that Dr. Dobb's assumption of the central authority's sovereignty, the absence of any specific aim for its economic activity, and the abolition of free choice of goods and employment, is far less unrealistic than those put forward in the suggestions of others taking part in this discussion.

Dr. Lerner has also denied that Dr. Dobb's conclusion follows logically from his premises. Dr. Lerner considers that economic calculation is not possible in such a case, and he adduces weighty arguments to assert the necessity of price- and competition-markets, whatever the form of the society.

Dr. Dobb's solution has also been strongly attacked by

---

[17] "Commodities must be adapted to human needs and not to the raw by-products of the heavy industry," wrote Leon Trotsky in *Soviet Economy in Danger*. In *Principles of Economic Planning*, G. D. H. Cole writes: ". . . it is for men—for all men—and not as an end in itself that production is carried on. The end is happiness, as well-being, and not output." And, again: "There will be 'workers' control'; only the inexorable discipline of the machine-system. There will be no freedom in industry, except for a few happy technical directors, free to manipuate their tools, human and inhuman, to their hearts' content. There will be no democracy; for political democracy will be stultified by the autocracy of the economic system."

What Cole says refers to the alternative of the worker's not having guild control. His comments on the possibility we are discussing here would, presumably, be still more pathetic.

Professor Hayek. Professor Hayek compliments Dr. Dobb on his courageous proposal, which constitutes a clear break with the opinion that is often put forward, that Socialism will not mean regimentation and barrack-life. Hayek grants that abolition of the consumers' free choice of goods and employment will simplify the problem in certain respects by eliminating one of the incalculable variables, but he says that Dr. Dobb seems to be under a "curious delusion," if he believes that it is only consideration for consumers' preferences that makes it necessary to have price-processes, and that categories of value would cease to have any significance. Prices would only cease to have significance, says Professor Hayek, if one could assume that production in the socialist state would have no specific aim whatever.

Professor Hayek ends his criticism by saying that changes in the public's taste is not the only unforeseeable variable with which a dictator will have to reckon. Climatic changes, alterations in the size of the population and in its state of health, technical changes and inventions, or exhaustion of mineral deposits, these and a hundred other changes that are continually taking place, will necessitate constant alterations in the plans. He says: "The distance of the really practicable and the obstacles to rational action will have been only slightly reduced at the sacrifice of an ideal which few who realized what it meant, would readily abandon."

The views and arguments put forward by Dr. Lerner and Professor Hayek in this connection are weighty ones, but they cannot be said to touch Dr. Dobb's solution in its pure, original form, and it is that which they are discussing. Dr. Lerner overlooks the strength of Dr. Dobb's logical position in his assumption of the central authority's sovereignty, its opportunity to neglect the wishes of the members of the community, and its omission to set up any goals. Professor Hayek is on safe ground with his criticism, in so far as he points out the possibility—mainly to reduce it *in absurdum*—that Dr. Dobb's socialist society has no aim at all. That, however, is the actual fact. Dr. Dobb does not state any ends for the activities of the society he is discussing. He merely points out that the public's free choice of goods and employment will have to stand aside for the benefit of the central authority's plan and sovereignty. There is one other reservation Professor Hayek makes:

> His attitude would only be tenable if costs determined value, so that so long as the available resources were used somehow, the way in which they were used would not affect our well-being, since the very fact that they had been used would confer value on the product.

Such an attitude to costs and values would not be unnatural in one who presumedly sympathizes with non-subjective theories of value, but that is not the point at issue. Dr. Dobb's point of view is tenable, whatever his view on formation of prices. By assuming the sovereignty of the central authority and freeing it from any necessity to follow goals, he makes it unnecessary to take extraneous prices into consideration at all.

As long as one sticks to more or less subconscious concepts of a "natural value," or those of a value determined by scarcity, labour-costs, by subjective value-judgments, or that value is created in the mind of the individual or in the market by barter-relationships, it is difficult to accept calculation on this basis, as *economic* calculation. Logically speaking, however, there is nothing to prevent "value" and what is "economic" being determined by the central authority. The only condition is, that one accepts the central authority as the only judge of value, and that there is no need for it to state its ends. It is, of course, highly doubtful whether the value-judgment of the central authority will coincide with that of the individuals, but one must not forget that discrepancies between different individuals' valuations of goods and services exist all the time. In reality this discrepancy is one of the necessary conditions for barter-activity (in communities where it is allowed).

Whether the official, communal valuation is expressed in market prices, monopoly-prices or in officially determined prices, it will not necessarily coincide with that of the individual. How often do you meet a person whose valuation of his own ability and contribution coincides with that of society and his employer? In a community where all forms of private exchange are forbidden, and where the central authority's valuation is the only lawful one, then that valuation is the value.[18]

The use of molybdenum for making toy swords, and of high-class lenses for microscopes to be used in elementary schools would be considered "waste" in a society where satisfaction of needs is considered as a matter of course, and where such a metal and such lenses would fetch a higher price for other uses. Yet, this would be considered neither wasteful nor uneconomic if the aim set were, for example, that children in the society in question should have only the best possible technical equipment, or that the lens-makers

---

[18] Since most of the economic theory assumes the existence of markets and prices determined by supply and demand, such a transition to official fixing of price and value means that the foundation for our present economic theory itself disappears in its essentials.

in that society should be favoured, in order, for instance, to maintain their numbers. When no ends are stated at all, as Dr. Dobb assumes, the matter grows even clearer; then, one can say that economic calculation has been accomplished, as long as calculations are made on the basis of the prices and scales of preferences laid down by the central authority.

From a logical point of view it must be conceded that the central authority in such a society will still follow "the economic principle," in that the result, according to the central authority's yardstick, will always be, or can (still according to the central authority's yardstick) be made greater, than the in-put. In these given circumstances the central authority can value the means of production as it will, produce what it will, and give the members of the society what, as many, or how few social goods it will, and yet still follow "the economic principle."

One can call it a caricature of "economic calculation," if the consumption of the individual is to be adapted to the whims of the central authority, and it can be asked whether one is not reducing the discussion to absurdity in suggesting the possibility of a society where goods, which strictly speaking are not necessary, are produced to subsidize a certain group of the population, or that a society's economic activity should not have goals, or not aim at satisfying the needs of its members. That is a matter of valuation. After all, in the world to-day you can find conditions not so very different from those just mentioned.

Underlying the tendency to characterize such a social order as absurd and meaningless is a humanistic, individualistic and, to a certain extent, emotional, respect for the individual. If socialism is regarded as an end in itself, to be preferred whatever form it takes and whatever its consequences (and many of the comments on capitalism in Dr. Dobb's book point to this), it is logical to put forward any proposal whatever, that can contribute to its realization.

It is, however, clear that the assumption of the central authority's sovereignty in matters of valuation brings us precariously close to absurdity, even if one manages to rid one's mind of individualistic points of view and accustomed categories of value. The central authority can, according to the assumption, say that it "calculates economically," if it makes more, for example, hats and beds, than the population can use. Similarly, if from material sufficient for 5 million suits, it only makes 4 million, it can still say that its calculation and use were "economic." The production of goods consists of the transformation of material, and the central authority can maintain that the four million suits in their final form have a value in excess of the costs involved —as estimated by the central authority. Valuation is its exclusive province. The central authority could also maintain that 5,000 small loaves are worth more than 5,000 large ones, if there is a difference in quality. Even if the quality were exactly the same, the central authority could say that 4,500 loaves have the same value as 5,000, if there were some difference in time or place. This, however, is to approach absurdity, and, if the central authority, in order to preserve the impression that its calculations and use were economic, should maintain that 4,500 loaves had the same value as 5,000 equally large loaves of the same quality in the same place and at the same time, that is, were it to say that a smaller quantity is larger than a larger one, one must, irrespective of "institutional" and "structural" points of view, admit that absurdity has been reached.

Dr. Felix Weil has expressed himself very decidedly[19] on the subject of such arbitrarily determined prices. He says that "any accounting made on the basis of such fictitious prices is a worthless gamble; without general denominators and, further, without automatic checking, such figures cannot be compared." It must be added that Dr. Weil is one of the few, in fact the only one of those who have taken part in this discussion, who, while granting that economic calculation is impossible in the socialist society, concedes that such a society can, nevertheless, exist. He says in a footnote that Mises is right, and not Polanyi and Leichter, when Mises says that economic calculation is impossible in such a society, but that he is wrong in concluding that a socialist society is impossible. He says: "This conclusion merely shows that it is beyond the comprehension of the modern bourgeois scientist to imagine such an economy." Dr. Weil announced that he would justify his view in a later essay, but this does not appear to have been printed, at least in the *Archiv*.

In the same number of the *Archiv* Dr. Polanyi remarks that Weil is alone in his opinion, and that he is not justified in his appeal to Marx, quoting one of Marx's sayings that in the socialist society value remains the decisive factor and that book-keeping will become more important than ever.[20]

It can also be questioned, as Dr. Lange has, whether a society where people could not choose their goods and occupation, would be tolerated by civilized people. This is a

---

[19] See "Gildensozialistische Rechnungslegung" in *Archiv für Sozialwissenschaft und Sozialpolitik,* 1924.

[20] Dr. Polanyi refers to *Das Kapital,* III, p. 388.

question which economic theory cannot answer. It is, fundamentally, a question of power, not merely of military power to prevent a possible uprising, but of the power to isolate and influence by propaganda. Man's sense of happiness depends only to a small extent on his standard of living and economic circumstances. Provided that the central authority manages to satisfy the people's physiological needs, there need not necessarily be any danger of dissatisfaction and rebellion. For this, however, the population must be isolated from other societies where conditions might possibly be unmistakably better, or, what from the point of view of leadership is the ideal, that it should be persuaded into thinking that just those conditions under which it is living, are the ideal. The technique of propaganda and cultural isolation has been so enormously developed and improved in the last few years, that Aldous Huxley's *Brave New World* can no longer be regarded as an imaginative *tour de force*.

Even though there are few theoretical and logical objections to Dr. Dobb's suggestion, it can be said with some justice that a society where activities can possibly be undertaken without any aim, is no society at all, and that the result must be anarchy and chaos. This seems to be the opinion of the majority of socialist economists (see Chapter I). In this connection it must be stressed that, *if* ends are stated, then Dr. Dobb's solution of the problem of calculation appears in a different light, for, in that case, the final products can no longer be valued arbitrarily. In that case, the economic principle requires that the input should be less than the produced result, judged from the ends accepted. In that case, there will again arise the need for a mechanism capable of registering the value and scarcity of resources in relation to the ends and to the changes of various kinds that will occur in a dynamic society. The problem of calculation will in that case still remain unsolved.

All the same, Dr. Dobb's solution is—logically—an advance on the others, because he eliminates the need to take account of the individuals' free choice of goods and occupation. Professor Hayek points out that his abolition only eliminates one of the variables that have to be considered: ". . . the changes in taste are by no means the only, and perhaps not even the most important, changes that cannot be foreseen."

Professor Hayek here seems to emphasize an unessential side of the question. The importance of eliminating free choice of goods and occupation lies not in having got rid of one variable (or two), but in having done away with this particular assumption. The greatest difficulties in the other solutions are created by just the specific demands inherent in this assumption. Not only is it difficult to obtain correct data on the (shifting) wishes of the individuals, but these wishes, in an industrialized society, must influence the valuation of a number of constantly changing intermediary products, in order to obtain a correct valuation (according to the end) and thereby a correct use of scarce resources. Dr. Dobb avoids this difficulty by his particular assumption—or lack of assumptions.

Even had Dr. Dobb set up ends for the activities of his society, the possibilities for economic calculation in it are considerably greater, because he has eliminated regard for the wishes of its members. If, for example, the society takes as its only aim the development of a war machine of a certain size within a certain time, a military central authority will, presumably, be able better than any other to determine the relative value of existing resources in the light of this particular aim. The military experts will determine what raw materials, power and labour are required to produce the various machines of war in the given space of time. The ideal economic calculation, naturally, demands that each of the variables, to which Professor Hayek rightly draws attention, should be taken into consideration; yet a plan of this kind will, presumably, *grosso modo,* be capable of attainment if one is content to judge it in the light of technical development in the armament industry only. The task of the military authorities will be considerably easier, if they can disregard questions of satisfying the wishes of the individuals. If so, the military central authority will only need to see that the production of armaments does not encroach so far on the production of foodstuffs, that the health of its forces is adversely affected.

The same conclusion (that the task will be easier) is reached if it is assumed that the sole aim of the society is to impress the world, e.g. with modern underground railways, or with a rapid development of its productive apparatus. Also, if one assumes the aim to be that of increasing the knowledge and capabilities of the society, which would mean a one-sided concentration on the building of universities, schools and libraries.

If, on the other hand, the aim were to create a foreign exchange reserve of a certain size, the problem would apparently be different. This implies, in fact, a new scale of preferences determined by the demand abroad, and there should then, strictly speaking, be a need for economic calculation in the usual sense. However, considering that the aim does not involve paying attention to the immediate needs of the members of the socialist society, it can be attained by exporting whatever can be sold abroad. In theory, there is nothing to prevent grain and foodstuffs being exported, even if this results in famine. The attainment of this goal, too, is made easier, because the central authority can neglect the needs and wishes of the individuals.

We have so far treated Dr. Dobb's solution as though it were far more consistent than it actually is. In later articles, as well as in his books, he concedes the necessity for certain competitive markets, and satisfaction of the needs and wishes of the individuals is also for him a desirable aim. It is in its pure, original form that Dr. Dobb's solution has the greatest theoretical interest.

We have already discussed the practical possibilities of his solution. From an individualistic point of view there are, of course, obvious objections to it. The validity of the other objections will depend on the degree of development of the society in question. In a society that can only produce enough to maintain its members on the bare existence level, objections to an official scale of preferences will have little weight. The *minimum* quantity of fats, carbohydrates, vitamins, etc., is more or less the same for everybody of the same age and sex. Needs of this kind can presumably be fixed by the central authority dieticians just as well as by the members of the community. (We are not competent to judge whether idiosyncrasies and unusually strong likes and dislikes in one individual are an indication of what his organism demands or cannot support.) If, however, the socialist society can produce more than the bare minimum—and it is generally asserted that it can—and it becomes a question of supplying conveniences and satisfying cultural needs, then this form of distribution is inadequate by reason of the variability and elasticity of the various needs of various individuals.

Where production takes no regard of what the public really wants, it will in practice easily become anarchic, and even though the central authority can—from a purely logical point of view—maintain that it is calculating economically, it can be objected with considerable justice that such calculation is just as arbitrary and valueless as accounting *in natura*.

15

Resume and Conclusions

If all the world were apple-pie,
And all the sea were ink,
And all the trees were bread and cheese,
What would we have for drink?

We have now discussed the possibilities of economic calculation, on the basis of generally accepted definitions and assumptions, in various types of socialist community. We have seen that one prerequisite for economic calculation was a monetary economy; also, that even in the socialist society one must calculate with factors such as risk-quotas, depreciation, interest on capital and ground-rent, as well as with the primary and produced factors of production, provided the end is maximum exploitation of existing resources with a view to satisfying the needs of the community.

We have seen that to reckon out the cost-quota mentioned will be difficult because, in the socialist society, there are no given prices for primary and produced means of production. We have seen that this lack will have far more serious consequences than the mere fact of being unable to calculate those quotas. If such prices cannot be obtained, it will exclude all possibility of economic calculation. We have seen that the socialist economists are themselves agreed that economic calculation is a necesary condition for rational economic activity and for achieving given ends. As a direct result of this, the view expressed by Professors von Mises and Brutzkus that the necessary data for calculation will not be obtainable has had a great effect, and many attempts have been made to refute it.

The question that naturally arises after such a survey of these proposed solutions is: are Mises and Brutzkus right in saying that economic calculation is impossible in the socialist society? This is not a question that can be answered "yes" or "no" out of hand. The answer depends, in the first place, on the definition used. If by calculation is understood computation of what a commodity costs, and by "cost" what the commodity is worth, and if it is taken that value can only be expressed by a price obtained in a market with competing buyers and sellers, then the answer is "yes." Mises and Brutzkus will be right, both in theory and practice, since in the socialist society there will, by definition, be only one owner of the means of production. This is, presumably, what Professor Mises meant, and it explains the force with which he puts forward his point of view. He has not, however, made it sufficiently clear that he assumes the existence of markets with several buyers and sellers, and therefore his assertion appears somewhat dogmatic and categorical.

If, however, calculation is defined as a computation of what an article "involves" (as has been done in this book) and it is held that "what it involves" can be expressed with the help of any commensurable and any kind of data whatever, irrespective of whether they have any content or not, then calculation may be said to be possible also in a socialist society, in which case the view of Professor Mises and Brutzkus is not correct.

Is there, though, anyone who will calculate with data that have no real content? As we have seen, many of the proposed solutions of the problem of calculation assume a planned economy with a central authority that will fix the values of both the means of production and of the final products, as well as determine the quantities to be produced. Must these decisions be arbitrary? Not necessarily. It will depend on the aim the society in question has chosen for its activities. If, however, the end is to satisfy the material and cultural needs of the community, difficulties in calculation will arise, unless one makes the unrealistic and unrealizable assumption that there are resources enough to cover at all times the combined needs of the entire community.

Several of those who have taken part in the discussion maintain that they have solved this problem of calculation, at any rate in theory. Having surveyed the more important of these proposals, it is difficult to accept this. It is significant that the various solutions are conflicting and partly irreconcilable, and that several of those who have put them forward have sharply criticized each other's solutions.

The dominant opinion at the present time is that the problem of calculation can only be solved in the socialist society, if it allows of conditions of competition similar to those to be found in the capitalist society. A few, but not all, put forward this proposal, well aware that it excludes the possibility of any planned economy. By doing this, they are tacitly admitting that the whole idea of socialism (with planned direction) is incompatible with economic calculation.

At the other extreme there is a small group of proposals, where the opposite conclusion is drawn: a planned economy is the main thing; the central authority, not the members of the community, must determine the scales of preferences and the order of needs. In the view of those putting them forward, the prerequisite of economic calculation in a socialist society is that the community's right to free choice of goods and occupation must be abolished. This, too, is a remarkable result.

Having once accepted the (non-economic) assumption that the central authority can dispose without regard to the wishes and needs of the community, this solution is logically the strongest and, perhaps, the most interesting in theory, for in its pure and original form it constitutes a break with the normal conceptions of value. If, on the other hand, the central authority does not need to have any aim at all for its activity, this could lead to results that will appear absurd to all whose idea of economic activity is that it should aim at satisfying the needs of the community, but this does not prevent the proposal from providing the best theoretic solution of the problem of calculation, and also the one that is least unrealistic.

If the central authority in such a society were to set itself an aim, the problem would appear in quite a different light. In that case, economic calculation would presuppose that the factors of production were valued, not only from the point of view of their usefulness in achieving this aim, but also that their valuation was continually being revised in the light of the changes that are constantly occurring in a dynamic society. The central authority would then meet with the difficulties that we have attempted to point out in this treatise. Whatever the circumstances, the solution of the problem will be easier, if it is assumed that the central authority does not need to consider the needs and wishes of the members of the community. Easier, not because one or two variables have been eliminated, but because valuation of the factors of production and the adaptation of production (when satisfaction of needs is aimed at) is not a thing that can be done by any technical experts, but will *ex hypothesi* be influenced by millions of individuals' valuations, and because the registration of these valuations and the adaptation of production to these and other variables meets with especial difficulties in the socialist society.

If one is to decide whether the problem of calculation has been solved, one must not only ask about definitions, but whether it is a theoretic or a practical solution that is intended.

Between the two extreme solutions just mentioned there is a number of others, which, according to their proposers themselves, are theoretic, but not practical solutions. Both Professor Hayek and Professor Robbins in commenting on the discussion have reached the conclusion that economic calculation is not impossible, in the sense of being theoretically impossible or inconceivable, but that in the socialist society it is impossible in practice. This judgment, both goes too far and not far enough. It does not go far enough, in so far as economic calculation must be said to be practically possible in a society where the central authority is powerful enough to make its valuations paramount at all stages of production without needing to set itself any aim. And, in the author's opinion, it goes too far in accepting various solutions as theoretically satisfactory.

Here arises the question of what are the criteria of a satisfactory solution of a theoretical economic problem.

To answer that question in detail would lead us outside the framework of this book, but one or two comments will not be out of place in view of the suitable examples provided by this discussion.

It is to a certain extent understandable that many of those who have proposed solutions should consider their task fulfilled, once they have pointed out a theoretical solution, even while admitting that it is impossible to put it into practice. Those who first took up the question, Pareto and Barone, drew a sharp distinction between the theoretical and practical usefulness (or uselessness) of their solutions. Professor Mises who has most clearly formulated the problem, on several occasions drew attention to the fact that what he had undertaken was a theoretic and scientific investigation. Without expressing here an opinion on Professor Mises' real intentions, or of the extent to which he has achieved them, one may say that it would be very natural to regard his statements as expressing the desire to see the problem treated theoretically and scientifically. What he says does not exclude the possibility of his having had socialist societies in the world of reality in mind when he denied that such societies can calculate economically. If this interpretation is right, one cannot say that the problem is solved by suggesting solutions that are notoriously impossible in practice.

In her *Lament for Economics* Barbara Wootton discusses what an economist can allow himself to assume. She has coined the term "apple-pie-ish" from the nursery rhyme used as the motto for this chapter and uses it to describe assumptions that have nothing to do with this world. If the writer records his agreement with Mrs. Wootton on this point, it does not mean that in principle he objects to discussions based on unrealistic assumptions. To select relevant factors, to discard irrelevant ones, and to construct model worlds, is in economic theory not only justified, but in certain cases necessary. Nevertheless, (and this should be emphasized) there must exist a methodological purpose, or necessity, for building on unrealistic premises. To use them, when not needed to simplify the discussion, merely to furnish a so-called theoretical solution is, in the author's opinion an abuse of a technical instrument.

In this discussion of economic calculation in the socialist society assumptions have been made that are highly "apple-pie-ish," particularly when one considers the nature of the problem. In some cases, the infinite velocity of reaction required by the static society has been assumed, in others a change in the psychological attitude of the individual (in his "egoistic-individualistic" attitude) that has characterized man throughout history, in others superhuman powers of vision, of omniscience and the gift of being able to get all relevant data and make a simultaneous solution of millions of equations that the mathematical solutions presuppose.

It must be added, that the extreme solutions are not based on unrealistic assumptions. Those that envisage competition, on the contrary aim at creating conditions that resemble most those to be found, or rather those that used to be found, in the capitalist societies. Nor is there anything unrealistic in assuming that economic calculation presupposes the concentration of all power in the hands of a central authority, and that men's right to free choice of goods and occupation be abolished. On the other hand, these groups of solutions imply a definition of price and calculation that robs those concepts of any reasonable meaning.

Finally, it must be pointed out that in this treatise we have purposely omitted to discuss various factors that bear on the possibilities of calculation in the socialist society. These are (1) possible fluctuations of trade cycles; (2) possible fluctuations in the value of money; (3) the form of society in other countries. (If there should still exist capitalist societies with competition it will be possible to obtain from them certain indications and data for calculation, which would not be there if all societies had adopted socialism); (4) the problems arising from foreign trade and exchange of goods and services with other societies; (5) the effect of managers with private ownership-interests being replaced by official functionaries, as the transition to socialism demands. Since the factors of production are, from the point of view of production, inanimate matter until they are combined by human endeavour, it would seem that it must lie within the scope of economic theory to discuss the conditions for maximizing that endeavour. It can, however, be objected that this is a question of social psychology, and, since it brings us into fields where opinions differ violently, we have not discussed it.

It must, however, be pointed out that the problem of calculation would not have been any easier to solve if we had assumed (1) fluctuations of trade cycles, (2) fluctuating value of money, (3) that all countries in the world were socialist, (4) that our socialist society was not autarchic, but dependent on foreign trade, and (5) that the abolition of private property would have psychological effects on the conduct of the managerial class.

The fact that, in practice, economic calculation is impossible in a socialist society whose aim is the maximum exploitation of existing resources in order to satisfy the needs of the community does not, of course, mean that a socialist society cannot exist—at any rate for a time. As Professor Robbins has pointed out in *Economic Planning and International Order*, it is obvious that a socialist society with workers, material and engineering ability can build factories, workshops, and power stations, and produce consumer goods. Nor is there anything to prevent the managers, whether impelled by force or reward, from conducting them with technical efficiency. A socialist society that lacks industries of various kinds can set about producing almost anything and for a considerable time whatever it produces will be regarded as useful by the members of the community.

The question, however, is not whether factories can be built and efficiently conducted, but whether the factors of production could have been put to a more advantageous use by employing them elsewhere. In a society whose aim is the maximum production of needs its resources must not be used for producing what may be momentarily lacking and so have a certain value, but for producing goods which, according to the ends stated, are of greater value than other goods. Each factor of production must be so employed as to give the greatest return according to the ends. This, and only this, is the criterion for rational economic activity. For determining this there is needed valuation apparatus, an apparatus with prices and costs varying with the variables with which one has to reckon in the world of reality, and it is here that there arise specific, and so far, unsolved difficulties for the socialist society.

The Price-Mechanism in a Private Capitalist Society

In private capitalist societies it is the more or less free formation of prices that provides the data necessary for calculation. Many objections are made against their price-mechanism, *inter alia* that it is unjust, because it is influenced by the distribution of income, which is itself said to be inequitable. This is an ethical, sociological question that we shall not discuss here. What interests us in this connection is the potential and actual efficiency of the mechanism which exists irrespective of the form of society and of the given, but continually changing, distribution of income. It may be stated at once (we shall revert to the question later) that the functioning and technical efficiency of the price-mechanism is in our day being undermined.

In spite of this, in the capitalist societies it is still prices, or rather, price-alterations, that act as the anonymous conductor of the economic orchestra. They play the same part as the central authority in socialist societies. It is price-alterations that keep production and business in capitalist societies from being conducted "blindly" and "without plan." It is price-alterations that provide the necessary indications that determine to what alternative uses "scarce resources" shall be allocated in order to satisfy consumers' effective demand. It is price-alterations that indicate what goods, what qualities and what quantities shall be produced and distributed.

A fall in prices may be caused by several factors: on the supply side, lower costs of production, new inventions, rationalization, greater competition, and *expectation* of a development in these directions. On the demand side, lower purchasing power or reduced interest in the commodity in question, or *expectations* of lower prices. The causal relationship is complicated, but the result is easily analysed: falling prices mean that there is being offered, or expected to be offered, more of the goods or services in question than the market can or will absorb at previous prices. Rising prices indicate the opposite.

If prices rise more than costs the result is greater profit. If prices fall more than costs the result is falling profit. The incentive to expand or reduce production, activity and demand will thus be increased or lessened. On the demand side the most important result of rising prices is a restriction in the number of those who can or want to buy. (This is not altered by the fact that rising prices and expectation of higher prices may temporarily stimulate demand and production.) Thus an automatic rationing is taking place without the use of ration-cards or official directives. This rationing, and the efficacy of price-alterations to restrict and expand consumption, however, vary greatly with the elasticity of demand of different goods.

Prices, or price-alterations, set in motion forces that tend to bring about equilibrium and harmony between supply and demand, between production and consumption. This point of equilibrium is not a constant level. The level itself is constantly shifting, but as long as free competition[1] and free price-formation are not entirely abolished, the tendency will be this: buyers will outbid each other and sellers will undersell each other, and both will be stimulated to make the deal, as otherwise they will risk someone else stepping in (see p. 299). The gap between actual market price and the "ideal" normal price, where consumption and production per time-unit are equalized, is likewise continually changing. The quicker the tendency towards the new point of equilibrium, the more effectively does the price-mechanism function. Provided the price-mechanism is allowed to work, even insignificant and finely graded alterations are registered, which makes the price-mechanism also a wonderful instrument for making quantitative comparisons.

The ability of price-formation to regulate is not confined to consumption goods, but extends to raw materials, semi-manufactured goods and means of production at every stage of production. That is to say, not only do there exist calculation-data for the factors of production and for consumption goods at every stage of production, but these data —with the reservations already taken and to be made— simultaneously register (1) the goods for which there is a demand (and in what quantities and of what qualities) and (2) the scarcity of the means of production in relation to

---

[1] J. E. Mead has given the following simple definition of perfect competition: "competition is perfect when two conditions are fulfilled; (1) when there is no artificial restriction upon the movement of factors of production from occupation to occupation in search of the highest reward, and (2) when no single unit of control—i.e. no single individual or company which is deciding to buy or sell something—can by its own action appreciably affect the price of the things bought or sold." *Economic Analysis and Policy,* London, 1936, p. 96.

the uses necessary for the production of the goods demanded. The dry price-datum is really the result of innumerable computations, measurements and valuations. It represents the final expression of a conflict between factors so different in nature as (on the supply side) costs in the form of scarcity of resources and man-hours used and (on the demand side) subjective valuation of needs. Professor Louis Baudin has written the following, almost poetical, description of prices' synthesizing ability:

> It (the price) synthesizes a number of factors, so that there is difficulty in identifying them and even more in foreseeing them: quantities, qualities, possibilities, calculations of interest, memories, fears, hopes. A price is not only the result of statistical figures. It includes all the vibrations of man's thoughts and soul, since ever they have exercised an influence on the market.[2]

Before continuing, let us just repeat that there is to-day in capitalist societies a tendency to do away with the price-mechanism, or at any rate to reduce its significance. This tendency takes various forms. That sector of the society's life in which activities are undertaken without regard to prices and markets, the so-called social sector, is continually growing. Fear of war, together with the policy of isolation adopted by the socialist communities, have forced other countries to put obstacles in the way of the international exchange of goods and services, which similarly hampers the free formation of prices (to say nothing of international division of labour). In addition business men have usually a tendency to interfere with the functioning of the price-mechanism, partly to assure themselves a fixed income,

---

[2] *La Monnaie et la Formation des Prix,* I. Paris, 1936, p. 591.

partly to protect "vested interests," and partly to eliminate competition and thereby the insecurity inherent in it. The natural tendency to take advantage of monopoly elements and to make cartels and price agreements has lately been strengthened because the authorities in some countries show a tendency to *order* the formation of cartels, or, at any rate, to punish those who sell cheaply or in other ways follow the rules of the price game. (U.S.A. under New Deal and Norway to-day.)

This means in fact that we have entered a new phase of economic development. For there is a great difference between a private monopoly or cartel and a legal-official one. Where an agreement regulating competition is voluntary, it is as a rule abolished, broken or modified, when conditions alter.[3] Competition, whose imperfection has so often been described, has in reality a quite astounding vitality despite all onslaughts. Competition may be camouflaged and go underground, but it is difficult to kill. If it is forbidden to compete in price, there will be competition in terms of credit and conditions of payment. Secret discounts and concessions may be given and even quite objectionable methods used.[4]

Therefore, the actual effect of private agreements to control competition is not so great as is usually assumed. The situation, however, becomes quite different when groups of

---

[3] See I. W. F. Rowe: *Market and Men, A Study of Artificial Control Schemes in some primary Industries,* London, 1936.

[4] There was a drastic example of this when *Norges Handelsstands Forbund* had to decide how many units go to the dozen, and pronounce a practice introduced by certain German firms as improper competition, namely to invoice thirteen units as a dozen. (See *Handelsstands Månedsskrift,* No. 9, 1937, p. 182.)

manufacturers and traders turn to the State to have a price-reduction forbidden by law. Laws which make alterations in price a crime or offence punishable with large fines are a much more effective and lasting method of hampering the functions of the price-mechanism, than any private attempts.

The propensity to control and regulate inherent in every government similarly tends to disturb the function of the price-mechanism. The last few decades have been characterized by an obvious tendency to switch from a price- and market-economy to interventionism and publicly fixed prices, also called "valuation-economy." The intervention of the authorities in the domestic production of goods by means of controlled prices, and in the international production of goods by means of agreement for quotas and clearing, marks the first stage in the abolition of the right of free disposal of the means of production and of the actual right of ownership to them. According to the definition of socialism given, this "valuation-economy" is an obvious step towards socialism.

The fact that price-formation and competition are in practice becoming more and more imperfect does not, of course, detract from their proverbial efficacy to regulate supply and demand. We shall not embark on a discussion of the theoretical possibilities of perfect competition, partly because this would involve a discussion of definitions and terms[5] which would take us too far away from our subject, and partly because any reference to ideal conditions would be irrelevant, since we are discussing the possibility of eco-

---

[5] See, *inter alia,* Joan Robinson: *Economics of Imperfect Competition,* and the subsequent discussion in the *Economic Journal.*

nomic calculation in a socialist community in the world of reality.

On the other hand, it may be mentioned in passing that it is illogical to demand the substitution of a socialist central authority for the price-mechanism on the grounds that the price-mechanism is becoming more and more imperfect, considering that this growing imperfection is mainly due to the development towards socialism.

For all its alleged imperfections the price-formation is still acknowledged as one of the chief factors in the economic activities of the capitalist society, and the terms "price-society" and "price-economics" are still used as synonyms for "capitalist society."

The importance of the price- and market-mechanism has even been affirmed by socialist economists.[6] Dr. Heimann writing (see also Chapter 4) of the price-system has said that:

> It records the least deviation in valuation with the accuracy of a seismograph, and directly by means of this occasions the adaptation of the processes of production to the new situation.[7]

---

[6] The expression "socialist economist" occasionally employed in this book, is in no way used to draw a distinction between "socialist economics" and a "bourgeois economics." As Sombart has rightly said, there are correct and incorrect economic theories, and it is here that the dividing line must be drawn. Nevertheless it is useful to use the term "socialist economist" of those who thus describe themselves, and "Marxist economists" of those who base themselves on the Marxist theory of value. The characterization has partly the advantage that it leads to economy in words, and partly prevents the views of such economists being dismissed as coming from "liberal economists," "Manchester economists," "orthodox" or "reactionary" economists. This may be important in a period, when these appelations have been invested with so much odium that the use of them sometimes seems to be regarded as a sufficient counter-argument in itself.

[7] *Mehrwert und Gemeinwirtschaft,* p. 169.

The decisive task of the economic system is to allocate labour and capital to the individual branches of production in proportion to the strength of the existing need for their products. In capitalist economic systems this task is fulfilled by the market, and no concentration in cartels and trusts can alter it. . . .

The market is what is really economic about the modern economic system. To do away with it would be a leap into the dark. . . .

The market, of course, is to-day capitalist in action. But is that alone reason enough to abandon it? Is Socialist Thought going to be so unhistorical and undialectic as to take over from Capitalism only its technological elements and its business organization, and to do away with its method of conducting its economy?[8]

Dr. Heimann considers that price-formation is the real heart and soul of the science of economics. He writes:

that order has been established and maintained in the seeming confusion of atomic industries, and how this effect has been achieved, this is the real object and kernel of economic science. . . .[9]

In *Lament for Economics* Barbara Wootton says that economic theory has been too much occupied with markets and equilibria, but in her *Plan or No Plan* she has given an admirably clear description of the potential efficacy of the price-mechanism. For all her later reservations about the fairness of the market-economy, the price-mechanism seems to enjoy her entire respect, especially when she says:

Here it may be said right away that no society which has attempted to dispense altogether with all use of the price

---

[8] "Sozialisierung" in *Neue Blätter für den Sozialismus,* Tübingen, 1930, Vol. 1, pp. 25–26.

[9] *Op. cit.,* p. 174, footnote.

mechanism has had any success sufficient to commend it to detailed study.[10]

And to quote Professor A. P. Lerner:

> But even if all decisions about what people should consume are made by a single dictator or by a very small oligarchy which can reach all decisions by agreement in the council chamber, an elaborate pricing mechanism will still be necessary to make possible the comparison of the marginal productivities of all original means of production and intermediate products in all stages of the manufacture of all commodities in order to achieve the purely technical maximization of the output of commodities in the proportions decided upon.[11]

and

> The proposition that I wish to establish is that when the State has decided what it is going to do as to fulfilment or nonfulfilment of individuals' choice, setting up its own system of priorities, it will not be able to achieve its ends with any reasonable degree of efficiency without the use of a price system.[12]

(Dr. Lerner on the price-mechanism is also quoted on p. 228.)

Dr. Felix Weil is of the opinion that fictitious, arbitrary prices are "a worthless gamble" (see p. 281), while Leon Trotsky succinctly puts it that "economic accounting is unthinkable without market relations."[13]

When the demands of producers and middle-men for raw

---

[10] *Op. cit.,* p. 55.

[11] "Economic Theory and Socialist Economy" in *Review of Economic Studies,* 1934–35, p. 60.

[12] See "A Rejoinder" in "Economic Theory and Socialist Economy" in *Review of Economic Studies,* 1934–35, p. 152.

[13] See *Soviet Economy in Danger,* New York 1933, p. 33.

materials, intermediate goods and means of production are met in the capitalist society, the former owners of the goods and means of production receive their share of the product. This does not mean that demand for consumer goods unilaterally determines the value of means of production and goods at earlier stages of production. There exists an interrelationship which is not confined to prices and incomes. The price of the product sold is only one of the factors with which producers and middlemen must calculate. There are, in addition, various costs. (See Chapter 2.)

Besides taking into consideration those data which are already given, a business man will, to a greater or lesser extent, also have regard to the future. The longer the period of production and turn-over, the greater attention he will have to pay to the possibility of future changes and thus of increased risk. In a progressive dynamic society with democratic rights the possibilities of such changes are both numerous and heterogeneous. Populations change both in size and composition; tastes alter; savings vary both in extent and rate of growth; the amount of investment varies and so does the pace of technical development.

There are other elements of uncertainty such as political developments, the possibility of alterations in the value of money itself as well as developments in the trade cycle (which is partly a result of these changes and of expectations of their effect). There exists a reciprocal relationship between several of these factors, which are themselves dependent on expectations about the future.

The anticipated attitude of competitors will also play its part; so that estimation of others' expectations also becomes a market-determining factor. To what extent such expectations will have any influence, the extent to which they will be based on irrelevant factors such as season of the year, state of the weather, glandular secretions or emotions like fright and hope, cannot be stated with any certainty, since the expectations vary in kind and strength from one individual to the other, and even with the same individual from period to period.

We shall not discuss here the interesting question of whether or not the economist should concern himself with motives of reason and emotion, and with the ethical or unethical motives that lie behind price-reactions and market phenomena, or whether he should be content to stick to the final price-data.[14]

The fact that price-determining motives and factors are varying and of many kinds, the fact that in all societies, irrespective of structure, estimates of the future contain elements of uncertainty, and the fact that the price-mechanism in our time is being more and more restricted in scope, should not obscure the fact that it is the price-mechanism which plays the part of the great conductor in the capitalist economy.

Further, it must be stressed that in capitalist societies there do exist markets where, despite more or less imperfect competition, prices are quoted that form a basis for economic calculation. Prices not only for consumer goods, but also for natural assets, raw materials, intermediate goods and means of production of all kinds, and not only "spot," but also "forward" prices. Forward prices make it possible not only to measure uncertainty in regard to the future, but also to eliminate it.

---

[14] See, *inter alia* Ludwig von Mises: *Grundprobleme der National-ökonomie,* Jena, 1933, pp. 168–169.

Price-formation also makes itself felt in respect of man-power. Here, its ability to regulate is, however, smaller. This is not only due to monopoly tendencies through labour unions, but because man-power differs in certain important respects from other objects dealt in. It is enough to mention its slow rate of reproduction. (It takes from fifteen to sixteen years before a new-born child becomes old enough to work, and in addition it is doubtful whether changes in wage-rates influence the birth-rate.) Another factor is the low mobility of manpower, partly due to emotional and psychological factors (dislike of breaking up a home and of leaving home and country), and partly to a political tendency towards self-sufficiency and isolation expressed in the growing number of obstacles put in the way of both emigration and immigration.

The importance of price-formation is also limited where it comes to credit, loans and the right to dispose of capital. Special factors enter into play when it comes to the formation of price for capital. A detailed discussion of this problem would result in a full-scale discussion of the theory of distribution and the trade cycle, upon which we cannot embark here, but the question of interest has been touched upon in Chapter 7. Here it must suffice to state that competition is less perfect, or, rather, still more imperfect, when it concerns credit, than when it concerns goods, but that interest rates exist in the capitalist societies as given data.

Many objections have been raised against private capitalism and the price-mechanism. They will be dealt with in Appendix B; but there is one that directly concerns the price-mechanism and should be discussed here.

We refer to the objection that in capitalist societies prices are used as indicators of profitability. People produce for profit, it is said. This statement is correct. If the commodity to be produced, or resold, is not demanded at a price that covers costs, it will not be produced or bought at that price. On the other hand, to imply that production for profit does not mean production to satisfy needs, is entirely false. The contrary is the case. The producers' and traders' every effort is directed towards anticipating and satisfying the needs of the buyers, in the last resort the needs of the public, such as they are expressed in effective demand. The success of producers and traders will depend on their ability to do this. Their ability to anticipate correctly will decide whether the result will be profit or loss, which in the long run will decide whether they can stay in business or not.[15]

In the discussion of the merits and de-merits of the price-mechanism it has been maintained that market economy is "democratic," inasmuch as every penny used for voluntary purchases represents a vote cast in the great election of what the public wants. This is a graphic, but misleading metaphor. The voting is not democratic; nor is it based on the principle of equality. The voting is not by heads, but according to the number of voting-papers, or banknotes. It is the amount of purchasing power at his disposal which determines the degree to which the individual consumer can influence the type and size of production. It may be said

---

[15] Professor Boris Brutzkus goes so far as to say that the producer and trader in a capitalist country, strictly speaking, does not need to keep books or to calculate, as prices will give him all necessary indications. If he does not take heed of prices, he risks losing his fortune and his position. In socialist countries where the state is the only owner of the means of production and the only distributing agency, this automatic purging process does not exist, so that, as Brutzkus says, "economic calculation is of far greater significance in the socialist, than in the capitalist society." (*Economic Planning in Soviet Russia*, p. 11.)

that this is unjust, but that is a moral judgment that we cannot go into here and which does not affect the price-mechanism's efficacy for regulating production and sales according to effective demand at any time and at any given distribution of income. (See p. 149, footnote 11.)

An additional word or two are still required about the view that there is an antithesis between production for profit and production to satisfy needs. If there is any point in this assertion (apart from its propagandistic value) it must mean that there is presumed to exist another scale of values than that of the buying public expressed by its demand. If we try to analyse that scale of values we generally find that it is a so-called "social scale of values" with the necessities of life at the top and expensive luxury articles at the bottom.

Such an order of preference would, perhaps, be right in a society where everybody was short of nearly everything. Once the demand for the necessities of life has been covered, people will, however, be found to have wishes and needs that vary from individual to individual and which no "social" scale can cover. In reality these special, individual desires make themselves felt long before the requirements of the primary physiological needs of life are satisfied. Even the physiological needs vary from individual to individual, and from season to season. A young man may be prepared to give up his lunch so that he can take his girl to the cinema; she may be prepared to sacrifice one or two meals in order to have a permanent wave; while a third may be ready to do without both girl and lunch in order to hear a symphony concert.

To use a given piece of ground for grain production is not necessarily a more "social" employment than to use it for a cosmetics factory or a farm for silver foxes. If there were overproduction of grain the first use would be quite irrational. Barbara Wootton, who has made use of an analogous example, says that this belief in an "intrinsic value" makes every university-trained economist see red, and that this relativity of all values is "extremely repellent" to non-economists, who find it incredible (to take the text-book example) that bread is not in some absolute sense more valuable that diamonds. Nor are they satisfied with the concession that existing monetary values may be compatible with moral principles or social needs, a concession which as she says "merely leads into the misty spheres of moral philosophy."[16]

This tendency to look at prices from a moral aspect is a contributory factor in the present-day trend of so many countries more or less consciously to prevent the price-mechanism from functioning. Market-economy is being replaced by valuation by price-regulators, which leads to values being determined not by the many, but by the few. The logical and psychological consequences of certain people having the power to determine values in the economic field is that they will also arbitrarily determine what is to be regarded as artistically and scientifically valuable. This retrogression to mediaeval *justumpretium* views is, in my opinion, one of the reasons why during the last decades the world has relapsed so rapidly into conditions of the Middle Ages in non-economic fields as well.

---

[16] *Op. cit.*, p. 39.

Alleged Defects of Capitalist Societies and the Chances of Eliminating Them in Socialist Societies

This is an appendix in the true sense of the word, in as far as it is not essential to the discussion of our subject. The objections to the capitalist market economy which will be considered here, are, strictly speaking, outside the scope of the book. Nevertheless there are good reasons for investigating them, if only because they have been advanced in several of the works dealing with economic calculation, and so introduced into the discussion. Moreover, many consider a description of the price-mechanism incomplete that does not state the more important objections.[1]

Here, there can obviously be no question of anything like a complete or systematic assessment of capitalism *versus* socialism. We shall merely take up those objections, essentially economic ones, which with greater or lesser relevance

---

[1] Mrs. Barbara Wootton asserts in *Lament for Economics* (pp. 159 and 162) that criticism of a "non-market economy" amounts to an implied defence of existing institutions. Such a conclusion is logically unjustified, as it is quite conceivable that a person may have objections to a market economy as well as to a "non-market economy." According to Mrs. Wootton's logic, her criticism of capitalist societies would amount to an implied defence of socialism. If her reasoning were correct, she herself would be guilty of the very thing for which she upbraids others.

have been brought into this special discussion. It is impossible to treat the objections systematically, for they are heterogeneous and have been advanced independently by different writers. The present writer's comments on these objections are subjective and not *"wertungsfrei."* This is due both to the nature of the subject and that of the objections.

It is alleged that the capitalist price-economy admits of simultaneous existence of unemployment, excess of goods and unexploited productive capacity; that the price-mechanism works too slowly, that producers' efforts to satisfy the needs of the community are fortuitous. Too little, it is said, is known about what is going on: rival investments are made in the same and in competing branches, and the extent of saving and investment are unknown.

It is objected that many "risks" are taken; that there is much "waste"; that factories are built only to be abandoned, that means of transport are made that prove unserviceable, with the result that workmen have to be dismissed. It is doubted whether economic progress is compatible with the maintenance of private capitalism. Advertising is said to be another form of waste, because competing industries employ enormous sums (much time and labour) on advertisements that neutralize each other; it is further objected that the advertisements appeal to the public's lowest instincts. Attention is drawn to the growing number of middlemen, traders, salesmen, and forwarding agents to show that the private capitalist society is tending to change from a productive society into a distributive society.

A further objection is that in certain respects the price-mechanism does not work at all, e.g. in cultural and social spheres. It is also maintained that the price-mechanism is imperfect in capitalist societies because of the existence of cartels and monopolies.

It is alleged that the technical optimum does not coincide with the financial optimum, and that in capitalist calculations no account is taken of the destruction of aesthetic values. Again, that the price-mechanism does not allow of the satisfaction of "negative preferences" and that it is not possible to pay for avoidance of the production of goods which one does not like.

Another objection, probably the one most frequently made, is that the distribution of income and capital is inequitable in the capitalist society; that the differences in the incomes of individuals is enormous, and that people who do nothing to benefit society receive huge incomes; that with such an unequal distribution of money, the society does not attain the maximum satisfaction of needs, because the subjective value of money differs between rich and poor.

Lastly, it is asserted that economic inequality, class differences, propaganda and factors of environment, prevent the masses in a capitalist society from enjoying real liberty of thought.

The most serious objections concern—and it is important to keep this in mind—conditions that are connected with, and partly the result of, the trade cycle. Unemployment, famine, distress, surplus goods, over-production, over-investment, under-production and under-consumption, are in reality all consequences of the ups and downs of the trade cycle (and, to a certain extent, of the price-mechanism not being allowed to function).

It is obviously impossible in a short appendix to discuss the complex of causes and preconditions which constitute the problem of the trade cycle. A certain light is, however, thrown on the problem by discussing the possibility of eliminating fluctuations in a socialist society. This possibility will depend on the form of socialism and planned economy that is attempted. Professor Mises reproaches the socialists for promising a society with rapid development, despite the fact that in their writings they are concerned with a static society. In their criticism of the capitalist society they refer to phenomena in a progressive society and paint in glaring colours the friction occasioned by economic changes which *must* occur in such societies.

We are still assuming a dynamic, progressive society, that is to say, a society that aims at progress and a rising standard of living and in which there occur changes of different kinds: changes in productive technique, in the accumulation of capital, in the size and age-composition of the population and in its tastes and needs.

Let us confine ourselves for the time being to a socialist society with a central authority equipped with sovereign powers. Such a society will in one respect have a better chance of eliminating trade fluctuations than capitalist and competitive societies, since the central authority can control investments and the rate of progress in such a way as to avoid those jerks in investment activity which are so characteristic of the capitalist society.

However, even in a socialist society with sovereign planned direction there will be variables that cannot be eliminated, such as the change between summer and winter, if the society in question is situated in the temperate zone. Nor can changes in the yield from crops be eliminated. Both are changes that alter the volume of production and the extent of employment (the two most important factors of the trade cycle). In an industrialized society with well-developed division of labour any alteration in economic activity will mean that the suppliers of tools, machinery and materials will also experience a change in demand. This will also affect the demand from the suppliers and *their* capacity to employ labour. Also dealers and the middle men will experience a reduction in their turn-over, which will lead to fresh readjustments.

There are variables which the central authority in theory should be able to eliminate, but which it will find very hard to do in practice, namely alterations in the size and age composition of the population. In theory there is nothing to forbid rearing of children or to have children being artificially bred *à la* "Brave New World," but it is unlikely that this would be tolerated in any society to-day.

There are further variables which a sovereign central authority could easily eliminate, but which would necessitate sacrifices of which only very few are aware and which are seldom formulated precisely. The central authority could put an end to the closure of factories and transfer of labour due to technical progress by preventing the use of modern methods of production and by shelving labour-saving inventions. But this would exclude technical progress, which is incompatible with the assumption of a progressive society.

The central authority could also eliminate readjustments due to alterations in taste and needs, but the price of doing so would be the abolition of consumers' free choice. It can be maintained that the consequences of the trade cycle are so serious, that they should be eliminated at any price. This decision is a political, not an economic, one, but it should be noted that the price in this case is retarded technical progress and the abolition of consumers' free choice and the free choice of occupation and place of work.

If the central authority should decide to disregard the desires and needs of the members of the community, it would also be able to eliminate the disturbances due to the fact that production in any modern industrialized society is round-about and time-consuming. In this case the central authority would fix the values of final products by decree, irrespective of whether the members of the community agreed to their valuations or not. Theoretically, there is nothing to prevent a central authority from producing goods which are not wanted by the community. A sovereign central authority can, in order to prevent readjustments and transfer of manpower, embark upon "wild" production, by which is here understood production of goods not desired by the members of the community. In this case "erroneous" investments could obviously be avoided.

If, however, the central authority aims at economic progress and production for needs, and further accepts free choice of goods and employment, this will introduce two of those variables which in capitalist societies cause changes in the volume of employment and production, in other words trade fluctuations.

But cannot a socialist community avoid the cumulative effects of trade depressions which are so typical of the capitalist market economy? The answer depends partly upon what kind of socialist society we assume: shall the central authority aim at progress or shall it continue production irrespective of whether there is a demand for the products or not? Another equally important factor is the degree of industrial development of the society in question. In a society with a natural economy and self-sufficient family-units a decline in production or employment in one quarter will presumably not make itself felt in other quarters. The epidemic nature and cumulative effects of the trade depression are inseparable from monetary economy, industrialization, and division of labour. It is often said that "a depression is the price paid for economic progress"; it can with equal right be said that the depressions are the price we pay for the advantages of monetary economy, industrialization, and division of labour. If we will do without these rational devices, the chances of eliminating the trade cycle are enhanced, but to do so will certainly entail a considerable reduction in our standard of living.

If it is held, as it is by many English socialist economists, that a prerequisite for economic calculation is that the socialist community should introduce competition, and if the competition is assumed to be between individual business units, the possibilities for eliminating trade fluctuations will *grosso modo* be equally slight in the socialist as in the capitalist society.

One argument in favour of the contention that socialist communities can eliminate trade fluctuations is that in such communities there will be no trade secrets. One "sits between glass walls," it is said. It is an interesting argument, but not convincing. In the first place the number of secrets kept by business-men in capitalist societies is not as large as is generally thought. For one thing there is much exchanging of technical and economic data among members of cartels. Even among pure competitors many examples of co-operation will be found, especially in the U.S.A., but also elsewhere. In Norway, for instance, there exists a bureau for extensive exchange of ideas between firms competing with each other. (Credit clearing, business research, exchange of data regarding technical progress and of ideas to reduce costs.) In the second place, even if we assume a society with a *sovereign* central authority, this authority will naturally be acquainted with its own plan, but in such a society this is of less importance since the central authority's valuation of the final result is the only one allowed. If, on the other hand, one assumes, as here, that there will be competition between the managers of the state trust and monopolies, data can undoubtedly be obtained and distributed, and perhaps more easily than in a capitalist society, but the control department cannot instruct the managers of these autonomous concerns to alter their production plans on the basis of what it learns from these data, for to do so would be to abandon the assumption of competition.[2]

Now, it can be objected that neither of the two extreme alternatives assumed can be accepted, neither a sovereign central authority with abolition of free choice of goods and employment, nor competition between autonomous business units. It may be said that one is more likely to get a

---

[2] Capitalist societies have means of eliminating the uncertainty inherent in the fact that managers of concerns have no knowledge of expansions made in other quarters. The expansion of the apparatus of production takes many forms, but the most important, such as the construction of ships and factories, can be ascertained without great difficulty even in a capitalist society. If the League of Nations or another international body would concentrate on the rapid collection and distribution of such data, not only through monthly publications, but immediately through the daily press, capitalist societies too might obtain the alleged advantage of "sitting between glass walls." At the same time there ought to be constant reminders that economic development is not linear, but wave-like. This would mean in practice that in boom-times the public would be reminded that recessions will come, and in times of depression that there are things called recoveries, a fact which politicians and business men are equally apt to forget.

planned society with a sovereign central authority which will *try* to pay some regard to the wishes of the consumers. If, however, the wishes of the consumers are to be considered at all, it will mean—in a dynamic society—that the central authority sooner or later *must* make transfers of labour. It should be stressed that there is unemployment even if the workers get subsidies. Even capitalist societies can—and partly do—support unemployed workers. The price paid for readjustments and necessary transfers of labour may in socialist societies take the form of a lower standard of living, deprivations, and confiscation by introducing new monetary units.

The fact that the development will *ex hypothesi* depend entirely on an individual person or a small group of persons whose word is law, may easily result in even larger disproportionate investments of capital, and thereupon larger readjustments than in the capitalist society. There is no reason to expect greater foresight regarding technical development and the future wishes of consumers from a central authority than from the thousands of autonomous concerns in the capitalist society where managers and owners are more or less dependent for their living on the correctness of their judgment. If a central authority should prove unwilling to admit to mistakes, the development will continue in the same false direction, so that the final readjustment may well be more painful than the trade fluctuations of the capitalist society.

Before turning to the objections made by that group of economists who can suitably be called "disharmonists," it must be mentioned that it is not only trade fluctuations that lead to the production of goods which no one wants to buy and to the destruction of food whilst people go hungry; these things are also due to the fact that the price-mechanism is not being allowed to work. The periodic accumulation of goods which were formerly a passing phase of the trade cycle, are, in part, being made permanent by state intervention and price subsidies. This creates an entirely new situation in which the possibility of adjustment and of mitigating fluctuations is considerably reduced (see p. 299).

No objection to the price-mechanism is more unjustified than the assertion that it causes accumulation and destruction of goods. The cause of these deplorable occurrences is not to be found in the price-mechanism, but in the fact that the price-mechanism is *not* allowed to work. That goes for wheat, pigs, coffee, fruit, and many other commodities, the production of which has been interfered with. Subsidies and prices fixed *by law* above market prices stimulate production and scare consumers away. The result is that the increasing stock, *unsaleable at those high prices,* must finally be destroyed.

In relation to this, it must be mentioned that there is a connection between the extent of unemployment and the creation of monopolies in the labour market. There is little reason to believe that a high price for man-power does not influence demand as for all other commodities. If it is held to be of decisive importance in eliminating trade fluctuations that there should be equalization of income and demand for consumer goods—in itself a highly doubtful contention—this can be achieved by other means than the payment of higher wages by employers.

It is worth noting that several of the young English socialist economists (see Chapter 13) hold that competition is a necessary prerequisite for economic calculation in the socialist society. They do not say precisely what degree of freedom in price formation and competition they claim for the socialist community, but what they desire seems to be a competition freer than that to be found in the capitalist society to-day. An insistence on this point from the socialist economists would be important in these days, when the weight of words to a large extent depends on the political label attached to those who speak them.

Another thing which is held against the capitalist market economy is that the efforts of producers to satisfy the needs of the community are haphazard.[3] There is no real foundation for this objection. The adaptation of production to the needs of the community is indeed the main concern of the private producer, and it is the constant subject of discussion between managers and their salesmen and agents. It is just the producers' ability to judge the needs of the consumers which determines whether or not he shall be able to keep in business (see page 308). Not only is the effort to satisfy existing needs not fortuitous, but the business man is constantly making experiments and investigations to determine the needs of the public, both in the laboratory and by means of the sample products he sends out in order to avoid fortuity.

On the other hand it is true that the capitalist society does not know exactly the extent of savings and investment. It is difficult to say what this ignorance implies. On this subject leading economists hold diametrically opposite points of view. A socialist community will have knowledge both of existing and future accumulation of capital. *If* this is an advantage, it must be balanced against the disadvantage that in a socialist society the individual members of the

---

[3] Among others, Barbara Wootton in *Lament for Economics.*

community have no influence on these decisions and that saving is compulsory.

Another objection made is that in the capitalist society there is waste because factories are closed down. Factually this allegation is correct. In the capitalist society factories are constantly being closed down, machines and means of production constantly being discarded. This can be a result of imperfect foresight, but it can also be, and in most cases *is,* an expression of progress. In a community with a changing population and ever varying needs and tastes, where methods of production change and the accumulation of capital varies, readjustments are inevitable if progress is the goal. Such readjustments involve transfer of labour from one factory to another, from declining branches of industry to vigorous ones, from badly managed factories to well-managed ones. It may be objected that progress is too quick. There are, indeed, many attempts being made to slow it down. Many of the activities of labour unions and other organizations demonstrate clearly their preference for security over progress. If it is true that inventions are sometimes bought up and laid aside, this is another expression that some people prefer slower progress in order to defend their vested interests.

While some reproach the market economy for too rapid progress, others maintain that progress and the raising of the standard of living can never be rapid enough. This is a question of valuation. One thing, however, is certain: the closing down of obsolete factories and the scrapping of means of production due to technical development is not waste, but the very opposite.

In crass conflict with the above objection is the allegation that the capitalist society is incompatible with economic progress. Dr. Oskar Lange writes, for example: "The real issue is whether the further maintenance of the capitalist system is compatible with economic progress."[4] He admits that "capitalism has been the carrier of the greatest economic progress ever witnessed in the history of the human race."[5] But, "The question arises . . . whether the institutions of private property of the means of production and of private enterprise will continue indefinitely to foster economic progress, or whether, at a certain stage of technical development, they turn, from being promoters, into becoming shackles of further advance. The last is the contention of the socialists."[6]

Dr. Lange's argument is that "A private enterprise, unless forced by competition to do otherwise, will introduce innovations only when the old capital invested is amortized, or if the reduction of cost is so pronounced as to offset the devaluation of the capital already invested. . . ."[7] Thus he does admit the existence of competition, yet omits to pay any attention to its consequences.

The actual situation is that competition does force concerns to introduce improvements and to modernize their plant even when the capital invested is *not* amortized. While most complain of too rapid development, the incessant scrapping of means of production and the ceaseless introduction of improvements and new methods, Dr. Lange is afraid of the opposite, and alleges that "interventionism

---

[4] "On the Economic Theory of Socialism" in *Review of Economic Studies,* 1937, p. 128.

[5] *Op. cit.,* p. 128.

[6] *Ibid.,* p. 128.

[7] *Op. cit.,* p. 129.

and restrictionism are the dominant economic policies."[8] He forgets to mention that the responsibility for the most objectionable interventions and restrictions, namely those imposed by law, must be laid at the door of the politicians. State intervention represents a step towards socialism, and socialist tendencies, at any rate, cannot be used as a reproach against the capitalist society.

One accusation against the capitalist society which seems to carry considerable weight in certain groups is that advertising constitutes waste and influences the consumers' choice by making them buy things contrary to their wishes and real interests. However, there are two forms of advertisement. There is that which points out new goods and new services; this must be regarded as a natural and useful service, and it has even been admitted that the socialist society will also have to avail itself of this kind of advertising. It should be stressed that the term "new" should not be confined to such goods and services which have not previously existed, but should also apply to those which can be produced at new prices which put them within the reach of new groups of buyers. The greatest advantage of modern mass production is that it gives the consumers the advantage of cheap buying, and it is self-evident that new possibilities for buying cheaply should come to the knowledge of the consumer.

The other form of advertisements are those which tell of goods already being offered in the market. The objections brought forward against this form are conflicting, but both imply an unwarranted criticism of the competitive market

---

[8] *Ibid.* 130.

economy. The first argument is that already mentioned, viz. that individuals are influenced to buy things other than those they desire. This seems to imply that the choice of goods is too limited. The other argument is that it would be only pleasant and soothing to the nerves to have prescribed what one should choose; it is troublesome for the consumer to have so many goods from which to choose, it is said. This argument implies the existence of a confusing and overwhelming number of commodities.

The decisive point is whether advertisements of existing goods represent waste or not. This is not a simple question. At any rate, it is quite obvious that the individual producer does not regard advertising as waste, for in that case he would not advertise. The business man's attention to the rentability of advertising is a factor of importance for judging the whole problem. The time and labour employed in advertising represent namely a partial saving on other accounts, among them personal selling. The increased production and turnover due to advertising further means lower fixed costs per unit.

From the public's point of view it would seem to be an advantage to have the widest possible choice, but on the other hand it must be admitted that the value of advertisements which merely hammer in a name, appears doubtful. The social utility of advertising becomes particularly doubtful when several undertakings in the same branch of industry each hammer in the name of their product. Professor Mises writes[9] that the socialist state would be saved all costs of advertising and all outlay for travelers and sales-

---

[9] See *Socialism*, p. 153.

men, but he thinks it likely that it would have to employ more people in distribution. Mises recalls now troublesome and expensive distribution was during the war, and also raises the question of whether ration cards will cost less than advertisements, and whether the huge apparatus and numerous personnel required for rationing is cheaper than the outlay on salesmen and agents.

Professor Mises concedes too much when he says that the socialist society will be saved all advertising. Announcements of new and cheaper goods will still be needed in socialist societies. Besides, agents and middle-men are needed for other things than selling, for example to speed up transport and to distribute goods rationally so as to avoid small parcels being sent over long distances.

Another criticism against the capitalist society is that advertisements are not always in accordance with the actual facts. It is hinted that the public is hoodwinked. This is a surprising accusation when one considers that advertising schools and textbooks teach that the precondition of successful advertising is that it is true and honest. Lies and exaggerations belong to the childhood of advertising, at any rate in the Northern hemisphere. It is a well-known fact that exaggerated and false advertisements militate against their purpose and destroy the reputation of the advertiser. In his speech opening the International Advertising Convention in Glasgow on 27th July, 1938, Lord Southwood of Fernhurst said, "Advertising has reversed Abraham Lincoln's dictum. Success on the scale achieved by these great advertisers is gained not by trying to fool some of the public all the time or all of the public some of the time, but only by keeping faith with all of the public all of the time. It is an exacting course—but reputable advertisers know that it is the only course."[10] How unfounded this broad accusation of false advertising is, would also appear from the investigations made by the American Federal Trade Commission during the fiscal year, 1937. It investigated 576,032 newspapers, periodicals and radio advertisements, and found that only one advertisement in every 160 "appeared to be false or misleading."[11]

Another objection of a slightly different kind is that advertising in the capitalist society appeals to the public's lowest instincts. Advertisements of this type cannot at any rate repel the majority of consumers; if they did, they would have soon disappeared. This rather Victorian objection is based on an aesthetic valuation which makes it difficult to discuss. In this age of psycho-analysis and behaviourism there is, besides, little reason to be incensed at advertisements containing sexual, eupeptic or olfactory allusions.

The allegation that the number of middlemen, salesmen, and forwarding agents is increasing in the capitalist society, and that this is changing it from a productive to a distributive society, is correct, but it does not constitute an objection. For the business community this development may be unwelcome because it means sharper competition, but for consumers an increase in the number of distributive agents means better service. When one considers the great advances that have been made in the sphere of pure production, it is perfectly natural that attempts should also be

---

[10] "See *The Influence of Advertising upon the Life of the Peoples*," 1938, pp. 4–5.

[11] See *Futurum*, Stockholm, No. 1, 1938, p. 56.

made to improve the distributive apparatus. It may be mentioned in passing that this objection conflicts with one made by the other disharmony economists, namely that the capitalist society produces too much and neglects the distribution of goods.[12]

It is quite correct to say that the price mechanism is imperfect in the capitalist society, especially in those where the law has introduced monopolies and cartels and restricted prices. Its growing imperfection due to price controls and state interference represents, however, a stage in the development towards socialism and can in no way be an objection against the capitalist market economy.

It is also true that the price-mechanism does not work in cultural and social spheres. This, however, is no argument for doing away with it in other spheres. Moreover, it should be kept in mind that the price-mechanism in the capitalist society does exert a certain influence even in cultural and social spheres, in so far as the market economy furnishes price data with which to calculate.

It is also correct to say that the "technical optimum" does not coincide in the capitalist society with the "financial optimum." Here as in many other cases, the statement is

---

[12] In *Britain without Capitalists,* London, 1937, written by a group of anonymous economists, the extension of the distribution apparatus in capitalist countries is called a form of "decaying capitalism" and "parasitism" (p. 84). On p. 133, however, it is stated that in the socialist community the number and size of shops will be determined by the demands of the consumers, and that shops will be able to remain open as long as is required "without any fear of sweating any distributive workers." Shift work can be employed just as well in shops as in factories, and if the workers desire it some shops may remain open throughout the 24 hours of the day (p. 135). What was a symptom of decay in the capitalist society has here become a sign of strength in the socialist community.

pointing to an existing fact, but, as in so many other cases, it does not amount to an objection. The preference for financial optima instead of technical optima is one of the capitalist market economy's greatest advantages, provided economical, and therefore rational, use of resources is the goal. The whole *raison d'être* of economic calculation is to find the "economic optimum" and to see that the input does not become larger than the output. If one aims at the "technical optimum," one runs the risk of such absurdities as, to take an example already used, molybdenum being used for making toy swords. (This question has been discussed in various parts of the book, particularly in Chapters 4 and 8.)

The assertion that in capitalist calculations no account is taken of the destruction of aesthetic values is not quite correct. If the aesthetic value of a piece of land is evident, nothing prevents the community from sacrificing something to preserve it. Nevertheless, it must be admitted that the demand for aesthetic values is not always expressed in terms of money in such a way as to make it available as a factor of calculation. However, it is just as possible in capitalist states, as in socialist ones, for the public, through preservation societies or other means, to stop open destruction of things of aesthetic value.

The objection that the price-mechanism cannot satisfy "negative preferences" and that one cannot pay to avoid things one does not like, was put forward by E. F. M. Durbin in his paper "The Social Significance of the Theory of Value."[13] Many of Dr. Durbin's views are most interesting, but some of the conclusions which Mrs. Wootton

---

[13] *Economic Journal,* December, 1935.

has drawn from them and enlarged on in her book[14] do appear rather far fetched. One can scarcely reproach a mechanism for not being able to do what it was never intended to do. A machine cannot produce pink roses. Mrs. Wootton laments that one cannot pay to have the difference between riches and poverty levelled out; she realizes that she can contribute to this by giving away her fortune, but complains that it is little use the individual person doing so "since the fortune of one rich man will not go far among the great multitude of the poor." This lament appears very artificial and not very fair either. If one regards equalization of income to be so great a blessing as Mrs. Wootton does, one must expect the price to be high.

The most frequent charge made against the capitalist market economy is that the distribution of income and fortune is unjust. It is not possible to determine objectively what is just and what is unjust. Some people understand by just distribution an equal *per capita* distribution. Others understand distribution according to needs (determined by age and sex). Others again think that distribution should be made according to contribution, that is to say according to the usefulness of each individual to the community. Others again think that distribution ought to be made according to "merit," which is a hazy idea to which we shall revert later.

There is no denying that differences in income and capital *at any one time* are very large in the capitalist societies, but it is not logical to infer that they are unjust (see p. 64). The discussion of socialism has shown that some advocates find difference in income more obnoxious than low in-

---

[14] *Lament for Economics.*

comes. Others, however, think that difference in income is of subordinate importance and that the main thing must be to raise the average as well as the lowest incomes as high as possible. Those holding this latter view will naturally consider the existence of large incomes and fortunes a low price for economic progress for all layers of society.

Whatever one's views on this question, there is no basis for adducing large differences in income as an objection against capitalism and an argument for socialism, unless it is certain that these differences can be eliminated in the socialist society. This appears extremely doubtful. In any kind of society the distribution of income will at any given time either be a matter of power or depend on the value set by his fellows on the services and goods provided by the individual. Both alternatives are thinkable in a socialist society. There can be a central authority which sovereignly determines the income of each social group or of each individual; under this assumption, arbitrary decisions are likely. If it were possible to introduce free competition (an unlikely assumption in a socialist society) income would be distributed according to a scale of value set by the consumers. Since the contribution will necessarily vary from individual to individual the second alternative will also mean that there will be wide differences in remuneration.[15]

Distribution of income "according to merit" is a misty goal, but it is surprisingly general, not least among artists

---

[15] We have assumed that individuals vary in respect of physical strength, intelligence, artistic and spiritual gifts, etc. One of the many paradoxes of our day is the tendency to disregard these differences when it comes to work, at the same time as a tremendous amount of time, energy and interest is employed to measure the least fractional difference in athletic accomplishments.

and scholars. The point of departure is that there must be something wrong with the distribution of income, when intelligent, gifted and industrious brain workers have small incomes, while ignorant manufacturers of pins or chewing gum may have huge incomes. One can understand and sympathize with this point of view, but it must be realized that it is really a strongly individualistic and "undemocratic" one. What really lies behind it is a desire for differentiated wages and to have one's own subjective valuation taken as the basis and not the valuation of the general public, which, as expressed in the effective demand, has already shown that products of the manufacturer of pins and chewing gum are in greater demand than those of the artists and scholars.

The third and most probable possibility is that in a socialist society income would be distributed according to the sovereign decisions of the central authority. When so much power is concentrated in the hands of a few, it is most likely that the matter will be decided entirely arbitrarily. Stalin has rewarded individual authors with high salaries and this, no doubt, accounts for the enthusiasm of many intellectuals for Soviet Russia, but it must be added that these high salaries are paid only on the condition that the author writes nothing but what is acceptable to the authorities. One of the results of our examination of the possibilities of calculation under different forms of distribution was to show that the distribution of purchasing power in a socialist community without competing markets must depend on power to an even greater degree than in other societies, where the income is distributed simultaneously with the production on the basis of more or less free formation of prices.

An investigation of wage relationships in Soviet Russia must surprise those who hold that differences in remuneration will be done away with in the socialist societies. Max Eastman has made a comparison[16] between wages in Soviet Russia and in the U.S.A., the capitalist state *par excellence.* Eastman refers to statistics given in the *New Republic* of 15th July, 1936, where the salaries of the heads of such large American companies as Chile Copper Company, Curtis Publishing Company, and Consolidated Oil are reported. He shows that their salaries are often 50 to 100 times higher than the relative average wage for non-skilled labour. For the Russian wages Eastman refers to an article by Leon Sedov in the *New International* of February, 1936, in which the author quotes, among other sources, from *Pravda* of February, 1933, where it is stated that while the miner who is not a Stakhanovist gets from 400 to 500 roubles a month, a Stakhanovist can receive 1,600 roubles. An assistant can get 160 roubles, if he is not a Stakhanovist, and 400 roubles if he is. Sedov also states that a certain named manager of a mine received 8,000 roubles a month and that engineers can earn from 800 to 100 times more than non-skilled workmen. In his review[17] of Barbara Wootton's book *Plan or No Plan* Professor Frank H. Knight asserts that on pp. 155–156 she states that wages can vary from 80 to 1,000 roubles a month.[18]

This may be countered by saying that there still remains the great difference that in the socialist societies income

---

[16] *The End of Socialism in Russia,* London, 1937.

[17] *Journal of Political Economy,* 1935.

[18] This reference to the height of wages is not to be found in the English edition, although the American edition is stated to be a photographic reproduction of the English.

from investments will not exist. This assertion, however, is
not correct. Incomes from investment are not necessarily
banned in the socialist state. Socialism means that the right
to private ownership of means of production is abolished,
but not that of interest-bearing securities. In Soviet Russia
it has been possible to buy State Bonds bearing 7 per cent
interest, and to pay money into a savings bank, where it is
free of both income tax and death duties. The interest has
been up to 10 per cent.[19]

When it is possible to earn from 10 to 100 times more
than the average wage and besides to invest one's money
at high interest rates, there will be good chances for making
fortunes.

In the discussion on unequal distribution of income and
fortune it is often said that the socialist society will be
classless. What has just been said makes it clear that this is
not the case. For other reasons—the concentration of
power inevitable when one or few persons manage all means
of production—the privileges will necessarily be greater
than in any competitive capitalist society. It is often said
that the alleged classlessness of the socialist society will
bring about far-reaching changes, the most important of
which is an alteration in people's mental attitude. This question of whether people's psyche will change under socialism
is of fundamental importance for the future of the socialist
society. It will be remembered that several of the solutions

---

[19] See *inter alia* Eastman's book. Barbara Wootton writes that the interest the public is generally given is "such as exceeds the wildest dreams of
fancy of the investor in the public loans of the capitalist countries." (*Plan
or No Plan*, p. 72.) L. E. Hubbard states that the interest on personal
savings accounts is 8 per cent plus 1 per cent on fixed term deposits.
(*Soviet Money and Finance*, London, 1936, p. 86.)

of the problem of calculation are simply based on the assumption[20] that such a change will take place (see p. 39).

Economists hold strongly divergent views both on the relationship between institutions and psychological attitude and on the particular consequences of the right to private ownership of property. On the one side there are those who hold that the right of private ownership is an institutionalist phenomenon in which one will find the roots of most social evils. On the other side are those who see in private ownership a great source of strength which forces us to undertake economic calculation and to minimize costs, and which acts as a stimulant to new enterprise, at the same time as the necessity of bearing losses provides the necessary brake. The right of private ownership is an institutionalist phenomenon in so far as it can be abolished under other forms of society, but it can also be said that the desire to acquire private property is bound up with the instinctive urge to protect one's mate and children and is thus linked with the reproductive urge. (See also the remarks on the instinct to save on p. 149.)

The argument that the right to private ownership is a necessary stimulant is often countered by saying that it is out-of-date.[21] It is said that the joint-stock companies of capitalist societies show that as far as means of production are concerned the right of ownership and that of disposal can be separated without injury. The analogy is too slight to have any value as proof. In the first place, many, and

---

[20] Professor Mises says succinctly: "It is an evasion of the problem to put one's faith in the hope that the moral purification of mankind . . ." *Socialism,* p. 217.

[21] See, *inter alia,* A. R. Sweezy: "The Economist's Place under Socialism" in *Exploration in Economics.*

probably most, limited companies were set up with the object of limiting responsibility. This means that in *most,* but not in the largest, companies, those who manage the means of production are in fact the owners. In the second place even in those companies where the right of ownership and disposal *are* separate, it will generally be found that (1) those who manage the means of production are shareholders, that is to say, they have a share in the ownership, and (2) that the managers are partly remunerated according to profit, that is to say, their incomes depend on the surplus, which is the same sort of stimulant as that of ownership. In the third place it must be kept in mind that the private ownership of a concern does not merely carry the right to the surplus, but also means bearing the risk of a loss. One can imagine socialist societies giving their business managers an incentive in the form of a bonus, but they are by definition prevented from giving them that special attitude that comes from risking one's own means. Finally, in the capitalist societies there are to be found in practically every branch of industry side by side with joint-stock companies concerns where management and ownership, formally or in actual fact, are in the same hands. This means that there exist privately owned concerns playing their part in determining the degree of efficiency and the tempo of modernization. The result is that even managers without owner-interest are forced to keep their concerns on the same level. In a socialist community there cannot possibly be competition from privately owned concerns.

The last of the objections mentioned—it is really not an economic one—is that there is no real freedom of thought in the capitalist society since the opinions and tastes of the masses are influenced by propaganda, the example of the upper classes and other factors connected with their environment.

This is to give a quite special meaning to the expression freedom of thought. In general usage we understand by freedom of thought the possibility of expressing opinions in speech and writing. Used in this sense, it is not correct to say that freedom of thought does not exist in the capitalist society. If, however, the expression is taken to mean the *capacity* for independent thinking without being influenced by one's surroundings, the argument is in itself correct. This, however, does not mean that it is an argument against the capitalist society. The opinion and tastes of the masses are influenced in any and every society by propaganda, by milieu and by the example of the ruling class. The criticism implied in the assertion is unjustified.

There is, indeed, little reason to believe that freedom of thought—in whatever sense—will be greater in the socialist than in the capitalist societies. In the first place, in both societies, since people live in social groups, they will be influenced by social factors. Secondly, socialist societies will also have their upper classes. In any modern industrialized society there will necessarily be superiors and subordinates, which of itself must lead to class divisions. Nor can the socialist community eliminate emulation. Even if one assumes both economic and athletic competition being eliminated, there will still remain rivalry in the choice of mate (at any rate as long as reproduction remains a matter for the two sexes). Irrespective of which faculties—intellectual, physical, or artistic—are rated highest in the community, there will always be individuals who get further than the others, and in the end they will form an *élite* or upper class which will set its stamp upon the others. The same will happen if an entire social group or a definite profession is made pre-eminent. When, after the revolution in Russia, the manual labourers were made the upper class, the former upper classes had to copy them in order to save themselves and obtain the same rights, such as, e.g., that of their children being allowed to attend school. Even if one gives the phrase "upper class" the restricted meaning of a social group having economic power (which is quite unreasonable) there will still be an upper class in the socialist society. The elimination of the right to own means of production is in this connection of minor significance. It is not the right of ownership as such that creates an economic upper class in capitalist societies, but the power and the opportunity to buy things which follow the right of private ownership. Social groups having this opportunity and kind of power will be found in the socialist state as well. The power of the leaders of a socialist society will indeed be infinitely larger than that wielded by an individual in a capitalist society, since they will have at their disposal the entire means of production in the community. If a socialist society, in a natural desire to achieve optimum division of labour and thereby maximum productivity, pays wages far in excess of the average, this would provide extensive possibilities for the formation of an economic upper class. If, in addition, there are facilities for investing money at high rates of interest free of tax and death duty (as in the Soviet Union) there will in fact be exceptionally good possibilities for the formation of an upper class.

With regard to the third factor which is supposed to destroy the masses' freedom of thought, propaganda, the danger is that in the socialist society it will be both more extensive and more intensive. There are many reasons for this. An individual, or group of individuals, invested with such large powers as the leaders of a socialist community will have, will naturally identify their own interests with those of the community. It is inevitable that they will believe that they are strengthening the state by suppressing all criticism of the system and of themselves. Besides, from a purely psychological point of view it is difficult for someone who has sovereign powers in one field (the economic) to be tolerant and liberal in others. From the technical point of view, the facilities for expressing divergent views will be either eliminated or greatly reduced in socialist societies, since the right to private ownership of the means of communication and dissemination such as printing machinery and halls for meetings, will by definition have been abolished. That this reasoning is correct is confirmed by developments in all socialist societies, both Marxist and national-socialist ones. Not only are certain views forbidden to be heard or read, but people are obliged to listen to chosen opinions. The leaders' fear of criticism is so great that they have also abolished the artist's right to free development and the scientist's freedom of investigation.

In a period when a question mark is affixed to all values and conceptions, when war is recommended as healthy training for youth and when the promptings of blood and instinct are given an equal value with the thoughts of the head, there is no objective foundation for denouncing such a policy. We shall, however, confine ourselves to stating that freedom of expression, freedom of artistic development and freedom for scientific investigation have been decisive factors in the development of mankind. One may consider this development as progressive or retrogressive, but it cannot be denied that the elimination of these factors will have

far-reaching effects that can change both the rate and direction of development. This, however, brings us to what
are the possible, or probable, consequences of socialism,
and that is a subject on which we shall not embark, for in
this work we have sought to follow the example of the
scientist, who, afraid of being accused of taking political
sides, omits to condemn even the forces which are destroy-
ing the very foundation of his work, namely his freedom to
investigate and explore. This is a form of objective passivity
which the author finds as admirable in its coolness, as it is
difficult to understand.

A Comparison between Our Conclusions and Experiences in Soviet Russia

The Soviet Union is to-day the only country which according to our definition is a completely socialist society. The National-Socialist countries have gone a long way towards this, but in them there still exists a formal right to possess means of production and a certain degree of free disposal.

It has been tempting, and would have been natural, to refer to developments and actual conditions in Soviet Russia on almost every point discussed in this book. This has not been done for many reasons, but especially because that might have aroused subjective reactions which could have detracted attention from the argument. Also, it might have been objected that references to Soviet Russia have little force as arguments, so long as it is not known what *aim* the Russian leaders have set themselves. Without that, we have no means of judging the efficiency or rationality of economic activity in Soviet Russia. If the aim has been merely to build up exactly that production apparatus which has been built, and *nothing else,* then the system cannot be said to have functioned unsatisfactorily. If it is correct, what the Soviet Courts pretend to have proved, that the

majority of the original leaders of the socialist movement
have in reality been saboteurs and secretly aimed at creating chaos, the system has not been bad. In such circumstances it is not a relevant objection to point out, as has
often been done, that rapid development of the productive
apparatus has involved a severe reduction in the standard
of living and that millions have died of starvation.

Nevertheless, this appendix will attempt a comparison
for these two reasons: (1) Soviet Russia from her socialist
experiments has harvested a crop of experiences which
should be of value to other societies, and (2) developments
in Soviet Russia shed light on problems discussed in this
book, *even though* there may exist no yardstick for judging whether the results have been good or bad.

The first experiment of the Communists on achieving
power was to nationalize the banks. They were taken over
on 14th December, 1917. At that time Lenin believed that
state socialism was three-quarters of the way to introducing socialism. This proved to be wrong. Nine months later,
in the summer of 1918, the attempt at state socialism was
given up. Lenin had overlooked the fact that in the private-
capitalist society banking is based on certain legal principles, including the right to own means of production, and,
if these are annulled, it also does away with banking in its
proper form. Its real contents disappear. Lenin had confiscated the banks' buildings, safes and books, but the banks
had really already ceased to function two months after the
communist revolution.[1]

In the period between the summer of 1918 and March,
1921, an attempt was made to introduce purely communist

---

[1] For a description and quotations, see Brutzkus, *op. cit.,* pp. 99–101.

principles, Lenin then considering money nothing but a capitalist tool for obtaining social goods, for speculation, and for exploiting the worker. In this period all goods were to be placed at the disposal of the central authority. The aim was to eliminate market transactions (a decree of 15th July, 1920, and elsewhere). No attempt was made to restrict the quantity of money, it being considered that the quickest way to destroy the remains of the bourgeois community was to destroy the value of money. The total amount of money in circulation on 1st November, 1917, was 22.4 milliard roubles, on 1st January, 1920, 225 milliards, and on 1st July, 1921, 2,346 milliards. During the war prices had not increased as quickly as the amount of money, but in this period they did so far more rapidly. Between November, 1918, and 1st July, 1921, the amount of money increased one hundred-fold, but prices rose till they were eight thousand times as high.[2]

In this period it was also decided not to require payment for use of the post, telegraph, gas, electricity, or other public services. People could travel by train or steamer for nothing. Wages were paid, at least in part, *in natura.* To get the workers to carry out the production programme, it became necessary in 1920 to set up committees in various districts to introduce forced labour.

The results of this period of no money and accounting *in natura* were such that these ideas had to be abandoned. Although the wretched results were partly due to the war, they were a clear object lesson that a natural economy in a modern community leads to chaos. The third congress of

[2] These figures are taken from Professor L. Jurowsky's book *Die Währungsprobleme Sowjetrusslands,* Berlin, 1925, p. 21.

the economic council announced in January, 1920, that a fixed unit of accounting would have to be introduced, and it was suggested that this should be a normal day's simple work with normal effort for a given working-day. This, in other words, was an attempt to put the Marxist theory of labour value into practice. Tschayanoff's ideas had to make way for those of S. Strumilin and E. Varga (see p. 75). Subsequent events of that hectic period make it difficult to ascertain how far the proposals of the congress were acted upon. Brutzkus maintains that no one took them seriously,[3] and Jurowsky tells us that the theorists discussed the problem, but never arrived at any result.[4]

The results were catastrophic. This was due to the natural economy, to practising the Marxist theory of labour value, or to other reasons. The Communists excuse themselves by saying that the Russian economic system was not ripe for socialism, but others maintain that Russian heavy industry was excellently suited to socialization, being highly centralized. The bread ration fell in the towns to about half what it had been before the war; there were 5½ million cases of typhus, railway traffic fell to 12 per cent of the pre-war figure and industrial production to between 10 and 15 per cent.[5] This amounted to a complete collapse and Lenin was forced to abandon his communist experiments.

In 1921 the so-called New Economic Policy, N.E.P., was introduced. In reality there was nothing new in it. It merely

---

[3] *Op. cit.*, p. 105.

[4] *Op. cit.*, p. 27.

[5] See Barbara Wootton's *Plan or No Plan*, in which she speaks of the "completeness of the collapse." Brutzkus gives (p. 100) industrial production in 1920 as being 13 per cent of pre-war. This is based on official statistics.

re-introduced a price- and market-economy. The results were good, and an obvious improvement was being felt as early as Autumn, 1922. The conclusion reached, however, was not that private enterprise and the price-mechanism should be retained, but that there was now a good enough basis for making a fresh dash for socialism. Private business men found their work made more and more difficult by the Communist authorities and at the end of 1923 it was obvious that they had no real legal security. At the beginning of 1924 most of the private capital earned under N.E.P. was confiscated and private undertakings were taken over by co-operative concerns whose managers were but little interested in profit and minimizing costs.[6]

The first prerequisite for centralization of business activity, as had already been discovered, was a comparatively stable currency, and it was only in February, 1924, when that had been achieved, that a plan could be worked out. This was done by the summer of 1925 and it was given the title "Economic Control-Figure for U.S.S.R. for the year 1925–1926." Space does not permit of any detailed description. We must confine ourselves to those sides of the development which throw light on our problems, but it may be mentioned that in putting this plan into effect they met with great difficulties which seem to have been connected with the abolition of markets.

Trouble was experienced first and foremost with the peasants, in the difficulty of obtaining their agricultural products. As their ability to sell freely at market was progressively restricted, the peasants received less and less for their products. According to official figures, at that period

---

[6] Brutzkus, *op. cit.,* p. 113.

they received (in industrial goods) what amounted to less than half of what they had got before the war. (Later they received far less still.)[7] There was also a tendency towards expropriation and compulsory surrender. The Institute for Economic Investigation drew attention to the dangers inherent in this tendency: "Any attempt to counteract discrepancies by the use of non-economic methods in a combined goods- and money-market must logically lead to the economic methods of early communism with all its characteristic features."[8] At the same time the Institute pointed to certain phenomena reminiscent of the early days of communism: illegal trading and the fact that the peasants were given low-quality goods; "This," said the Institute, "will lead to a serious drop in the production and sale of agricultural products." Memories of the early days of communism were still so fresh that this warning aroused a storm of indignation as a result of which the institute had to cease its activities. Events, however, proved the prognosis right. The government met with increasing difficulties in obtaining agricultural products; the peasants refused to give up their corn for low prices, and in 1927 almost no corn crops were grown at all.[9]

As the government had destroyed the trade in grain, it had to assume responsibility for feeding the people. In January, 1928, it decided to close all markets and to go over

---

[7] See *Collectivized Agriculture in the Soviet Union,* Monograph No. 2 issued by School of Slavonic and East European Studies, University of London, 1934.

[8] Institute for Economic Investigation's *Bulletin* No. 11–12, 1927, p. 52. (Brutzkus, *op. cit.,* p. 120.)

[9] See Brutzkus: *Op. cit.,* p. 121.

to compulsory surrender of products and an economy of coercion. The last pillars of the N.E.P. had thus fallen. The first result was that for the first time since 1922, according to official figures,[10] the acreage under corn decreased.

The economic ideology of the early days of communism was now again in vogue due to the fact that the non-political experts were at this period replaced by young communist orthodox economists. These still believed in communism and natural economy. In their opinion money could be eliminated without risk, as money was merely a symbol of accountancy, and if the Soviet economy required a yardstick of value, the most suitable one was the working day. In connection with the Gosplan for 1929–30 they said that:

> the expression of the national income in value form (in price) begins to lose its universal significance.

That they had at least some doubts appears from the following:

> This gives rise to new problems of economic analysis in general and for the analysis of the conditions of distribution in particular—problems which are solved neither by the theory of Soviet economics, nor by our statistics.[11]

Their doubts were more justified than their faith. The communist ideas proved to be just as difficult to put into practice now as they had been previously.

One result of the new policy of "economic planning" was that the government, despite the bad harvest, exported

---

[10] See Brutzkus: *Op. cit.,* p. 136.
[11] Brutzkus: *Op. cit.,* p. 153.

wheat in order to obtain foreign exchange to carry out the plan. It is estimated that the famine this entailed cost about six million lives in the years 1931–32.[12]

Those who, despite criticism of the "welfare concept," also take account of human factors must, when judging Soviet collectivization, remember not only this extraordinary large loss of life, but also the fact that it turned the peasants into serfs. The workers on collective farms are forced to work under particularly severe conditions and have no more chance of getting away from the collective farm than their forefathers had of escaping from their village before the emancipation of the serfs in 1861.[13]

Agriculture was not the only sector in which the attempt to revert to natural economy and communist principles created difficulties. It was accompanied by a renewed laxity in the granting of credit and by certain inflationary phenomena. At a conference of managers held in Moscow in 1931 many depressing statements about the economic situation were made, and it was obvious that the Soviet economic system was on the verge of a new general collapse.[14]

Under N.E.P., when means of production had to be acquired in the markets, all concerns calculated in money and sought to be economical and to make ends meet. Now, however, the acquisition of means of production no longer depended so much on money, as on the decisions of various boards. Once the decision had been made, the money could

---

[12] See Professor K. A. Wieth-Knudsen's *Hvad vet vi om Sovjetrussland?* Olso, 1935; pp. 42–43.

[13] See *Collectivized Agriculture in the Soviet Union*, pp. 24–25. This also gives quotations from official decrees concerning labour on collective farms.

[14] See Brutzkus: *Op. cit.*, pp. 162–163.

always be obtained from the state bank. Thus managers became accustomed to carry out their plans without economizing either on labour or means of production.[15] What really happened was that the economic plan, originally set out in money, degenerated into a kind of economy *in natura,* although that system had already been proved unworkable in practice.

A new conference was held in secret and Stalin made a speech (on 23rd June, though it was not published till 5th July) that decided the Soviet government's policy for the following period. Even though Stalin neither abandoned the idea of a planned economy, nor showed himself in any way in favour of private trade, he admitted that certain capitalist institutions were indispensable for implementing their communist plans. He strongly denounced any idea of a moneyless economy, which he called a "Trotsky-ist" idea (rather unjustifiably in view of Trotsky's opinion, see p. 263). Economic calculation was now to be recognized as the chief principle of the Soviet economy, and Stalin coined the expression "Soviet distribution" to take the place of "socialist distribution." Contact with consumers was to be made and wholesale undertakings were to be set up in the provinces to avoid distribution in small lots, and irrational and superfluous transport. During the course of 1931 it was further decided that half the profit should be retained. The system of rationing was to be avoided, if possible. A widely varied scale of price-rates was introduced to increase the efficiency of labour. The choice of managers for concerns was no longer to be dictated merely by party-member-

---

[15] *Za industrializaciu,* 19th December, 1930 (quoted in Brutzkus: *Op. cit.,* p. 163).

ship, but qualifications had also to be taken into consideration. Finally, a number of credit reforms were introduced, the purpose of which was to force managers to adopt better methods of calculation.

Professor Brutzkus maintains that this attempt to introduce certain capitalist institutions within the socialist framework was not without effect and that it saved the Soviet economy from final collapse.[16] Professor Louis Rougier has reached the same conclusion:

> If one summarizes the lesson to be drawn from the Soviet experiment, one could say: the experiment was successful where it was unfaithful to its principles; it has failed where it has been faithful to them.[17]

What is of greatest interest for our purpose is to examine whether these directions to introduce economic calculation were feasible in a socialist society like Soviet Russia.

Economic calculation presupposes a certain stability in the value of a currency. "Without a firm monetary unit," writes Trotsky, "commercial accounting can only increase the chaos".[18] There is no disputing the fact that the value of money in Soviet Russia has been unstable, but that is not where the greatest difficulty has lain. The greatest difficulty has been that prices have been arbitrary and that after the abolition of markets there have existed simultaneously— irrespective of time and value of money—*several different levels of prices* (for goods at the same place and stage of production, and of the same quality). Trotsky, who is fully

---

[16] *Op. cit.,* p. 170.

[17] *Peut-on savoir la Vérité sur l'Expérience Soviétique?* Besançon, 1937, p. 45.

[18] *Soviet Economy in Danger,* New York, 1933, p. 31.

alive to the consequences of abolishing markets, said:

> By eliminating the market and by installing instead Asiatic bazaars the bureaucracy has created, to consummate all else, the conditions for the most barbaric gyrations of prices, and consequently has placed a mine both under the plan and under commercial calculation. As a result, the economic chaos has been redoubled.[19]

Most of those who have studied the question either in Soviet Russia or from existing literature, state that the result of abolishing markets has been to make price-formation in Soviet Russia arbitrary.

Though references will follow later, it can be stated in advance—and this is of decisive importance for the problem under discussion—that the basis for economic calculation disappears the moment prices are fixed arbitrarily and become void of real significance.

R. L. Hall, who is in sympathy with socialism and planned economy, has made a study of most of the literature in English on Russian prices. Of his conclusions the following will throw light on our problem:

> Russian writers made constant reference to the control of processes with reference to prices and costs; but these do not yet mean what they do in ordinary economic language.[20]
>
> Until this is general (that prices do represent the relations of supply and demand) the state cannot have any prices of finished goods in which it can place any confidence, and it is difficult to know in what units it can make its calculations, since its money is to a large extent meaningless (because of the variety of price-levels).[21]

---

[19] *Op. cit.*, p. 34.

[20] *The Economic System in a Socialist State*, London, 1937, p. 236.

[21] *Op. cit.*, p. 238.

When the final prices are not representative of any particular supply-demand relationship, costs cannot be imputed from them.[22]

It is difficult to know how the Planning Commission gets its statistics.[23]

On the whole, then, it seems unlikely that the costs at present can be reliable indices. They serve to control the operations of the directors of industry, but do not really measure the alternative possibilities of the productive resources.[24]

. . . the danger would be that the Russians might allow themselves to be influenced by their prices and costs under the impression that these had some validity.[25]

It will be seen from this account . . . planning does not mean the careful adjustment of means to ends . . . There can be little doubt that this causes what would be considered fairly large losses of welfare in price economics, both through the production of goods which are not wanted so much as others would have been if the consumers had a free choice: and through the lack of knowledge about the relative costs of productive resources.[26]

One example of the chaotic state of prices in Soviet Russia is the existence of several different pricing systems for retail prices. L. E. Hubbard mentions seven:[27] (1) Normal (i.e. ration) town prices at which limited quantities of goods are sold to that part of the population possessing ration cards. (2) Country prices at which the peasants buy manufactured goods at the village co-operative shops. (These are sometimes equal to the town "commercial

---

[22] *Ibid.*, p. 244.

[23] *Ibid.*, p. 246.

[24] *Op. cit.*, p. 249.

[25] *Ibid.*, p. 252.

[26] *Ibid.*, p. 255.

[27] *Soviet Money and Finance*, pp. 138–140.

price," but sometimes not, because the peasants receive fewer manufactured goods than townspeople.) (3) Commercial prices at which unrestricted quantities of consumption goods (except bread and cereals), are sold. The "commercial" level is several times higher than the "normal," and there has never been a constant ratio between the two. (4) Conventional prices at which the peasants sell their surplus produce to the state collecting organizations and to enterprises. (5) Open-market prices at which the town consumer buys direct from the peasants. (These prices are determined by supply and demand, but Government action prevents prices rising to an exorbitant level.) (6) The single bread price. Since the abolition of bread cards on 1st January, 1935, bread, flour and other cereal foods and fodder have been sold by the State at prices roughly midway between the former rationed and "commercial" prices. (7) Torgsin or "gold" rouble prices which apply to the foreign shops. This is classed as external trade and has no bearing on paper rouble prices. Hubbard adds that it is clear that the purchasing power of a given sum of roubles is not constant, but depends on the privileged position of the individual.

These different values for the one sum of money when possessed by different individuals mean that two nominally equal sums received by the government (in the form of taxes or by sale of government bonds) have a different value even for the state (and hence for the community), depending on the greater or lesser privileged class to which the tax-payer or purchaser of bonds belongs, on which depends the larger or smaller quantity of goods which the amounts in question could have been used to acquire.

A practical example of how little importance is attached
to pricing in Soviet Russia is given by Barbara Wootton.[28]
She visited a large home for rescued street children outside
Karkov. Attached to the home were extensive workshops
in which the children made electrical gears. The authorities
told her with pride that, though the actual building had
been given them by OGPU, the institution was otherwise
"entirely self-supporting." As the children worked four
hours in school and four hours in the workshops daily, and
as they were obviously unskilled when they came, this certainly seemed remarkable. Further enquiry elicited, however, that the gears were not produced anywhere else in
Russia, and were sold exclusively to certain state-trusts.
This put the statement that the home was self-supporting
in a different light. Obviously the term had no real meaning (we are quoting Mrs. Wootton), since the planning
authorities could both give the home a monopoly and at
the same time see that the purchasers of its products were
provided with funds to pay what was asked, notwithstanding the high price.

Elsewhere in his book L. E. Hubbard says:

> Since the test of an experiment is how it works, we must try
> to answer this question in relation to the Soviet monetary sys-
> tem. The theory that prices fixed on a basis of production costs
> can serve the same purposes with equal efficiency as prices fixed
> by supply and demand on an open market has been proved a
> fallacy. It also seems that when arbitrary price-fixing interferes
> with a currency's function as a measure of value it also im-
> pairs its utility as a costing unit. The Soviet argument is that
> the value of an article to the community does not necessarily
> agree with its value as determined by the price obtainable under

28 *Plan or No Plan*, p. 91.

open-market conditions. . . . This theory, carried to its logical conclusion, would mean the abolition of money.[29]

The most serious consequence of using prices without meaning and real contents is that there is no basis for calculation.

In a lecture given to the American Economic Association on 28th December, 1935, Alexander Gourvitch voiced his doubts about the accuracy of Russian data for calculation. He described the sharp rise in prices and the cost of living in Soviet Russia and said that investment undertaken without regard to costs had resulted in resources being tied up in incomplete and unprofitable activities.[30]

In the subsequent discussion Michael T. Florinsky had the following to say:

> The question of prices is one of the most important and also one of the darkest in the entire field of communist economics. The few articles dealing with this fundamental subject which have appeared in Soviet periodicals throw practically no light on the actual process of price-making in Soviet-Russia.[31]

Florinsky also said that one of the few discussions of the subject of which he knew was to be found in *Planovoe Khozyaistvo* (Planned Economy) No. 4, 1932. In this number the Soviet economist S. Turetsky points out that even for goods of the same class there is often no connection between production costs and the price. He revealed that with production costs equalling 100, the prices of machinery,

---

[29] *Op. cit.,* pp. 308–309.

[30] *American Economic Review,* 1936, pp. 270–271, 276 and 280 (Suppl.).

[31] *Op. cit.,* p. 289 (Suppl.).

machine-tools and metal goods varied between the wide limits of from 65 to 200.[32]

L. E. Hubbard has this to say:

> The notion is more or less that the price of any article should correspond with its production cost in labour-time. On attempting to put this theory into practice prices have been reduced to a mere formula which lacks reality.[33]
> The difficulties, if not impossibility, of correlating production planning and financial planning when neither plan is definitely subordinate to the other, the only link being provided by arbitrary fixed prices, has been demonstrated.[34]

Nicolaus Basseches, an engineer and the *Neue Freie Presse's* correspondent in Moscow, put the matter in a nutshell:

> It is not to be expected that any considerable improvement will occur in this regard. For the reasons for the rise in self-costs—and this rise will certainly be far higher than what the official figures give—lie in general conditions. First and foremost Soviet industry has no possibility of calculation. . . . There can be no ordered calculation in the Soviet Union.[35]

In this treatise the importance of economic calculation has been stressed. This view is shared by all those who have taken part in the discussion (with the exception of Dr. Weil). The fatal consequences of lack of calculation are explained by L. E. Hubbard:

> . . . accounting is of greater necessity to a Soviet economic enterprise than to a capitalist undertaking. A capitalist entre-

[32] *Ibid.,* p. 289.
[33] *Op. cit.,* p. 166.
[34] *Ibid.,* p. 322.
[35] From "Die Industrie", supplement to *Die Rote Wirtschaft,* p. 95.

preneur can carry on with a bare minimum of bookkeeping, and the state of his bank balance indicates whether he is losing money or making profits. . . .

The manager of a Soviet enterprise may continue an untroubled course of squandering practically indefinitely, unless his activities are subjected to a very searching and thorough periodical scrutiny. And even this will only show whether his enterprise is operating more or less efficiently than others of the same sort.

The fact that a Soviet enterprise is making paper profits or losses is no real criterion of its efficiency or of its utility to the community. For instance an enterprise may consume a quantity of a comparatively scarce raw material, also needed by another enterprise manufacturing something else of greater utility.

The fixed price of the material may be low and the first enterprise may show a paper profit, but the real cost of its products, measured by the quantity of the second commodity which is not produced, will be greater than the nominal production cost.[36]

Waste and irrational use of resources (irrational in relation to the objective) are not the only consequences of there being no real basis for calculation. Real planning becomes difficult or impossible, and, also, there is no basis for control. To quote from *Contemporary Russia* (which set out to throw light on developments in Russia on the basis of documentary reports):

Price control was lax and indifferent, and in any case the multiplicity of price levels hindered effective supervision. Some types of shop even sold the same sorts of goods at different prices.[37]

In W. B. Reddaway's short, but interesting book we find this:

---

[36] *Soviet Trade and Distribution*, London, 1938, p. 323–324.
[37] See Vol. I, No. 1, October, 1936, p. 70.

. . . production has been planned on a somewhat arbitrary basis and without much conscious consideration of the principles of interpreting demand; indeed the Bolshevik planners seem to have very little conception of demand *at a price,* but regard it as something absolute.[38]

If these shortcomings were simply due to failure of the personal element, there would be little more to say on this subject, since this essay is not concerned with elaborate calculations of the degree of success attained in practice; but it is fairly clear that the system itself is at least partly responsible.[39]

A long article by Dolnikov in *Za Industrializaciu* of 19th March, 1933, contains the following:

It is disquieting that factory managers do not seem to be interested in reducing production costs. This unfortunate fact is in no way due to indifference or sabotage, but quite simply to *the system prevailing in the Soviet Union.*[40]

and also this:

the costs of production may be 50 per cent above the decreed selling-prices. . . . The factory managers lose interest in doing their best to reduce the costs of production, since they know beforehand that whatever happens they will lose 80–90 roubles a ton on the goods they produce because of the large difference between production costs and the selling-price fixed by law.[41]

It would be possible to quote many other similar statements confirming the arbitrariness of prices in the Soviet Union and the ensuing impossibility of real economic calculation, but there are other aspects of the problem of cal-

---

[38] *The Russian Financial System,* London, 1935, p. 84.

[39] *Op. cit.,* p. 85.

[40] From *Russland i Sovjetpressens Speil,* quotations collected by Victor Mogens, Oslo, 1933, p. 23.

[41] *Op. cit.,* p. 24.

culation we wish to compare with experiences in Soviet Russia.

We have previously asserted that a socialist society has the means of satisfying its members' urge to save. In Soviet Russia this has only been partially exploited. W. B. Reddaway has this to say:

> Both classes have suffered somewhat from the lack of any reliable means of accumulating a store of value. It is possible for the individuals to save by hoarding cash, or depositing it in savings banks, or by subscribing to the State loan—the last being virtually compulsory. But all these involve exposing his wealth to the vagaries of the rouble, and the State loan is not even readily saleable in case of need nor useable as security for a loan from a bank or pawnshop. As a result the individual generally tries to do his saving, so far as he does any, by purchasing durable consumption goods which he can, if necessary, pawn or sell through the State Commission shop.[42]

and further on:

> . . . it is almost unnecessary to say that private money-lending is a cardinal sin.[43]

There is ample confirmation that interest-rates in a socialist society become arbitrary and unconnected with either savings or investments. Barbara Wootton has had this to say:

> In the absence of any capital market in the Soviet Union, however, the true cost of abstinence cannot be tested out . . . The Planning Commission stint the present for the sake of the future up to the point at which *they* presumably think that the increased future return justified the present sacrifice. . . . In a

---

[42] *Op. cit.*, pp. 69–70.
[43] *Op. cit.*, p. 70.

society whose savings were regulated by the price mechanism
the correctness of this judgment would soon be checked by the
response of the savers to varying stimuli . . . it is quite hope-
less to expect this to be shown in measuring the balance of out-
goings and incomings of any particular enterprise.[44]

W. B. Reddaway tells that there is:

little or no use of the rate of interest, either as a controller
of the volume of saving, and so a judge of the optimum total
amount (a function which it (the State) performs very in-
differently), or as a selector of the most eligible schemes
(which it does better); in the distribution of raw materials,
land and other factors between different industries; and indeed
in the whole system of planning.[45]

Calvin B. Hoover has stated that:

as important economic categories both rent and interest have
disappeared.[46]

Now, this does not mean that interest does not exist.
Soviet Russia, too, has reckoned with interest of a kind, but
the rate is clearly quite arbitrary and takes no account of
fixed principles. According to Wilhelm Keilhau[47] the bank-
rate for a number of loan-operations in 1922 was fixed at
30 per cent per *month*.

Hoover himself says later in his book that *Prombank* (the
bank for long-term industrial loans) takes from 6 to 8 per
cent plus certain additions. He also says that the interest
varies with the profitability of the industry in question

---

[44] *Plan or No Plan,* pp. 98–99.
[45] *Op. cit.,* pp. 71–72.
[46] *The Economic Life of Soviet Russia,* New York, 1931, p. 2.
[47] *Europeiske Pengesystemer,* Oslo, 1930, p. 148.

(whatever is meant by that), but does not explain whether the most profitable industries are regarded as the best credit objects and so given the lowest rates, or whether they are penalized with high rates in order to help less profitable concerns. However, he does tell that the oil and textile industries pay 6 per cent, while the coal and metallurgical industries pay 2 per cent.[48]

What the other writers have had to say is rather contradictory. Arthur Feiler explains that loans are in many cases granted without interest being charged.[49] Against this L. E. Hubbard (1936) says that the interest on all kinds of loans is generally 6 per cent, which perhaps means that Soviet Russia is now trying to revert to greater unity in interest rates.[50] In a later book Hubbard said that "Soviet enterprise pays no interest on borrowed capital, only on a short-term credit."[51]

It will be noticed that there has been no talk of anything but interest on *loans*. Dr. Maurice Dobb who with his Marxist views tries to reduce the significance of interest as an element of cost and factor in calculation (though he makes considerable concessions) tells us that no interest is charged on a concern's original capital. This, too, will obviously entail serious difficulties not only because capital items are not subject to turn-over and market valuation, but also because of the inflation and the fact that at all times there exist different levels of prices. Dr. Dobb says:

---

[48] *Op. cit.,* p. 190.
[49] *Das Experiment des Bolschevismus,* Frankfurt, 1930, p. 116.
[50] *Soviet Money and Finance,* p. 59.
[51] *Soviet Trade and Distribution,* p. 202.

Under the New Economic Policy in Russia the original capital assigned to be industrial trusts carried no interest charge, and accordingly no such charge entered into business accounting.[52]

How uncertain are the socialist economist's views on interest charges appears from the following quotation about S. Strumilin who seems in many ways to have influenced economic development in Soviet Russia. In *Geld, Kredit und Banken*[53] Malcolm Campbell says:

According to Strumilin interest on capital is not to be taken into account, although to do so would also be both possible and perhaps useful in a socialist economy.[54]

Regardless of whether interest is charged or taken into account in Soviet Russia, it is obvious that interest rates are fixed more or less haphazardly, that the imposition of interest charges is arbitrary, and the burden of them considered of subordinate significance as a factor of cost and calculation. In order to throw additional light on the subject it might be mentioned—under reference to what has been said on *lending rates*—that *borrowing* rates lately carried interest of up to 7 percent for government bonds and 10 per cent for saving accounts. (See Appendix B.)

There is little about calculation of rent to be found in accounts of Soviet Russia. What there is tends to show that rent is charged even more seldom and more arbitrarily than

[52] *Russian Economic Development since the Revolution,* London, 1929, 2nd Edn., pp. 174–180.
[53] Supplement to *Die Rote Wirtschaft,* Königsberg, and Berlin, 1932.
[54] *Op. cit.,* p. 119.

interest on capital. Reddaway only mentions the subject *en passant* and rather evasively.[55] Hoover says:

> A limited right of rental of land was permitted with the dual purpose of providing some income for landholders who were unable to cultivate their land and of increasing the harvest of grain by making it possible for the richer peasants to farm more than their own allotment.[56]

It seems improbable that this possibility still exists after the purge of the *Kulaks*. (Hoover's book is based on studies made in 1929–30.)

Hubbard has this to say:

> The State (Soviet Russia) really gets in addition to economic rent a monopoly profit from its power to exploit the peasant. Even so, the similarity to capitalist rent is somewhat artificial.[57]
>
> Thus there appears to be little resemblance even between rent in a Soviet economy and rent as determined in practice in a capitalist economy.[58]

Barbara Wootton came to a similar conclusion:

> The Soviet economy, which recognizes no private ownership of land, and refers in most uncomplimentary terms to the payment of rent, has no similar scale by which to reckon. So far as I can learn, rent has no part, even as a purely accounting item, in the budget of Soviet institutions.[59]
>
> I have never been able to find any evidence that a quantitative monetary comparison of the utility to be derived from its various possible uses influences these allocations.[60]

---

[55] *Op. cit.,* p. 24.
[56] *Op. cit.,* p. 73.
[57] *Op. cit.,* p. 271.
[58] *Ibid.,* p. 272.
[59] *Op. cit.,* p. 71.
[60] *Ibid.,* p. 71.

Failure to take account of ground rents, and thus of differences in composition and suitability of the soil, excludes the possibility of economic calculation and hence full rational use of existing resources. To charge ground and farm rents is, in Soviet Russia, generally considered one of the grossest forms of exploitation; for that reason it is interesting to see that Hubbard ends his chapter "Agricultural Rent" with the following:

> It seems that the introduction of a free-price system must very considerably lessen, if not entirely end, the exploitation of the peasant in favour of the industrial proletariat.[61]

When both prices and interest-rates are fixed arbitrarily there remains no real basis for calculating depreciation. This does not preclude attempts being made. At the end of 1931 a "Price Committee" was set up under the "Council for Labour and Defence" to determine and control price-formation in retail and wholesale trade. Among the factors of calculation mentioned by *Contemporary Russia*[62] as figuring in the standard rules there was depreciation or, in Soviet terminology, "accumulation." (However, this is not necessarily the same as depreciation; it might also mean reserves.)

Professor Hoover tells us that there were regulations for the depreciation of various categories of buildings: the average was 6.5 per cent. In his opinion the rate of total depreciation in Soviet Russia must be considered a reasonable one, when the accumulation of capital (development of the productive apparatus) is taken into consideration.

---

[61] *Op. cit.*, p. 274.
[62] Vol. I, No. I, October, 1936, p. 70.

This is a social view that may appear natural, especially for a socialist society, but Hoover's assertion raises serious problems. Amongst other things one must know the *aim* of the society in question if we are ever to get a yardstick for determining (1) the value of the capital to be depreciated, and (2) the value of the capital goods which are supposed to represent the depreciation quota. It is self-evident that means of production which possibly have no value (if the products are not in demand or have no contribution to make towards the end to be achieved) can *not* be reckoned as depreciation quota. Also, the mere setting up of an end to be achieved does not automatically provide a yardstick for valuation that can be used in practice.

This question of depreciation is discussed in but few of the economic works on Soviet Russia. Barbara Wootton and Reddaway have not touched on it, as far as can be seen, and L. E. Hubbard dismisses it with the following sentence:

> It is true that every enterprise is supposed to set aside from its revenue each year a certain sum for amortization, but this, as far as is known, has no direct connection with the original construction costs.[63]

Dr. Dobb's book stands alone in that he has discussed the question with considerable thoroughness from the theoretical aspect. He has besides provided valuable practical illustrations. When it comes to the question of calculating with amortization quotas, Dr. Dobb is admitting more than when he was discussing interest. He says:

---

[63] *Op. cit.*, p. 316.

> Ordinary wear and tear of plant and buildings is, of course, an ordinary cost, like the use of stocks of raw materials, to be covered by assignments to a depreciation fund and included in commodity prices.[64]

To justify this charge Dr. Dobb adds:

> In a socialist society that problem becomes solely a technical question of accounting, to be settled according to accounting convenience, and no more. The charging of interest on capital here loses its wider class significance as a payment to a rentier class without the rendering of any equivalent effort-service in return.[65]

Perhaps it was necessary to add this characteristic sentence for Marxists, but from the point of view of accounting theory it is unnecessary and irrelevant. If amortization is an *"ordinary cost,"* then whether one reckons with an amortization quota or omits to do so, is *not* "solely a technical question".

Dr. Dobb gives many examples of the use of amortization charges in Soviet Russia.[66] They give the impression that the theoretical conception and the practical use of amortization quotas have both been uncertain and unstable.

R. L. Hall also has little to say about amortization in Soviet Russia, but his discussion of the theory throws considerable light on the problem, especially when it is remembered that Hall believes in the possibility of economic calculation in the socialist society.

After saying that "estimates" have been obtained for labour and capital, Hall continues:

---

[64] *Op. cit.,* p. 175, footnote.
[65] *Ibid.,* p. 175.
[66] *Ibid.,* pp. 293–294.

A further guess must be made at the annual depreciation of the plant, and we have finally the net earnings, which are the quasi-rent of the plant. Capitalizing these at the assumed rate of interest, we have an estimate of the value of the fixed capital, erroneous to an unknown extent owing to the various guesses which have been made.[67]

Many people seem to believe that it is irrelevant to discuss *profit* as a factor in calculation when dealing with a socialist society. Profit is nevertheless a well-known calculation factor in Soviet Russia. Arthur Feiler says:

A normal profit-and-loss account, as in private undertakings, is also prescribed.[68]

The Price Committee which was abolished by the Council for Labour and Defence in 1931 (see p. 364) laid it down in its basic regulations that retail shops should calculate to make a profit. It is, indeed, very natural that the question of profit and loss should come up whatever the nature of the undertaking, and it is also discussed in most economic works on Soviet Russia.

That profit does not seem to have any *real* significance in Soviet Russia is a different matter. As a risk-factor it has disappeared, since economic activity is based on quite different motives (*what* they are is usually very difficult to discover). That a concern works with a deficit is not in itself a reason for curtailing or giving up activities, if its continuation is otherwise considered feasible.

Nor is profit (or the maximalizing of profit) in any way a criterion by which efficiency of the managers can be judged. Stalin's recommendation (see p. 349) shows how

---

[67] *Op. cit.,* p. 91.
[68] *Op. cit.,* p. 116.

much more important political colour and sympathy have been. His recommendation may have been due to political considerations, but also to the fact that profit is a quite unreliable measure of a manager's capabilities, when price and costs are fixed arbitrarily as in Soviet Russia.

Many of the attempts to solve the problem of calculation are based, as has already been shown, on the assumption that consumers' preferences, and thus production, can be determined in the socialist society from statistics supplied by the retailers, or what amounts to the same thing, from information on which goods are in demand, and which not. We had various objections against these proposals, one of which was that such data would only be reliable under conditions which it would be highly unrealistic to assume existing in a socialist society.

An investigation of conditions in Soviet Russia shows that the prerequisites for useable data have not existed in that country. In telling of what actually had taken place, Reddaway says:

> there is no automatic device to secure the application of this test, and the shortage of goods has tended to stultify it. For if more of one commodity is being produced than is economically desirable the manager of the commercial shops will not insist on reducing their purchases of it simply because they cannot make such a big profit on selling it as they do on other things—they will be too afraid of not getting an adequate substitute: whilst it is a decidedly cumbrous process to secure an increased amount of an article which is in particularly short supply. In the absence of a system whereby relative over-production was made painfully obvious—e.g. by the appearance of a loss in the accounts of the producing organization—it is probable that decisions on what to produce will continue to be made somewhat at hap-hazard.[69]

---

[69] *Op. cit.,* pp. 85–86.

Contemporary Russia says:

> The ration system itself had a deteriorating effect on retail trade. The closed shops became little more than issue depots; the shop managers and assistants had little incentive to study the desires of their customers since all they had to do was mechanically to hand out the quantities of bread, sugar, tea, etc., marked on the ration books. And, since the workers could only buy at the shops to which they were attached there was no question of competing for their customers.[70]

And Hubbard has this to say:

> every consumer, individual or enterprise, made a point of buying up to the last unit of the goods they were entitled to purchase at the fixed prices because these prices were lower than the natural market price. . . . Under open-market conditions prices would have afforded a much more sensitive as well as earlier sign of over-planning. Added to this was the fact that the various price systems impaired the reality of cost accounting and caused all sections of the community, including enterprise administrators, to lose confidence in and respect for the currency.[71]

In his other book Hubbard gives another example of how the fact of there being a superfluity or scarcity of consumer goods is by no means necessarily an indication for production. He says:

> The practical importance of these turnover periods is that no trading organization should at any time hold larger stocks of any goods than can be sold during the turnover period.[72]

When the goods in theory and according to the plan are

---

[70] Vol. I, No. 1, October, 1936.
[71] *Soviet Money and Finance,* p. 318.
[72] *Soviet Trade and Distribution,* p. 131.

to be sold out during the turnover period, which is the ideal generally aimed at, it is self-evident that there can be no statistics of remaining stocks to serve as basis.

In reality the fact that shops in Soviet Russia were sold out did not only mean that sales had gone according to the plan, but that there was actual scarcity. To quote Hubbard again:

> . . . during the last quarter of the year an inspection of 260 shops in the Province of Voronezh disclosed that 69 shops were bare of sugar, in 49 there was no confectionery, in 36 no salt, in 26 no cigarettes.[73]

M. Yvon, a French communist who worked for eleven years in different places in Soviet Russia has confirmed that it was not only difficult to get the goods, quantities, and sizes one wanted, but difficult to get goods at all. The result was that people took what they could get in the hope of being able to swap it later for something they did want.[74]

The existence of this state of affairs is confirmed by Barbara Wootton. She writes:

> . . . one constantly hears it said by those who have lived in the Soviet Union that any Russian who has more than the lowest pay may be quite at a loss to know on what to spend his money. Thanks to the rationing system and the practice of fixing prices at lower levels than serve exactly to match demand to supplies, the goods run out before the money to buy them is exhausted. Consequently demand may be oddly distorted into certain channels which represent, not the true preference of consumers over the whole field of possible consumption, but their reaction to a situation in which a large part of their con-

---

[73] *Op. cit.,* p. 203. The author refers his reader to *Financial Programme for the U.S.S.R. for* 1937, p. 18.

[74] *Ce qu'est devenue la Révolution Russe,* Paris (no date), pp. 16–18.

sumption is decided for them by authority, and in which, for the rest, they have to buy, not what they want, but what there is.[75]

Under such conditions it is self-evident that statistics of sales are valueless, giving no indication of the consumers' preferences, nor of what should be produced to meet their demand. The discussion of the degree in which price-formation and competition must be free before turnover figures can be of any practical use, will not be repeated here.

The supposition that the socialist society will also have need of middlemen, is borne out by experience in Soviet Russia. *Vide* Stalin's recommendation (quoted on p. 349) that wholesale depôts should be established to avoid uneconomic sending of small quantities over large distances. Also lack of rolling stock and deficiencies in the organization of transport led to the establishment of a kind of middleman called "pusher," whose job was to push forward deliveries.[76]

Stalin's order dividing activities among smaller units is, however, not merely an admission that the middleman has a logical place in a rational economic system, but also that it is difficult to control large concerns. It was, too, a symptom of the reaction against the *gigantomania* that had obtained such a hold on Soviet Russia.

It would take us too far from our subject to do more than touch on the question of how far variations in the trade cycle are eliminated in Soviet Russia. It can be said that the volume of production is a very uncertain criterion for judging variations in the trade cycle in a socialist society,

---

[75] *Op. cit.,* pp. 93–94.
[76] *Russland i Sovjetpressens speil,* p. 49.

since it can be determined arbitrarily by the planners according to non-economic considerations. (This can, of course, be considered an advantage in the system, but that would be to bring up the question of whether we are dealing with a society of plenty or of scarcity, and, if the latter, what is the aim of its activity.)

As far as Soviet Russia is concerned the question appears in a special light, since its production apparatus was but slightly developed, a fact to which Barbara Wootton also draws attention. When the Russian revolution was over, there was a shortage of factories of practically every kind. Under such conditions there is no risk of "exaggerated and unco-ordinated" expansion of the productive apparatus. It is the adjustment after such exaggerated or unco-ordinated activity that in a capitalist society brings the depressions. It must be considered highly probable that Soviet Russia will be faced with similar problems when the rate of expansion eventually comes to be reduced. In any event, it will be necessary to have adjustment in the form of transference of labour to different employment.

Hubbard has the following to say on this point:

> If an economic crisis be defined as an unpredicted disturbance in the orderly development of production and consumption, resulting either in a shortage of goods or a shortage of effective demand—that is, in the phenomena usually termed underproduction or overproduction—then the economic history of the Soviet Union, since planning superseded the relatively free market of N.E.P., has been a succession of crises, for at practically no period during that time has there not been a shortage of something, in 1932, for instance, a real shortage of food of all sorts, in latter years shortages of boots, sewing thread, matches, etc. If planning is immune from some of the

defects of capitalism, it seems to possess peculiar faults of its own.[77]

It is often claimed that unemployment has been eliminated in Soviet Russia. That is not the case. In Brutzkus' book[78] there is a section "The Problem of Unemployment" in which he refers *inter alia* to countless hordes who besiege Soviet-Russian railway stations and who are continually moving from one place to another. Later, it is explained that even in periods when manpower was in great demand, it was not possible to make use of this enormous mass of "raw workers." Also, it should be noted that the unemployment statistics pre-eminently refer to towns. Brutzkus draws attention to the paradoxical phenomenon that in the towns where the possibilities of finding work are least, there is the least unemployment, since people leave the towns and go into the country where they have a slightly better chance of making a subsistence. Brutzkus also says the object of the passport law was to keep the peasants from the towns. "It was much more convenient to let them starve in the country.[79]

These pass regulations were introduced by the Soviet Government on 27th December, 1932, and it is stated that as a result 800,000 people were discovered in Moscow who had no right to a pass and so had to take to the broad highway. As those who had work received a pass, this should mean that in reality there were 800,000 unemployed in Moscow alone, which is in crass contradiction with the as-

---

[77] *Soviet Trade and Distribution,* pp. 344–345.
[78] *Ibid.,* pp. 222–226.
[79] *Op. cit.,* p. 225.

surances that there is no unemployment in Soviet Russia.[80]

Before passing judgment one must also take into consideration the fact that it is obviously easier to have people employed when they can be forced to accept wages as low as the employer cares to give. That forced labour and "compulsory enrolment" of workers exist to a greater or lesser extent in Soviet Russia is apparent from most accounts of conditions there. Such compulsion does not necessarily involve military compulsion. When a state is the one and only employer it has all the economic powers of compulsion it requires.

Hubbard throws considerable light on this problem of unemployment and forced labour in Russia:

> A large proportion of the forced labour, employed in the undertakings referred to above, consists of peasants deported to the labour camps. It is believed that the total number of convicts and other forced labour is probably some four to five millions, though naturally no official figures are ever published. In any case, the peasants were presumably rendered superfluous to the needs of agricultural labour by the introduction of machinery and the rationalization accompanying the amalgamation of peasant holdings into collective farms. . . .[81]
>
> A large amount of free labour also is employed at a remuneration that cannot be regarded by any standard as a satisfactory wage.[82]
>
> There is no unemployment relief and the Trade Unions do nothing towards securing a decent minimum living wage nor to prevent the dilution of labour. . . . This is exactly the same state of affairs as prevailed in Great Britain at the beginning of the industrial revolution. It is evident that in the Soviet Union either a large proportion of the Workers are terribly exploited,

---

[80] See *Russland i Sovjetpressens speil*, p. 52.
[81] *Soviet Trade and Distribution*, p. 328.
[82] *Op. cit.*, p. 329.

or that the work they perform is so sterile that their output does not yield a living wage.[83]

Hubbard also has much of interest to say about the problems of unemployment and the trade cycle in Soviet Russia. In his first book he says, *inter alia,* that unemployment is not a condition likely to occur in a community in which there is a general shortage of commodities. He also points out that Russia is a country where climatic conditions cause wide variations from year to year in the crops of food-stuffs and raw products. A bad harvest will not affect the agricultural population alone, but also reduce the demand for industrial goods. Hubbard suggests that the same causes would have much the same effects even where output of consumers' goods is supposed to correspond exactly with the demand. As a matter of fact, the reaction of the harvest on industry should be even greater than before the war, since a much larger proportion of the raw materials for industry is now produced internally instead of being imported.

> The more self-sufficient a country the more national consumption depends on national production, and if for any reason production permanently or temporarily declines, consumption must be reduced.[84]

Hubbard ends his examination of the subject from which we have quoted only very briefly, by saying:

> In such circumstances if planning is to prevent unemployment, or more accurately prevent conditions arising which in a

---

[83] *Ibid.,* p. 331.
[84] *Op. cit.,* pp. 281–282.

capitalist system would result in unemployment, it will need to be carried out with almost superhuman prescience; in fact, with a perfection that human organization can scarcely attain. Of course, absolute unemployment can always be avoided by employing surplus labour at a loss on the principle of relief works in capitalist countries. But to substantiate the claim that planning can overcome unemployment it must be shown that it is capable permanently of finding remunerative employment for the whole body of workers.[85]

This statement is of theoretical interest and has also general validity, i.e. it applies to non-socialist societies as well.

This brings us to the end of our comparison between deduced conclusions and the experience of Soviet Russia.

We have done little more than touched on the human factor, which many will consider as the most important of all. There is, however, little evidence that regard for the human factor has ever influenced the Soviet Government's plans; and so, strictly speaking, we are not justified in judging the result of economic activity in Soviet Russia by the degree to which the needs of the consumers have been satisfied.

To start taking the human factor into account would mean concentrating on aspects that lie outside the scope of this book. We would have to ask the numbers of those who have been "liquidated" and who have died of starvation and under-nourishment. Not only that, but also the psychological results of spying, informing, forced labour, concentration camps, and other deprivations of liberty. Such things cannot be measured quantitatively, but there is available a fairly comprehensive literature on this aspect written by

---

[85] *Op. cit.*, p. 283.

Russians and foreign socialists, or, rather, *quondam* socialists, and communists.[86]

"If the first duty of a government is to provide its population with food, leisure and clothes," says Professor Rougier,[87] "then the Soviet Government has defaulted on that three-fold duty." This statement given after a trip to Russia in September, 1932, has since been corroborated by M. Dorgelès, correspondent of *L'Intransigeant,* in January, 1937. Professor Rougier sums up Moscow in the one word "misery" ("La misére").[88]

One objection frequently made is that you cannot compare conditions in Soviet Russia with the countries of Western Europe, because Soviet Russia has remained such a long way behind. Professor Rougier in answering this, made a very interesting suggestion.

He pointed out that the division of Russia which took place after the Great War really provides unique data for a comparison between the respective merits and demerits of the capitalist and socialist systems. On the conclusion of peace large portions of Russia were transferred to Finland, the Baltic States, Poland and Roumania. Professor Rou-

---

[86] Professor Rougier's *Peut-on savior la Verité sur l'Expérience Sovié-tique?* already mentioned, provides a good general picture and names most of the books that have been published in French and English. Professor Pierre Pascal who was in Russia as a member of the Bolshevik Party from 1917 to 1939, and then Professor of Russia at Lille University, says in an introduction to M. Yvon's book that those one can most safely believe are the foreign communists who have earned their living in Soviet Russia for several years. They do not much like talking about it, says Professor Pascal, but when they do, it is astounding how their accounts agree.

[87] *Op. cit.,* p. 42.

[88] *Op. cit.,* p. 42.

gier's suggestion was that an impartial committee should be set up to examine conditions in the districts lying 20 kilometres to the west of the Soviet-Russian frontier and 20 kilometres to the east of it. This would enable one to see what differences, if any, developments had brought to the different groups of people who twenty-five years earlier had lived under like conditions.

There is one other point relating to the human factor that might have been discussed in more detail, and that is the rise of bureaucracy in Soviet Russia. Even economists like Dr. Lange, who otherwise have no great objection to the socialist society, are anxious on this point and of the opinion that bureaucracy is a danger to Soviet Russia and socialist societies generally.

In giving vent to such fears the word "bureaucracy" must be used in its pejorative meaning, for the introduction of socialism necessarily involves setting up a large bureaucracy. That is an inevitable consequence when concerns formerly run by private enterprise are to be managed by officials. In other words it follows from the definition that a socialist society will require an enormous bureaucratic apparatus.

The fear that a socialist community can easily get a bureaucracy also in the pejorative meaning of the word, seems to be borne out by what has happened in Soviet Russia. Arthur Feiler adduces as one reason for this, the fact that the severe punishments meted out in countries where there is a dictatorship, make people inclined to shift responsibility on to others.[89] This leads to more and more officials being employed and to work being unconscion-

---

[89] *Op. cit.*, p. 104.

ably delayed. As an example he mentions that during a reorganization of the Russian Finance Commissarist (R.D.F.S.R.), further dividing responsibility, it appeared that the number of officials[90] could be reduced by over half, from 43,000 to 19,000.

Hubbard has this to say on the subject:

> A serious drawback to State bureaucratic administration is that officialdom as a whole always plays for safety. This is peculiarly the case in Soviet Russia, where the results of errors of initiative are apt to be gravely unpleasant.[91]

Hoover speaks of a factor that is not a direct outcome of bureaucracy, but which is due to the state ownership in the socialist community. He tells us that a huge proportion of a manager's time goes on Party work and that much of his energy is expended on endless committee meetings.

> The drain on the energy of the executive personnel and the tendency to consider talk a substitute for work, which is occasioned by these meetings, is a serious handicap on Soviet Industry.[92]

Just as there are disharmony-economists who consider it wrong to discuss the market-economy without adducing its defects, so there are socialists who consider it wrong to discuss Soviet Russia without mentioning the alleged advantages of its Five-year Plans.

Now, such production plans give little material on which to judge the problem we are discussing: the possibility of

---

[90] *Ibid.,* p. 105.
[91] *Soviet Trade and Distribution,* p. 106.
[92] *Op. cit.,* pp. 6–7.

economic calculation. It has never been denied that a society with sufficient resources can undertake a technical expansion, especially when other societies give it the advantage of their experience and experts. The question is
whether a socialist community can calculate *economically,*
so that its resources find the best and most rational use.
Here we again come up against the question of the aim of
its economic activity.

It can be claimed that this aim is clear as regards the
Five-year Plans in Soviet Russia, namely to achieve a certain industrial expansion. However, there is one fundamental distinction between the setting up of such an aim
in a socialist as opposed to a private capitalist society. In
the capitalist society the major part of activity will automatically be directed to satisfy the effective demand of the
population, as that is the way in which most members of
the community earn their daily bread. But when a socialist
society, where by definition the central authority is the one
and only employer and entrepreneur, sets up such a single
aim as technical expansion, there may be a risk that other
aims, such as satisfying the demand of the people will be
neglected. Acceptance of a single aim in a socialist society
means that the central authority can, if it likes, depress the
standard of living down to, or even below, the minimum
for physical existence. Logically speaking, however, no objection can be advanced against accepting such a single aim,
so from a theoretical point of view there is still good reason
to discuss the results of the Five-year Plans.

On paper the first Five-year Plan was a success. According to the report of Gosplan industrial production was to
have been increased by 133.3 per cent in the course of five

years. 93.7 per cent of this increase was achieved,[93] and that within a shorter period than envisaged, namely four and a half years.

This report, however, has one important flaw. The figures on which it is based are figures of value. This simply means that no importance can be attached to them at all, since prices in Soviet Russia are fixed quite arbitrarily.

> No reliance can be placed upon these figures, which are based on prices; such calculations belong to the sphere of that 'statistical demagogy' which is a feature of all reports issued in Soviet Russia under the Five-year Plan. The authorities want to show for the benefit of foreign countries, the successes achieved by the planned economy; and it is possible to prove anything by manipulating prices in an economy in which there is no ordered currency and no regular market business.[94]

The inflationary rise in prices that took place during that period is in itself sufficient to make all calculation based on results measured in money quite unreliable. It was a standing joke in Soviet Russia during the Five-year Plan that the activity which had increased most and exceeded all expectations was that of the printing presses. The Plan had aimed at a maximum in circulation of R.3,200 million, but the actual figure was R.6,800 million.[95]

Thus if we are to be able to judge the success of the Five-year Plan we must disregard statistics, based on prices, and confine ourselves to the volume of production. Not even the figures given for quantities can be relied on, for as

---

[93] Brutzkus, *op. cit.*, p. 199.
[94] *Ibid.*, pp. 199–200.
[95] Hubbard: *Soviet Money and Finance*, pp. 303–304.

Brutzkus says[96] at that time Soviet-Russian statistics were
becoming more and more unreliable. The Institute for
Economic Research had been closed, and later, in 1930,
Gosplan and the Central Statistical Administration were
"purged" of non-party experts. As a result, most of the
economic periodicals ceased publication, while those that
continued were filled with attacks against "saboteurs," etc.
The statisticians had received their orders and were now to
"play a practical part in Communism's fight against capitalism."[97] While the Five-year Plan had originally been
worked out by the best brains Soviet Russia had at the time,
these same people were now forbidden to express their views.
However, it must be said that the Russian papers showed
considerable liberality in the space they gave to complaints
about the results of the Five-year Plan. It was even permissible to criticize the statistics. For example, *Isvestia* on 1st
March, 1930, disclosed that the actual figures for crops in
certain districts were 40 per cent lower than the official
ones.[98]

There is also another reservation to be made: a percentual
rise in the total production does not tell much about the
fulfilment of a plan, even if you are reckoning in quantities.
A plan that aims at doubling the production of two commodities, is not fulfilled merely because the average increase is 100 per cent, if the production of one has increased
by 20 per cent and that of the other by 180 per cent. To
exceed the increase aimed at is just as contrary to the plan
as *failure* to achieve it. To produce in excess of what is

[96] *Op. cit.,* p. 24.
[97] *Op. cit.,* p. 134. Hubbard says the same.
[98] Rougier: *Op. cit.,* p. 34.

planned means that transport, warehouse-space, etc., are taken up to the detriment of other uses planned.

Even though the first Five-year Plan was not wholly accomplished, the rise in production was enormous. To give an exact valuation, however, many factors have to be considered. If production in the basic year was exceptionally small, a percentual rise says correspondingly little. What is really required is a knowledge of the country's existing resources and possibilities, and to know how far they were exploited both in the basic and in the final year. Brutzkus says:

> We must remember that Russia is still a young country, industrially. In such a country, assuming favourable trading conditions, industrial development can proceed at a much more rapid pace than in a country which has long been industrialized.[99]

As far as the speed of development is concerned, we may mention that the rise in production for the three years 1910–1913, that is when Russia was still under the Tsar, was nearly as large as under the Five-year Plan: 45 per cent for coal (from 25 to 36 million tons), 57 per cent for pig iron (from 3.1 to 4.8 million tons), and 51 per cent for copper (from 22.3 to 33.8 thousand tons).[100]

Then we must remember that the figures on which the statistics are based refer to the places where production took place, not to where the products were received. In a capitalist society the two sets of figures ordinarily coincide. It

---

[99] *Op. cit.,* p. 203.
[100] *Ibid.,* p. 203, where the sources are given. The figures relate to Russia's former territory.

appears that this is not necessarily the case in Soviet Russia. The explanation lies in transport condition. Complaints about the deficiencies of transport in Soviet Russia are legion. To give one example, in 1930, a year when there was a bumper harvest, of the total 22.2 million tons some 5.5 million, that is circa 25 per cent, failed to reach the railway stations, having been either spoilt, stolen, or just never arrived.[101]

These in themselves serious objections to the alleged success of the Five-year Plan become minor ones when we come to consider the quality of the goods produced. The Soviet Press is literally swamped with complaints about the poor quality of industrial products and the large quantities of commodities destroyed.[102] The figures given are such that one would consider them incredible, had they not been reproduced in the Soviet Press. "The percentage of substandard goods is enormous," says *Light Industries* of 4th June, 1933, ". . . in the stocking industry the wastage is 37–50 per cent." And in the issue of 23rd June, 1933: "The industrial trusts and factories give such extraordinary figures (of wastage) as 80–90 per cent.[103]

A report from the People's Commissariat dated 28th July, 1933, draws attention to the fact that several quarters had sent in reports about agricultural machinery being delivered without motors, magnetos, and other essential parts.[104] In his *Soviet Trade and Distribution* Hubbard says the People's Commissar of Agriculture had admitted that

---

[101] *Op. cit.,* p. 147. Taken from *Sovietsk ya toyovlya,* No. 55, 1931, p. 12.
[102] *Ibid.,* p. 205.
[103] *Ibid.,* p. 205.
[104] *Russland i Sovjetpressens speil,* p. 28.

the productive employment of tractors was no more than between 40 and 50 per cent of their technical capacity.[105]

One more example, which shows how the system of fixed selling prices can make it more advantageous to produce poor quality goods, than those of the best quality. In his article in *Za industrializaciu* of 17th March, 1933,[106] Dolnikov says:

> They (metallurgical factories) can often sell to outsiders, e.g. building firms, coal trusts, etc., second quality rails at a higher price than they receive for fixed high quality rails from the People's Commissar for Traffic.
>
> Thus certain workshops and even entire factories often find it in their interests to produce poor-quality rejects or goods below the contract standard. They get a specific premium for their inferior work or the poor quality goods they purposefully produce.
>
> In 'Serp i Molot' rejected scrap-iron sells at twice the price of mill-iron. Thus it is in the interests of the factories to produce scrap-iron or to sell mill-iron as scrap.
>
> The 'Zlotoust' Factory sells second- and third-class products at a very high price to smaller factories, artisans and combines, which pay cash for it. It happens that first-class goods are sold as second-class, and such transactions are on a very large scale.

Considering that the figures for the value of production are useless for judging the Five-year Plan (since prices are fixed arbitrarily), that both the percentual and the absolute increase in the quantitive figures depend on the extent of production in the basic year, that in most cases the target quantities were far from being reached, and that the quality of the products supplied was very low, there is little reason to claim either that the Five-year Plan was accom-

---

[105] *Soviet Trade and Distribution*, p. 328.
[106] *Russland i Sovjetpressens speil*, p. 25.

plished, or that it was in any way a triumph for "the system."[107]

That quality did not improve during the second Five-year Plan is shown by the following quotations. There are many more available:

> *Pravda,* 8th August, 1936, reports that of 9,992 motor cars examined, 1,958 proved to be defective.
> *Pravda,* 23rd September, 1936, reports that of 2,345 chairs 1,300 were unusable.
> *Pravda,* 18th November, 1936, reports the main factory for gramophone records in Nojevik should, according to the plan, have supplied four million records during 1935. It delivered 1,992,000, of which 309,800 could not be used. There was an increase in the number of scrapped gramophone records during 1936: 156,200 in the first quarter; 259,400 in the second quarter; 614,000 in the third quarter; and in the month of October itself 607,000.
> In *Pravda,* of 23rd September, 1936, Professor Bourdenko complains of the bad quality of surgical instruments.
> *Pravda,* of 4th November, 1936, reports that 99 per cent of the copybooks produced by the factory "Labour's Heroes" were unusable.
> *Isvestia,* of 12th December, 1936, reports that eight million copybooks had to be scrapped in Rostov.[108]

An article by the New Commissar for Domestic Trade, Smirnov, that appeared in *Pravda,* during December,

---

[107] It is quite a different matter that the rapid expansion of the apparatus of production achieved by the Five-year Plans has aroused enthusiasm both in Soviet Russia and among socialists all over the world, at any rate during the first Five-year Plan, and that this enthusiasm has had great advertising value. Whether the outlay has been worth the advertisement is a matter on which we shall not attempt to express an opinion.

[108] These quotations are taken from Andrè Gide's book: *Retouches à mon Retour de 'U.S.R.R.,* Paris, 1937.

1937,[109] provides a certain picture of the second Five-year Plan and particularly of the course developments were tending to take. According to him the Soviet Government intended in 1938, that is the first year of Stalin's third Five-year Plan, "to make great changes in all spheres." The Bureaucracy was to be done away with and the Soviets were to go over to "the same trading principles as are employed in capitalist countries."

Trade, says Smirnov, 'remains the problem child of Russia's people's economy'. The Commissariat for Domestic Trade and the entire trading apparatus had hitherto been a complicated bureaucratic machine that had merely interfered with and hampered the expansion of trade. 'Trotskyist spies and noxious vermin' had been everywhere at work deliberately undermining the trade of Soviet Russia. Industry had produced goods that the consumers neither liked, nor wanted. In many districts there were far too many goods, which it was impossible to get rid of, while elsewhere there was nothing to be had. . . .

For example, furniture was sent from Moscow and Minsk to Krasnojarsk, where there was a surfeit of timber and wooden commodities, while Moscow and Minsk lacked timber for furniture factories. In many places goods to the value of millions of roubles rotted, while elsewhere the same goods were not to be had for love or money. . . .

Hitherto Soviet trade had not functioned with the suppleness that is absolutely essential in the world of trade, and customers were often frightened from buying by the brutal impoliteness of the shop-assistants. . . .

Before the simplest matter could be arranged the papers had to pass through ten different persons' hands. . . .

Customers had been given short weight and measure in shops. The foodstuffs supplied for the canteens in factories, schools, etc. had often been rotten, and there had been many cases of food-poisoning, especially in the Donetz area. . . .

---

[109] Quoted from *Dagens Nyheter,* 9th January, 1938.

In the course of the next few months thousands of smaller shops were to be opened all over the land, in which trade would be done on the new principles.

Competition in a socialist society can be no more than a pseudo-competition, but the fact that Commissar Smirnov wanted to return to the principles of price and competition which are found in capitalist societies, is interesting for our investigation.

There are many signs that this is the direction the Soviet Government wants to take. Hubbard has told us that when rationing was abolished and people allowed to buy in whatever shop they liked, the Government exhorted the managers of shops to compete with each other, if not in price, then in service, quality, cleanliness of the shop, etc.

> The form of competition was in fact specifically recommended by government spokesmen and in the newspapers. It is possible that when the idea of competition on these lines has been assimilated, some latitude will be allowed in the matter of price.[110]

and he also says that

> it would be surprising if the open-market principle was not in due course extended to wholesale trade.[111]

On monetary development Hubbard has this to say:

> The path travelled by the rouble since the beginning of 1935 has shown a remarkable convergence towards orthodox capitalist principles. Even as politically the Soviet Government is visibly tending to become more democratic as the younger

---

[110] *Soviet Money and Finance*, p. 326.
[111] *Op. cit.*, p. 322.

dictatorships become more despotic, so Soviet economic theory may soon be considered reactionary by the advanced advocates of social credit schemes and the manipulation of credit in Western countries.[112]

We began this treatise by saying that the present tendency in most countries is in the direction of socialism, controlled prices and restrictions on competition. This statement requires to be modified. We must conclude by saying that this tendency exists in all countries, except the one wherein socialism has been tried, Soviet Russia.

---

[112] *Ibid.,* p. 330.

Bibliography

I

Books and treatises exclusively or mainly concerned with economic calculation in the socialist society.

BARONE, ENRICO: "The Ministry of Production in the Collectivist State" in *Collectivist Economic Planning,* London, 1935.

BRUTZKUS, BORIS: "The Doctrines of Marxism in the Light of the Russian Revolution" in the first part of *Economic Planning in Soviet Russia,* London, 1935.

DICKINSON, H. D.: "Price Formation in a Socialist Community" in *Economic Journal,* June, 1933.

DOBB, MAURICE: "Economic Theory and the Problem of a Socialist Economy" in *Economic Journal,* December, 1933.

———— "Economic Theory and Social Economy. A Reply," in *Review of Economic Studies,* 1934–35.

DURBIN, E. F. M.: "Economic Calculus in a Planned Economy" in *Economic Journal,* December, 1936.

———— "A Note on Mr. Lerner's 'Dynamical' Propositions" in *Economic Journal,* September, 1937.

FRASER, T. H.: "The Price Mechanism under Capitalism and under Communism" in *Al Quanoun Wal Iqtisad,* No. 6, November, 1935, Cairo.

GOURVITCH, ALEXANDER: "The Problem of Prices and Valuation in the Soviet System" in *American Economic Review,* 1936, suppl.

HALL, R. L.: *The Economic System in a Socialist State,* London, 1937.

HALM, G.: "Ist der Sozialismus wirtschaftlich möglich?" in *Wirtschaftsprobleme der Gengewart,* Berlin, 1922.

—————— "Further Consideration on the Possibility of Adequate Calculation in a Socialist Community" in *Collectivist Economic Planning,* London, 1935.

HAYEK, F. A.: "The Nature and History of the Problem" in *Collectivist Economic Planning,* London, 1935.

—————— "The Present State of the Debate" in *Collectivist Economic Planning,* London, 1935.

KALDOR, N.: Review of Carl Landauer's *Planwirtschaft und Verkehrwirtschaft,* in *Economic Journal,* June, 1932.

KERSCHAGL, R.: "Die Möglichkeit einer Wirtschaftsrechnung in der sozialistischen Planwirtschaft" in *Ständisches Leben,* Vol. 2, 1932.

KNIGHT, F. H.: "The Place of Marginal Economics in a Collectivist System" in *American Economic Review,* 1936, suppl.

LANGE, OSKAR: "On the Economic Theory of Socialism, I" in *Review of Economic Studies,* Vol. IV, No. 1, October, 1936.

—————— "On the Economic Theory of Socialism, II" in *Review of Economic Studies,* Vol. IV, No. 2, February, 1937.

LEICHTER, OTTO: *Die Wirtschaftsrechnung in der sozialistischen Gesellschaft,* Vienna, 1923.

LERNER, A. P.: "Economic Theory and Socialist Economy" in *Review of Economic Studies,* 1934–35.

———— "A Rejoinder to Mr. Dobb" in *Review of Economic Studies,* 1934–35.

———— "A Note on Socialist Economics" in *Review of Economic Studies,* No. 1, October, 1936.

———— "Statics and Dynamics in Socialist Economics" in *Economic Journal,* June, 1937.

LIPPINCOTT, BENJAMIN E.: *On the Economic Theory of Socialism,* Minneapolis, Minnesota, 1938.

MARSCHAK, J.: "Wirtschaftsrechnung und Gemeinwirtschaft. Zur Mises'schen These von der Unmöglichkeit sozialistischer Wirtschaftsrechnung" in *Archiv für Sozialwissenschaft und Sozialpolitik,* Vol. 51, 1923/24.

MISES, LUDWIG VON: "Die Wirtschaftsrechnung im sozialistischen Gemeinwesen" in *Archiv für Sozialwissenschaft und Sozialpolitik,* Vol. 47, 1920.

———— "Neue Beiträge zum Problem der sozialistischen Wirtschaftsrechnung" in *Archiv für Sozialwissenschaft und Sozialpolitik,* Vol. 51, 1923/24.

———— "Neue Schriften zum Problem der sozialistischen Wirtschaftsrechnung" in *Archiv für Sozialwissenschaft und Sozialpolitik,* Vol. 60, 1928.

———— "Economic Calculation in the Socialist Commonwealth" in *Collectivist Economic Planning,* London, 1935.

NEURATH, OTTO: "Geld und Sozialismus" in *Kampf,* XVI. Jahrg. Heft. 4/5.

PIERSON, N. G.: "The Problem of Value in the Socialist

Society" in *Collectivist Economic Planning,* London, 1935.

POLANYI, KARL: "Sozialistische Rechnungslegung" in *Archiv für Sozialwissenschaft und Sozialpolitik,* Vol. 49, 1922.

———— "Die funktionelle Theorie der Gesellschaft und das Problem der sozialistischen Rechnungslegung. (Eine Erwiderung an Prof. Mises und dr. Felix Weil)" in *Archiv für Sozialwissenschaft und Sozialpolitik,* Vol. 52, 1924.

RHIJN, A. A. VAN: "De economische Calculatie in het Socialism" in *De Economist,* s'Gravenhage, 1932.

ROPER, W. CROSBY, JR.: The *Problem of Pricing in a Socialist State,* Cambridge (Mass.), 1931.

STRUMILIN, S.: Articles in *Ekonomitscheskaja Shishni* Nos. 237, 284 and 290, of 23 October, 17 December, 24 December, 1920, respectively.

TAYLOR, FRED M.: "The Guidance of Production in a Socialist State" in *American Economic Review,* Vol. XIX, 1929, also published in *On the Economic Theory of Socialism,* Minneapolis, Minnesota, 1938.

TISCH, CLARE: *Wirtschaftsrechnung und Verteilung im zentralistisch organisierten sozialistischen Gemeinwesen,* Wuppertal—Elberfeld, 1932.

TSCHAYANOFF, A. W.: "Zur Frage einer Theorie der nichtkapitalistischen Wirtschaftssysteme" in *Archiv für Sozialwissenschaft und Sozialpolitik,* Vol. 51, 1923.

VARGA, E.: "Die Kostenberechnung in einem geldlosen Staat" in *Kommunismus,* II. Jahrg., Heft, 9/10, 24.3.1921. Originally published in *Ekonomitscheskaja Shishni.*

WEIL, FELIX: "Gildensozialistische Rechnungslegung. Kritische Bemerkungen zu Karl Polànyi: 'Sozialistiche Rechnungslegung' in diesem Archiv 49/9, S.377 ff." in *Archiv für Sozialwissenschaft und Sozialpolitik,* Vol. 52, 1924.

ZASSENHAUS, HERBERT: "Uber die ökonomische Theorie der Planwirtschaft" in *Zeitschrift für Nationalökonomie,* Vol. 5, 1934.

—— "Neuere Planwirtschaftsliteratur und die Theorie der Planwirtschaft" in *Zeitschrift für Nationalökonomie,* Vol. 7, 1936.

II

Books and papers concerned with economic calculation in the socialist society.

ANONYMOUS: *Britain without Capitalists,* London, 1937. *Grundprinzipien Kommunistischer Verteilung und Produktion,* Berlin, 1930. Published by Allgemeine Arbeiterunion Deutschlands.

BASSECHES, NICOLAUS: *Die Industrie,* supplement to *Die Rote Wirtschaft,* Königsberg and Berlin, 1932.

BAUER, O.: *Der Weg zum Sozialismus,* Vienna, 1919.

BEVERIDGE, WILLIAM H.: *Planning under Socialism,* London, 1936.

BOURGUIN, MAURICE, *Les Systèmes Socialistes,* Paris, Troisième édition, 1933.

BOWEN, J.: *Conditions of Social Welfare,* London, 1926.

BURROWS, RAYMOND: *The Problems and Practice of Economic Planning,* London, 1937.

COHEN, A. W.: *Kann das Geld abgeschafft werden?,* Jena, 1920.

Contemporary Russia: "The Soviet Price System," Vol. I, No. 1, October, 1936.

DICKINSON, H. D.: "The Economic Basis of Socialism" in *Political Quarterly*, September–December, 1930.

———— "Freedom and Planning. A Reply to Dr. Gregory," in *Manchester School*, Vol. IV, 1933.

DOBB, MAURICE: *Russian Economic Development since the Revolution*, 2nd Edition, London, 1929.

———— *Political Economy and Capitalism*, London, 1937.

DOBBERT, GERHARD: *Soviet Economics*, London, 1933.

DURBIN, E. F. M.: "The Social Significance of the Theory of Value," in *Economic Journal*, Vol. 45, 1935.

GERHARDT, J.: *Liberalismus und Wirtschaftsdemokrati*, Berlin, 1930.

Unternehmertum und Wirtschaftsführung, Tübingen, 1931.

GOSSEN, H. H.: *Entwicklung der Gesetze des menschlichen Verkehrs und des daraus fliessenden Regeln für menschliches Handeln*, 3rd Edition, Berlin, 1927.

GREGORY, T. E.: "An Economist Looks at Planning" in *Manchester School*, Vol. IV, 1933.

HALM, G.: *Die Konkurrenz, Untersuchungen über die Ordnungsprinzipien und Entwicklungstendenzen der kapitalistischen Verkehrswirtschaft*, Munich and Leipzig, 1929.

———— "Uber Konkurrenz, Monopol und sozialistische Wirtschaft" in Jahrbücher *für Nationalökonomie und Statistik*, Vol. 133, 1930.

Kapitalismus und Sozialismus, Berlin, 1931 (with L. POHLE).

HAWTREY, R. G.: "Collectivism" in *The Economic Problem*, London, 1926.

HEIMANN, EDUARD: "Die Sozialisierung" in *Archiv für Sozialwissenschaft und Sozialpolitik*, 1918–19.

Mehrwert und Gemeinwirtschaft, Berlin, 1922.

———— "Zur Kritik des Kapitalismus und der National-ökonomie" in *Blätter für den religiösen Sozialismus,* 7, Jahrg., 1926.

———— *Soziale Theorie des Kapitalismus. Theorie der Sozialpolitik,* Tübingen, 1929.

———— "Uber Konkurrenz, Monopol und sozialistische Wirtschaft" in *Die Arbeit,* 1929.

———— "Sozialisierung" in *Neue Blätter für den Sozialismus,* Jahr. I, Heft 1, 1930.

———— *Sozialistische Wirtschafts- und Arbeitsordnung,* Potsdam, 1932.

———— "Planning and the Market System" in *Social Research,* 1934.

Uber gemeinwirtschaftliche Preisbildung, Köln Vierteljahrsh. Bd. I, 2, S.

HORN, E.: *Die ökonomischen Grenzen der Gemeinwirtschaft,* Halberstadt, 1928.

HUBBARD, L. E.: *Soviet Money and Finance,* London, 1936.

Soviet Trade and Distribution, London, 1938.

LANDAUER, CARL: *Grundproblem der funktionellen Verteilung des wirtschaftlichen Werts,* Jena, 1923.

———— *Planwirtschaft und Verkehrwirtschaft,* Munich and Leipzig, 1931.

———— "Value Theory and Economic Planning" in *Plan Age,* October, 1937.

LANGE, OSKAR: "Marxian Economics and Modern Economic Theory" in *Review of Economic Studies,* 1934.

MACHLUP, FRITZ: "On the Meaning of the Marginal Product" in *Exploration in Economics, Notes and Essays*

Contributed in Honour of F. W. Taussig, New York, 1936.

MANDELBAUM, K. and G. MAYER: "Planwirtschaft" in *Zeitschrift für Sozialforschung,* Bd. III, 1934.

MARTIN, P. W.: "The Present Status of Economic Planning" and "The Problems Involved" in *International Labour Review,* February, 1937.

MAYER, G., see K. MANDELBAUM.

MEYER, GERHARD: "A Contribution to the Theory of Socialist Planning," in *Plan Age,* October, 1937.

MISES, LUDWIG VON: *Socialism,* London, 1936.

Liberalismus, Vienna, 1927.

Grundprobleme der Nationalökonomie, Jena, 1933.

MORREAU, G.: "De Economische Struktur eener Socialistische Volkshuishouding" in *De Economist,* s'Gravenhage, 1931.

MOSSE, ROBERT: "Monnaie, Capitalisme et Économie Planifiée" in *Annales du Droit et des Sciences Sociales,* Numéro 6, 1936.

——— "The Theory of Planned Economy" in *International Labour Review,* September, 1937.

NEURATH, OTTO: *Durch die Kriegswirtschaft zur Naturalwirtschaft,* Munich, 1919.

——— *Vollsozialisierung,* Jena, 1920.

——— *Gildensozialismus, Klassenkampf, Vollsozialisierung,* Dresden, 1922.

——— *Wirtschaftsplan und Naturalrechnung,* Berlin, 1925.

PARETO, VILFREDO: *Cours d'Économie Politique,* Lausanne, 1897.

——— *Les Systeme socialistes,* Paris, 1902 and 1903.

——— *Manuel d'Économie Politique,* Paris, 1909.

PIGOU, A.: *Socialism versus Capitalism,* London, 1937.

POHLE, L.: *Kapitalismus und Sozialismus,* Berlin, 1931 (with G. HALM).

POLLOCK, F.: *Die Planwirtschaftlichen Versuche in der Sowjetunion, 1917–1927,* Leipzig, 1929.

REDDAWAY, W. B.: *The Russian Financial System,* London, 1935.

ROBBINS, LIONEL: *The Great Depression,* London, 1933. *Economic Planning and International Order,* London, 1937.

SCHIFF, W.: *Die Planwirtschaft und ihre ökonomischen Hauptprobleme,* Berlin, 1932.

SWEEZY, A. R.: "The Economist's Place under Socialism" in *Explorations in Economics. Notes and Essays Contributed in Honour of F. W. Taussig,* New York, 1936.

TROTSKY, LEON: *Soviet Economy in Danger,* New York, 1933.

WEBER, MAX: *The Theory of Social and Economic Organization,* London, 1947. (Originally published in German, Tübingen, 1922.)

WEGLIN, W.: *Tauschsozialismus und Freigeld,* Munich, 1921.

WOOTTON, BARBARA: *Plan or No Plan,* London, 1934. *Lament for Economics,* London, 1938.

Index

Biographical Note

Trygve J. B. Hoff, born in Oslo in 1895, began his study of economics with "an original sympathy for socialist ideals." He was graduated from Oslo University in 1916 and received his Ph.D. from the Harvard Graduate School of Business Administration in 1920. At Harvard he became intrigued with Ludwig von Mises' contention that rational economic calculation under socialism was impossible. Investigating the problem on his own earned him a doctorate from Oslo University whose faculty was predominantly sympathetic to socialism. He became a convinced advocate of free markets and was a founding member of the Mont Pelerin Society. He served as editor of the prominent liberal Norwegian journal *Farmand* from 1935 to 1960. In 1945 he authored *Peace and the Future, The Way of Liberocracy*, a summation of his economic and political philosophy.

Karen I. Vaughn is Associate Professor of Economics at George Mason University and is author of *John Locke: Economist and Social Scientist,* University of Chicago Press, 1980.

This book was set in the Times Roman series of type. The face was designed to be used in the news columns of the London *Times*. The *Times* was seeking a typeface that would be condensed enough to accommodate a substantial number of words per column without sacrificing readability and still have an attractive, contemporary appearance. This design was an immediate success. It is used in many periodicals throughout the world and is one of the most popular textfaces in use for book work.

Printed on paper that is acid-free and meets the requirements of the American National Standard for Permanence of Paper for Printed Library Materials, Z39.48-1992. ⊚

Book design by JMH Corporation, Indianapolis, Indiana
Typography by Typoservice Corporation, Indianapolis, Indiana
Printed and bound by Thomson-Shore, Inc., Dexter, Michigan